D0707549

Theorizing Citizenship

SUNY Series in Political Theory: Contemporary Issues
Philip Green, editor

Theorizing Citizenship

edited by
Ronald Beiner

State University of New York Press

Published by
State University of New York Press, Albany

© 1995 State University of New York

For information, address the State University of New York Press,
State University Plaza, Albany, NY 12246

Production by Christine Lynch
Marketing by Dana E. Yanulavich

Library of Congress Cataloging-in-Publication Data

Theorizing citizenship / edited by Ronald Beiner.
    p.   cm. -- (SUNY series in political theory. Contemporary
issues)
   ISBN 0-7914-2335-2 (alk. paper). -- ISBN 0-7914-2336-0 (pbk. :
alk. paper)
   1. Citizenship.   2. Civil society.   I. Beiner, Ronald, 1953-
II. Series.
JF801.T465   1995
323.6--dc20   94-10401
                                                        CIP

10 9 8 7 6 5

To Charles Taylor

Contents

Acknowledgments

The following articles were originally published as indicated. I would like to thank both the authors and the publishers for their permission to reprint these essays.

"The Ideal of Citizenship Since Classical Times," by J. G. A. Pocock, originally appeared in *Queen's Quarterly*, Vol. 99, No. 1 (Spring 1992), pp. 35–55.

"The Myth of Citizenship," by Michael Ignatieff, originally appeared in *Queen's Quarterly*, Vol. 99, No. 4 (Winter 1987), pp. 966–85.

"Who Needs a Theory of Citizenship?" by George Armstrong Kelly is reprinted by permission of *Daedalus*, Journal of the American Academy of Arts and Sciences, from the issue entitled "The State," Vol. 108, No. 4 (Fall 1979), pp. 21–36.

"Citizenship and Authority: A Chastened View of Citizenship," by Richard E. Flathman, originally appeared in *News for Teachers of Political Science*, No. 30 (Summer 1981), pp. 9–19, and is reprinted by permission of the American Political Science Association. It was previously reprinted (with revisions, reproduced here) in Richard E. Flathman, *Toward a Liberalism* (Ithaca, NY: Cornell University Press, 1989), pp. 65–108. The original essay was supported by a grant from the National Endowment for the Humanities.

Michael Walzer's Gunnar Myrdal Lecture was originally published, under the title "The Idea of Civil Society," in *Dissent* (Spring 1991), pp. 293–304, and is reprinted by permission of the Foundation for the Study of Independent Social Ideas, Inc. It was previously reprinted, under the title "The Civil Society Argument," in Chantal Mouffe ed., *Dimensions of Radical Democracy: Pluralism, Citizenship, and Community* (London: Routledge, 1992), pp. 89–107.

"Polity and Group Difference: A Critique of the Ideal of Universal Citizenship," by Iris Marion Young, originally appeared in *Ethics*, Vol. 99, No. 2 (January 1989), pp. 250–74, and is reprinted by permission of the University of Chicago Press.

"Is Patriotism a Virtue?" by Alasdair MacIntyre was first published by the Department of Philosophy, University of Kansas, as an E. H. Lindley Lecture. Copyright 1984 University of Kansas.

"Aliens and Citizens: The Case for Open Borders," by Joseph H. Carens, originally appeared in *The Review of Politics*, Vol. 49, No. 2 (Spring 1987), pp. 251–73.

"Citizenship and National Identity: Some Reflections on the Future of Europe," by Jürgen Habermas, originally appeared in *Praxis International*, Vol. 12, No. 1 (April 1992), pp. 1–19, and is reprinted by permission of Basil Blackwell, Ltd.

"Return of the Citizen: A Survey of Recent Work on Citizenship Theory," by Will Kymlicka and Wayne Norman, originally appeared in *Ethics*, Vol. 104, No. 2 (January 1994), pp. 352–81, and is reprinted by permission of the University of Chicago Press.

As always, I am much indebted to Joe Carens for his ever-helpful advice and encouragement. Finally, I wish to express my appreciation for generous assistance received from the Research Committee of the Department of Political Science at the University of Toronto.

Introduction

Why Citizenship Constitutes a Theoretical Problem in the Last Decade of the Twentieth Century

Rousseau, writing books addressed mainly to a reading public in France, as well as a larger European audience, took care that the title pages drew attention to his identity as a *"citoyen de Genève."* Following this illustrious precedent, I shall, in this introduction, allow myself the presumption of writing as a Canadian, since it seems to me that Canadians have especially good reasons to be anxious about whether modern citizenship is in a sound condition.[1]

The topic of citizenship is of course a large one, and it seems to grow larger day by day, as more and more theorists are drawn to reflect on the many-layered crises that are rendering citizenship ever more problematical. In a brief introduction, it is necessary that I limit myself to highlighting only a few aspects of the problem that seem to me salient, especially in the light of contemporary concerns as well as the events that have provoked them. Nationalism, ethnic strife, the fragmentation of previously united multinational political communities such as Yugoslavia, the Soviet Union, Czechoslovakia, and perhaps even my own political community place the problem of citizenship—of what draws a body of citizens together into a coherent and stably organized political community, and keeps that allegiance durable—at the center of theoretical concerns. But once we put it on the agenda, and begin to examine the problem with some attention, we soon see that manifold difficulties start to unfold. As far as North American society is concerned, we are committed socially and economically to capitalism, whether in a milder or harsher version, and we are committed intellectually to some variety of liberalism. But capitalism is certainly no respecter of civic boundaries; on the contrary, to the extent that our lives today are shaped by the modern corporation, we are driven to attend to market imperatives that transgress and subvert civic boundaries.[2]

(This is so pervasive that in Canada a new fringe party like the "National Party" needs to arise in order to protest against this.) As for liberalism, it is a philosophy concerned with upholding the dignity and inherent rights of individuals, understood as instantiations of a *universal* humanity, and so it is unclear why this philosophy would accord any special moral status to the claims of citizenship. Why concern ourselves with the quality of civic life within *our own* national boundaries rather than with, say, human rights violations within some society halfway around the globe?[3] So we see that the two defining commitments of our modern, more or less capitalist, liberal society tend to render the meaning of citizenship deeply problematical, rather than help to dispel what puzzles us here.

In the first part of this introduction, I want to draw attention to a few of the salient challenges to the idea of citizenship in the modern world, and then subsequently come back again to the question of a principled theoretical response (or perhaps the lack thereof).

I.

Let me begin with Jürgen Habermas's very helpful summary of three contemporary developments that have rendered deeply problematical the relation between national identity and citizenship:

> First, the issue of the future of the nation state has unexpectedly become topical in the wake of German unification, the liberation of the East Central European states and the nationality conflicts that are breaking out throughout Eastern Europe. Second, the fact that the states of the European Community are gradually growing together, especially with the impending *caesura* which will be created by the introduction of a common market in 1993, sheds some light on the relation between nation state and democracy, for the democratic processes that have gone hand in hand with the nation state lag hopelessly behind the supranational form taken by economic integration. Third, the tremendous influx of immigration from the poor regions of the East and South with which Europe will be increasingly confronted in the coming years

lend the problem of asylum seekers a new significance and urgency. This process exacerbates the conflict between the universalistic principles of constitutional democracies on the one hand and the particularistic claims of communities to preserve the integrity of their *habitual* ways of life on the other.[4]

These political crises identified by Habermas are indeed central to an understanding of why the problem of citizenship is especially salient in our day. Ethnic and sectarian conflict in northeastern and southeastern Europe; a redefining of national states at the heart of Europe, in a post-Cold War epoch that might have been expected to diminish political turbulence but seems instead to have generated *more* of it; dislocating shifts of identity provoked by mass migration and economic integration, accompanied by defensive reactions to bolster these jeopardized identities: all these political dilemmas have raised anew deep questions about what binds citizens together into a shared political community. To these formidable challenges may be added what is probably the greatest challenge of all to contemporary citizenship, namely, persistent mass unemployment, which offers the surest prospect of excluding tens of millions of people even within the richest nations on earth from a sense of full membership in civic community.[5]

As regards the issue of national identity, the basic problem as I see it is that national citizenship is being simultaneously undermined by not only globalizing pressures but also localizing pressures. But these two opposing challenges are by no means unrelated. In fact, particularistic identities assert themselves most forcefully just when globalist tendencies present real threats to such identities. It is no accident, for instance, that nationalism rises up again in Europe simultaneously with a movement towards European integration.[6] Nationalism is typically a reaction to feelings of threatened identity, and nothing is more threatening in this respect than global integration. So the two go together, and although they push in opposite directions, *both* undercut the integrity of the state, and the civic relationship it defines. This is what I elsewhere refer to as the dialectic of globalism and localism.[7] By calling this a "dialectical" relationship, what I mean is that the two are inseparable tendencies; they are opposites that nonetheless mirror each other, two sides of the same coin.[8] Hence there is an unsuspected correlation between liberalism and nationalism. This thesis, I believe, admits of a more generalized formulation, namely, that the attraction of ideologies generally is a function of deracination; as deracination spreads in modern societies, individuals are increasingly exposed to the grip of ideologies of all kinds (whether universalistic or antiuniversalistic).[9]

I want to return later to this question of "nation" in the civic sense, as opposed to "nation" in the ethnic sense, and of how the latter subverts the former. So let me turn now to some other issues that pose contemporary challenges to the idea of citizenship. Since my space is limited, let me concentrate on three (related) challenges to the idea of citizenship:

1. what Michael Walzer has called "the civil society argument";

2. what I call "groupism," or "groupist" ideologies, but which might also be called "radical pluralism" (not the old liberal pluralism, but a new, trendy left wing pluralism);

3. as a generalization of 1. and 2. above: the post-modernist challenge.

1. *Civil Society.*

In the 1970s and 1980s, "civil society" was raised as one of the most prominent banners in the struggle against the Stalinist regimes of Eastern Europe. The basic idea here was that active involvement in an autonomous civil society composed of a multitude of voluntary associations separate from (or opposed to) the sphere of the state, represents a superior form of citizenship as compared with the decayed citizenship of subservience to an all-pervasive paternalistic state. More recently, this slogan of East European intellectuals has been picked up and embraced by theorists in the West.[10] These theorists argue that given the character of the modern state, with its anonymity, its bureaucratic remoteness, its imperviousness to democratic agency, the modern state is, not the vehicle of citizenship, but a bar to genuinely democratic citizenship. Citizenship, then, must be *localized*. This is of course a new formulation of an old argument, for all forms of liberalism invoke some version of the civil society argument.

This kind of argument certainly has a lot of force to it. Michael Walzer, in his contribution to this volume, explains the force of this idea, but also traces its limits. As Walzer rightly argues:

> Here is the paradox of the civil society argument. Citizenship is one of many roles that members play, but the state itself is unlike all the other associations. It both frames civil society and occupies space within it. It fixes the boundary conditions and the basic rules of all associational activity (including political activity). It compels association members to think about a common good, beyond their own conceptions of the good life. Even the failed totalitarianism of, say, the Polish communist state had this much impact upon the Solidarity union: it determined that Solidarity was a Polish union, focused on economic arrangements and labor policy within the borders of Poland.[11]

Although Walzer is plainly sympathetic to the civil society vision, he understands that, as he puts it, "citizenship [i.e., political, state-centered citizenship] has a certain practical preeminence among all our actual and possible memberships."[12] It is surely highly significant in this connection (as is noted by Walzer as well) that the Solidarity movement in Poland, the most sensational model of the civil society vision, and the one that helped most to inspire this line of theorizing, did *not* confine itself to civil society once the totalitarian state had collapsed, but went on to turn itself into a political party, quickly assuming the reins of government, and the leader of the original Solidarity movement is of course today the president of Poland. This was not a sellout by Solidarity, but a natural response to the "built-in" insufficiency of the kind of "localized" citizenship made available to us at the civil society level alone.[13]

2. *Pluralism.*

A more radical version of the same argument is made by theorists like Iris Marion Young in the name of group identity, invoking popular slogans like "the politics of difference."[14] Here the cultural fragmentation of citizenship is seen not as a danger, but as a positive advantage. Debates about multiculturalism in Canada and the United States obviously draw upon this sort of radical pluralist argument. Will Kymlicka has pointed out the central perplexity to which we are led when we follow through this way of thinking to its ultimate limit:

> On the one hand, many of these groups are insisting that society officially affirm their difference, and provide various kinds of institutional support and recognition for their difference, e.g., public funding for group-based organizations...On the other hand, if society accepts and encourages more and more diversity, in order to promote cultural inclusion, it seems that citizens will have less and less in common. If affirming difference is required to integrate marginalized groups into the common culture, there may cease to be a common culture.[15]

The pluralist vision poses a threat to the idea of citizenship because groupism taken to its logical conclusion amounts to a kind of ghettoization; that is to say, a tendency on the part of each group in the society to withdraw behind the boundaries of its own group, its own groupist identity, with no need to acknowledge a larger common culture. Citizenship would then be reduced to an aggregate of subnational ghettoes.[16]

In order to clarify the range of theoretical options, I want to distinguish three basic possibilities:

(1) The first of these options I will call "nationalism." In a provocative essay entitled "In Defense of the Nation," Roger Scruton defines national identity in terms of ethnic-cultural identity.[17] According to Scruton's argument, groups must assimilate to the "national idea," or if they cannot, ought not to belong to the political community but instead should belong to one that offers them a sense of home and rootedness. The thrust of Scruton's argument is that what ultimately sustains the liberal state is not a sense of *political* membership in the state but the *social* loyalties and allegiances that define nationhood, and therefore that citizenship as a political concept is ultimately parasitic upon nationhood as a social concept. In other words, a relation to the nation as a prepolitical community is more basic than any relation to the state precisely because the former is

situated on the social side of the social/political dichotomy. For instance, Scruton's argument is that America "works" as a liberal state, not on account of a sense of shared political commitment to the Constitution, but rather, because it has successfully instilled the sense of itself as a genuine "nation," albeit one defined nonethnically.[18] It is at the social level, the level at which national identification reposes, that one secures the sense of prepolitical community without which the liberal state, no less than any other kind of state, dissolves. While Scruton defends the liberal state, he attacks liberals because liberalism, as he conceives it, is defined by blindness to or willful ignorance of this essential truth.[19]

Scruton repudiates any association between nation and race. Rather, "nation," as he defines it, refers to the development of a people's destiny, preferably within definite territorial boundaries, embracing shared language, shared associations, shared history, and a common culture (including, often but not always, the culture of a shared religion). The idea of a multinational state, on this conception, is inherently unsustainable, for such states either move in the direction of forging a unitary sense of nationhood, or cease to exist. Admittedly, the sustainability of multinational states appears at present to warrant a great deal of pessimism. (Scruton refers to Lebanon, Cyprus, and India, but he seems to have been premature in his judgment that Czechoslovakia had solved its problem of common nationhood).[20]

(2) In various writings, Bhikhu Parekh offers a strong defense of multiculturalism.[21] According to his argument in its most robust version, the state is obliged to serve the pluralistic identities of subgroups, not vice versa. In one passage, he goes so far as to argue that immigrant communities in Britain are bound by no obligation to conform to a larger host culture, on the grounds that British society not only admitted but positively recruited them to help rebuild its postwar eeonomy, "in full knowledge of who they were and what they stood for."[22] How far is a society really obliged to go in order to accommodate minority cultures? Is a liberal

society required to condone the wearing of veils by Islamic schoolgirls forced by their families to do so? Should France exempt North Africans from French military service and allow them to substitute service for countries that in given circumstances may be militarily opposed to France? Should Rastafarians in Britain be exempt from marijuana laws that apply to the rest of the population? Should the Hispanic population in the U.S. not be required to adapt to English as the primary language of daily life? If there is no limit whatever to cultural pluralism, then clearly we approach the point where the very notion of common citizenship as an existential reality dissolves into nothingness.[23]

(3) Having summarized Scruton's nationalist option and Parekh's multicultural option, I want to propose a third possibility, which I would develop under the heading of citizenship. According to this third conception, there is a requirement that all citizens conform to a larger culture, but this culture is national-civic, not national-ethnic.[24] It refers to political, not social, allegiance, or, to employ the classical liberal dichotomy, it identifies membership in the state, not membership in civil society. I think this conception is captured very well in Jürgen Habermas's notion of "constitutional patriotism."[25] Admittedly, it can be quite tricky to separate out these two senses of nationhood, for the social and the political, culture and state, unavoidably overlap in all kinds of ways. Still, I think this approach offers a helpful way of mediating the debate between nationalists like Scruton and multiculturalists like Parekh. As I try to spell out at further length below, what I'm searching for under the title of citizenship is an elusive middle term between opposing alternatives that I find unacceptable.[26]

3. Post-modernism.

In recent years, certain French intellectual fashions have caught on in North America, and the most familiar umbrella term for these new theoretical tendencies is "post-modernism."[27] The basic theoretical challenge here is that the philosophical universalisms that we know from the canonical tradition of the West all involve what we might call a "hegemonic function," which is to suppress various particularistic identities. Appeals to universal reason typically serve to silence, stigmatize and marginalize groups and identities that lie beyond the boundaries of a white, male, Eurocentric hegemon. Universalism is merely the cover for an imperialistic particularism. If all of this is correct, then the debunking of Western rationalism, and the universalism it presupposes, serves to liberate oppressed groups who are then free to express and articulate their authentic, but suppressed, identities. Post-modernism, thus defined, is actually an encompassing theoretical statement of the claims of localism and pluralism reviewed above. But if we were right to criticize the idea of a localizing and pluralizing citizenship, then we ought to be disturbed by the claim by post-modern social theory that *all* social reality is untranscendably local, plural, fragmentary, episodic, and infinitely rearrangeable.

Post-modern philosophy has sought to do for social theory what the post-modern movement has done in art and architecture: to turn pastiche into a distinctive style; to splice and tape cultural identities so that any comforting sense of fixity or essence is subverted— perhaps to turn the necessities of our modern condition into virtues.[28] In Salman Rushdie's phrase, this involves seeing cultural "mongrelization" as a positive and enriching thing.[29] I certainly agree that there is something attractive and refreshing about this notion that we are all hybrids. Still, there is something worrying here as concerns the possibility of sustaining a coherent idea of citizenship. This worry is captured very well in the following response by John Pocock:

> A community or a sovereign that demands the whole of one's allegiance may be foreclosing one's freedom of choice to be this or that kind of person; that was the early modern and modern danger. A plurality of communities or sovereignties that take turns in demanding one's allegiance, while conceding that each and every allocation of allegiance is partial, contingent, and provisional, is denying one the freedom to make a final com- mitment which determines one's identity, and that is plainly the post-modern danger. . . . It is one thing to decide that being a Canadian—or, like me, a New Zealander—offers one an open

range of identities, and that freedom consists in retaining one's
mobility in choosing between them. It is quite another when the
sovereign or quasi-sovereign powers of this world get together to
inform one that there is no choice of an identity, no commitment
of an allegiance, no determination of one's citizenship or personality that they regard as other than provisional (or may not
require one at any moment to unmake). Under post-modern
conditions we do confront these alliances of unmakers,
deconstructors, and decenterers, and our citizenship may have
to be our means of telling them where they get off.[30]

So one might hope; but more and more we find today that it is the
deconstructors who tend to be successful in telling citizenship where
it gets off.

It is doubtless true that the primary motivation behind the
politics of difference is to secure inclusion for traditionally excluded
groups and marginalized voices. But does it make sense to speak
of inclusion if all is particularity, and there is no possibility of rising
above the contest of rival particularisms? Inclusion in what? If
citizenship doesn't involve a kind of universality, how can there be
a community of citizens to which the hitherto excluded and
marginalized gain entry? Here, post-modernism leaves us at a loss,
and to recover a coherent idea of citizenship we must go back to
older categories of political thought (available from Aristotle,
Rousseau, or Hegel, for instance, rather than from Nietzsche or
Foucault).[31]

One hopes that pillars of the republican tradition such as
Aristotle and Rousseau were mistaken in thinking that ethnic and
cultural homogeneity is a necessary condition of civic identity. On
the other hand, it should be clear that the more that citizens become
fixated on cultural differences within the political community, the
more difficult it becomes to sustain an experience of common
citizenship. In other words, what is shared as citizens must have
a power to shape identity that at some point overrides, or is more
salient than, our local identities. Consider as an example the recent
controversy concerning gays in the U.S. military. The argument here,
surely, (viz., the Clinton argument) is that the willingness and
capacity of gay soldiers to contribute to the defense of the American
nation pertains to a shared civic identity that is larger, is more

comprehensive, and possesses a more egalitarian foundation than the more local allegiances of homosexual identity or heterosexual identity. From this point of view gay activists or gay theorists who want to lay such emphasis on their partial identity as gays that it excludes the possibility of a more general ("sex-blind") citizenship cannot help but undermine the egalitarian argument that Clinton is trying to make on their behalf. Shared citizenship entails egalitarianism, and this egalitarianism is undercut by too much emphasis upon particularistic identity insofar as the egalitarian conception presupposes an appeal to what is shared across divergent cultural or ethnic groups. An obvious parallel is the nonconscription of Arab Israelis into the Israeli army. I think that there is a compelling egalitarian argument for the full participation of Arab-Israeli citizens in the I.D.F. But such an argument presupposes that what Jews and Arabs share as citizens transcends their ethnic identity. One would not be at all surprised if many or most Arabs were unwilling to embrace this egalitarian argument, precisely for the sake of giving priority to their Arab identity (which mirrors perfectly the Jewish motivation that denies them equal citizenship in the first place). This would simply be another way of saying that for them Israeli citizenship is impossible. Yet one would like to think that a citizenship that transcends ethnicity *is* a possibility.[32]

The affirmation of particularity is by no means limited to the sphere of ethnic conflicts and national identity. Certain brands of feminism present the appearance of a kind of "gender nationalism"; that is, they seem to suggest the same kinds of narrow particularism that one encounters in the realm of ethnic divisions. Another example would be identification with one's own social class, to the exclusion of other classes within society.[33] Yet I think the events of our day entitle us to give special attention to national particularism. After all, no feminists so far as I know are proposing a gender equivalent of ethnic cleansing, and even in the days when class warfare was being waged on behalf of class-based ideologies in Russia and China, this was done in the name of a higher universalism that was supposed to be the ultimate outcome of the struggle of one class against another. But today nationalists are indeed killing one another, and doing so without any appeal to a higher trans-

national universalism; on the contrary, they do so in brutal rejection
of any kind of universalism. Let us, then, probe further the relation
between citizenship and nationalism.

II.

Our problem today is that we seem to be locked into a choice
between two mutually exclusive alternatives, neither of which strike
me as satisfactory. On the one hand, there are the various kinds
of universalism that exalt the inviolable moral worth of individuals,
seen as human beings *as such*, above and beyond any collective or
civic identity that would "particularize" human beings, so to speak.
This universalistic vision, as we discussed early on in this essay,
tends to render morally dubious any privileging of citizenship,
which implies, after all, an exclusive and particularistic identity. On
the other hand, we have the forces of exclusivity and particularism
that celebrate and affirm just those forms of group identity that
distinguish sets of individuals from one another, and which tend,
again as we referred to at the outset, to generate the kind of ethnic
and nationalistic outbursts whose outcome, as we have seen more
and more in the last few years, is the self-dissolution of citizenship.
So we are left with two competing visions—liberal universalism and
antiliberal particularism—*both* of which tend to subvert, from
opposing directions, the idea of a civic community. Mutually
exclusive, but not—one hopes—exhaustive. However, in order to
show that these alternatives do not exhaust the possibilities, one
would have to make available a full-fledged theory of citizenship.
And here, I'm sorry to confess, I simply don't have in my possession
such a theory of citizenship. (I wish I did.)

Lying at the heart of this dilemma is what I would call the
"universalism/particularism conundrum." To opt wholeheartedly
for universalism implies deracination—rootlessness. To opt
wholeheartedly for particularism implies parochialism, exclusivity,
and narrow-minded closure of horizons. Yet it is by no means clear
that a viable synthesis of particularistic rootedness and universalistic
openness is philosophically or practically available. In practice, and
perhaps even in theory, we always seem to get drawn to one

unsatisfactory extreme or the other. This elusive synthesis of liberal cosmopolitanism and illiberal particularism, to the extent that it is attainable, is what I want to call "citizenship."

The conundrum sketched here is the same conundrum that we find Rousseau struggling with at the end of the *Social Contract*, where we are left with two unhappy alternatives: political particularism, which is false and inhuman, and moral universalism, which is morally and religiously true but is politically useless and ultimately uncivic.[34] Rousseau criticizes that phony cosmopolitanism that allows individuals to "boast of loving everyone in order to have the right to love no one."[35] Yet by the same token, Rousseau is as critical as any universalist liberal of the spirit of national exclusivity and parochialism. In the *Second Discourse*, the very thinkers who are, in the *Geneva Manuscript*, condemned for their cosmopolitanism, are praised as "great cosmopolitan souls, who surmount the imaginary barriers that separate peoples"![36] Rousseau is anti-cosmopolitan *and* anti-particularist.[37] The *via media* between universalism and particularism remains inaccessible. The key here, of course, is to distinguish genuine cosmopolitanism from phony cosmopolitanism (or: to distinguish "the liberal spirit," in the sense of openness to the real diversity of social experience, from "liberal tolerance" in the sense of a shallow acceptance of whatever the existing social order happens to have cast up), but to draw these distinctions is by no means easy, at least theoretically.

In order to help clarify the alternatives here, I want to distinguish three theoretical perspectives:

1. liberal: emphasizing the individual, and the individual's capacity to transcend group or collective identity, to break the shackles of fixed identity (social station, hierarchy, traditional roles, etc.), to define and redefine one's own purposes, and so on.

2. communitarian: emphasizing the cultural or ethnic group, solidarity among those sharing a history or tradition, the capacity of the group to confer identity upon those otherwise left "atomized" by the deracinating tendencies of a liberal society.

3. "republican":   emphasizing "civic" bonds. From my point of
                            view, *both* of the above two competing
                            perspectives (No. 1 and No. 2) jeopardize the
                            idea of a political community that is reducible
                            neither to an aggregation of individuals nor to
                            a conjunction of identity-constituting groups.
                            That is, both liberal and communitarian
                            theories pose threats to the idea of citizenship
                            as I understand it. The decisive question, of
                            course, is whether there really exists some third
                            possibility that is theoretically coherent and
                            practically viable. I think that Jürgen Habermas
                            is groping in the direction of such a theoretical
                            perspective with his idea of "constitutional
                            patriotism," an idea of citizenship that is
                            intended to be neither individualist nor com-
                            munitarian, neither liberal nor anti-liberal. But
                            it remains highly uncertain whether one can
                            give sense to such an idea relative to the
                            realities of life at the end of the twentieth
                            century (or indeed whether such an idea of
                            citizenship has *ever* made sense).

My threefold schema yields two instrumental approaches to
citizenship, and one non-instrumental approach to citizenship:
According to perspective No. 1, political community is instrumental
to the strivings of individuals to give to their lives an authentic
meaning or sense that they are happy with as individuals. For
example, the idea here would be that membership in "Canada" is
justified by the Charter of Rights and Freedoms. According to
perspective No. 2, political community is instrumental to the
strivings of communities to elaborate a collective identity that can
be constitutive of the selfhood of its members (to use Sandel's
terms). Here, the idea would be, for example, that membership in
"Quebec" as a quasi-state would be justified by the state's promotion
of the collective identity of Québécois (understood as a linguistic-
ethnic category rather than as a category of citizenship equally
applicable to anglophone or allophone citizens of Quebec).

According to perspective No. 3, political community is a good in itself: political traditions constitute living totalities that are not reducible to the purposes of individuals or the goals of subcommunities, and our humanity would be diminished if our lives lacked a focus for this civic dimension of existence, even if it were somehow possible to satisfy all of our individual and group purposes without participation in a larger political community. This ambitious claim is a modern (and no doubt watered down and liberalized) version of Aristotle's ancient claim that human beings are by nature political animals, that without full membership in some kind of polis, we live a life that is less than fully human.[38]

Allowing myself now to speak freely in my Canadian voice, I will call perspective No. 1 the "Pierre Trudeau" vision of citizenship (with its uncompromising appeal to individual rights), and we can call perspective No. 2 the "Jacques Parizeau" vision of citizenship (with its invocation of "old stock" Québécois).[39] I find both of these two accounts of citizenship radically deficient, but I lack any confidence that I can come up with a third account that will satisfy readers or satisfy myself, a third perspective that supplies the deficiencies of No. 1 and No. 2, and retains (in a higher synthesis) the strengths of each (relative to the other). The convincing "NO" that issued forth from the citizens of my political community in the 1992 referendum, some of whom voted no for "Pierre Trudeau" reasons and some of whom voted no for "Jacques Parizeau" reasons, brings home to us in a very concrete political fashion the difficulty of conceptualizing the experience of citizenship in a way that doesn't get drawn into the unhappy either/or enforced by the polarizing alternatives of perspectives Nos. 1 and 2.

Let us summarize our analysis by specifying three models of political community:

1. Political community in the service of individual identity (liberalism)
2. Political community in the service of communalist identity (nationalism)
3. Political community as an expression of "civic" identity (?)

The closest I can come to filling in this question mark is Václav
Havel's appeal to the idea of "Czechoslovakia" as a civic union.
But of course, as we all know, both the political movement that
Havel founded and the idea of Czechoslovakia to which he
appealed have recently succumbed to liberalism in Bohemia and
nationalism in Slovakia. The now departed Czechoslovak federation provides one example, and my own polity provides another,
of a more general syndrome whereby citizenship gets squeezed
out between the opposing imperatives of liberalism and nationalism:
Just as Czecho-Slovak citizenship gets squeezed out between
Czech liberalism and Slovak nationalism, so Canadian (Anglo-
Gallic) citizenship gets squeezed out between Anglo liberalism
and Gallic nationalism.[40] Needless to say, these formulas represent a gross simplification of complex societies.[41] But theory
typically involves radical simplification, in the interests of
sharpening our sense of fundamental alternatives in the midst
of complexity.

My basic thesis is that liberalism is correct in its diagnosis of
what's wrong with nationalism, and nationalism is correct in its
diagnosis of what's wrong with liberalism. Therefore we are left
deprived of a suitable vision of political community unless we can
come up with a third possibility that is neither liberal nor nationalist,
and that somehow escapes the liberal's arguments against
nationalism and the nationalist's arguments against liberalism.[42] The
problem, as my examples are intended to convey, is that this other
possibility tends to get squeezed out between universalizing and
particularizing antipodes. In his essay "Nationality," Lord Acton
wrote: "The co-existence of several nations under the same State
is a test. . .of its freedom."[43] The fate of what was until not long ago
the state of Czechoslovakia proves how difficult it is for contemporary states to pass this test—notwithstanding the huge
advances of liberal democracy that we have witnessed since 1989.
Indeed, paradoxically, these advances of liberal democracy appear
to have made it *more* difficult for contemporary states to pass this
test! What I've been trying to suggest here is that the fate of a country
like Czechoslovakia (alas, no longer a country!)—or for that matter
the fate of a country like my own—constitutes a philosophical
problem.

III.

Reflection on citizenship is occasioned by certain commonplace experiences; in my case, reflection on the experience of being a "rootless cosmopolitan." Being a Jewish intellectual in an economically advanced, socially liberal, culturally diverse, and politically very marginalized society, it was virtually unavoidable that I would turn out to be a rootless cosmopolitan. The pressures towards rootless cosmopolitanism are so strong that an intellectual (a cosmopolitan intellectual!) like Michael Walzer has to devote the full force of his energies as a theorist to showing that the moral and intellectual claims of rootless cosmopolitanism are illegitimate.[44] When Kant set out his ideal of the "world citizen," considering politics in the light of a *"weltbürgerliche Absicht,"* he articulated something genuinely attractive, but I suspect that even Kant himself realized that there is at the same time something not entirely attractive in this point of view. (Consider, for instance, what Kant says concerning the sublimity of war in the *Critique of Judgment.*) So, cosmopolitanism is morally and intellectually deficient. But what are the alternatives? Are we to resist rootless cosmopolitanism through the vehicle of something like Canadian nationalism, with all the ludicrous parochialism that this entails? Or do we opt for, say, Québécois nationalism, which is no less ludicrously parochial? All nationalisms are driven by the urge to resist rootless cosmopolitanism, but they do so at the price of embracing various stifling parochialisms in relation to what one might call the "ideal of an open humanity." So, cosmopolitanism is unsatisfactory, and anti-cosmopolitanism is unsatisfactory. This inevitably forces upon us the question: Can there be an ideal of citizenship that is neither deracinating nor parochializing, or is such an ideal nothing but a chimera?

Let us illustrate what we have in mind in referring to the pettiness of nationalism. Consider the following exchange during a conversation between Salman Rushdie and Edward Said:

> SAID: . . . A close friend of mine once came to my house and stayed overnight. In the morning we had breakfast, which included yogurt cheese with a special herb, *za'atar.* This com-

bination probably exists all over the Arab world, and certainly in
Palestine, Syria and Lebanon. But my friend said: "There, you
see. It's a sign of a Palestinian home that it has za'atar in it." Being
a poet, he then expatiated at great and tedious length on
Palestinian cuisine, which is generally very much like Lebanese
and Syrian cuisine, and by the end of the morning we were both
convinced that we had a totally distinct national cuisine.

RUSHDIE: So, because a Palestinian chooses to do something it
becomes the Palestinian thing to do?

SAID: That's absolutely right.[45]

These discussions of the real or imagined uniqueness of national
cuisine may seem innocent enough, but in the fevered world in
which we live, there is no telling when such benign reflections may
turn ugly. In a documentary film by Michael Ignatieff entitled *The
Road to Nowhere*, depicting the shambles that the former Yugoslavia
has become, Ignatieff suggests gently to his interlocutors, members
of a Serbian paramilitary unit in a village outside Vukovar, that the
wine they are drinking is Croatian wine. This draws the vehement
retort, "*Serbian* wine!"

This kind of thing is inherent in all nationalisms.[46] On the other
side, I agree with Joseph Carens's argument in chapter 8 of this
volume that there is something in the very logic of liberalism that
carries one towards cosmopolitanism. If one follows this through
all the way, one eventually arrives at a point where all national (civic)
boundaries become meaningless; that is, where citizenship itself
becomes meaningless. These strike me as not very satisfactory
alternatives. Thus, my concern with citizenship is centrally motivated by the feeling that there must be a third alternative beyond
liberalism and nationalism, which represent two opposing extremes
in the relationship between the individual and group identity.
Liberalism seeks to give the individual primacy over the group, even
(if necessary) at the price of an alienation from any and every group
identity. Nationalism seeks to give the group primacy over the
individual, which—as we see with more and more stark evidence
today—contains the seeds of real human evils. As one of the neo-
fascist thugs in the film *My Beautiful Launderette* says, "You have to
belong to something." Extrapolating from the film, this statement

about the need for belonging can be interpreted in two possible ways: Either fascism is a uniquely evil expression of an otherwise benign human need for belonging; or there is a kind of latent fascism implicit in any impulse towards group belonging. I find myself unable to dismiss the element of truth expressed in the second interpretation. Again, given this choice between alienating liberalism and the latent evil in any fully consistent nationalism, my response is that there has to be another alternative.

In the preceding section, I proposed a name for this desired alternative, and it takes no more than the display of this banner ("republicanism") to be plunged into the swirling controversies that animate contemporary citizenship theory (as the exemplary essays in this collection so well illustrate).[47] Of course, the term "republican citizenship," conjuring up images of robust civic involvement and citizenly commitment, necessarily implies a rebuke to liberalism, with its minimalist conception of the duties and responsibilities of citizenship (preferring to define citizenship in terms of rights and entitlements).[48] These two opposing visions of what citizenship requires are nicely encapsulated in Richard Flathman's contrast between "high citizenship" and "low citizenship," and the contention between them remains one of the central debates carried on by theorists of citizenship. The republican vision is associated with the enthusiasms of theorists like Hannah Arendt, Benjamin Barber, Skinner and Pocock, Charles Taylor, and myself, and these enthusiasms get a sceptical reception from Flathman, Michael Ignatieff, Kymlicka and Norman, and George Kelly, among the contributors to this volume.[49] But as Kelly rightly emphasizes, we are not in a position to determine what intensity of human energies to invest in the activities of citizenship until we have established the character of the civic relationship, and the nature of the political community whose legal and ethical bonds define the idea of citizenship. Theorizing citizenship requires that one take up questions having to do with membership, national identity, civic allegiance, and all the commonalities of sentiment and obligation that prompt one to feel that one belongs to *this* political community rather than *that* political community; and as this introduction has sought to sketch, precisely these questions remain as puzzling as ever, perhaps considerably more so in an age when the planetary scope of politics makes the national state appear more like a municipal arena. In this sense, the choice between "high citizenship" and "low citizenship" waits upon a better understanding of the civic community that presumes to make claims upon us as citizens.

Notes

1. Cf. J. G. A. Pocock: "I recall reading, a couple of months ago, an article in the *Economist* forecasting that Canada might become the first postmodern democracy, and wondering whether this was an encouraging prospect." This volume, p. 47.

2. Of course, this aspect of the contemporary world economy is a direct entailment of liberalism as applied to the realm of economics. For a good recent statement of the connection between political liberalism and economic liberalism, see James Fallows, "What Is an Economy For?," *The Atlantic Monthly*, January 1994, pp. 76–92. As Fallows makes clear, the Western liberal commitment to the primacy of universal markets over national borders necessarily undermines the claims of citizenship in the formation of economic policy. (Thus, Western nations typically treat their citizens as consumers first and foremost, whereas Asian societies like Japan typically require that the welfare of consumers be subordinated to their interests as members of a distinct political community.)

3. For an account of the globalizing, and therefore implicitly anticivic, thrust of the liberal tradition, see Joseph H. Carens's contribution to this volume (chapter 8).

4. This volume, pp. 255–256. The crisis of immigration and the crisis concerning European integration are clearly connected. The nature of this connection is nicely summarized by Jean-Marie Colombani, editor of *Le Monde*: "Just when we need a sense of strong nationhood to help integrate and absorb a new generation of immigrants, with different races and religions, the French are asked to transfer their allegiance to some vague European idea. This contradiction is feeding an identity crisis and undermining trust in our political leadership." Cited in *The Washington Post*, Sunday, 21 Mar. 1993, p. A32.

5. As Michael Ignatieff lays out with great lucidity in chapter 2, the modern welfare state was intended to embody a definite *civic* ideal, in the sense that it grew out of the conviction that the state would have to guarantee a modicum of material security in an insecure world if it were

serious about giving a content to citizenship that a relentlessly market-based society would otherwise betray without limit. In this respect, the willingness of contemporary Western democracies to tolerate a much greater flux in the structures of economic life, entailing a greatly reduced security of employment, cannot help but be symptomatic of a profound crisis in the idea of citizenship. (This volume, p. 69; George Kelly's critique of what he labels "Civil II," in chapter 3, strikes me as failing to appreciate sufficiently this civic aspiration at the root of the expansion of the welfare state.)

6. For an elaboration of this phenomenon with respect to the European Community (viz., European federalism as a source, paradoxically, of Le Penism), see Conor Cruise O'Brien, "Pursuing a Chimera: Nationalism at Odds With the Idea of a Federal Europe," *Times Literary Surplement*, 13 Mar. 1992, pp. 3–4.

7. Ronald Beiner, *What's the Matter With Liberalism?* (Berkeley: University of California Press, 1992), p.109.

8. Cf. Ernest Gellner, "From the Ruins of the Great Contest," *Times Literary Supplement*, 13 Mar. 1992, p. 10: "A modern society is a mass, anonymous one in which work is semantic not physical, and in which men can only claim effective economic and political citizenship if they can operate the language and culture of the bureaucracies which surround them. The socio-econonic processes which helped establish a liberal and consumerist society in the West also engendered nationalism, for men can only live comfortably in political units dedicated to the maintenance of the same culture as their own. So in the West, the emergence of modernity was accompanied by the emergence of nationalism."

9. On nationalism as a reaction against deracination, cf. Isaiah Berlin, "Nationalism: Past Neglect and Present Power," in *Against the Current*, ed. Henry Hardy (London: Hogarth Press, 1979), pp. 349, 351–352.

10. See, for instance, John Keane, "The Limits of State Action," in Keane, *Democracy and Civil Society* (London: Verso, 1988), pp. 1–30. While Keane is certainly a proponent of the "civil society argument," he fully appreciates why traditional leftists are uneasy about promoting the autonomy of civil society at the expense of the state.

11. This volume, p. 169.

12. This volume, p. 170.

13. See G. M. Tamás, "The Legacy of Dissent," *Times Literary Supplement*, 14 May 1993, pp. 14–19, for a good account of the reasons for

the appeal of the antipolitical slogan, "civil society," and of its sorry consequences in post-Communist Eastern Europe. For another useful critique of the civil society argument, see Elizabeth Kiss, "Democracy Without Parties?," in *Dissent* (Spring 1992), pp. 226–231.

14. See chapter 6 in this volume, as well as Iris Marion Young, *Justice and the Politics of Difference* (Princeton, New Jersey: Princeton University Press, 1990). See also chapter 10 in this volume, pp. 301–309.

15. Will Kymlicka, *Recent Work in Citizenship Theory*, A report prepared for Multiculturalism and Citizenship Canada, September 1992, p.24. (This is a fuller version of chapter 10 in this volume.)

16. A good analysis, in the Canadian context, of what the "politics of difference" does to citizenship, and of how civic solidarity becomes hopelessly fragmented when each interest group puts in its own distinct claim for recognition, is offered in an unpublished paper by Reg Whitaker entitled "What is the Problem With Democracy?". At its worst, the politics of difference is really just a new, trendier version of the old liberal interest group politics, not less cynical for all the leftist patina that accompanies it. For a fuller analysis of the Canadian situation with respect to citizenship, see Alan C. Cairns, "The Fragmentation of Canadian Citizenship," in *Belonging: The Meaning and Future of Canadian Citizenship*, ed. William Kaplan (Montreal & Kingston: McGill-Queen's University Press, 1993), pp. 181–220.

17. Roger Scruton, "In Defense of the Nation," in Scruton, *The Philosopher on Dover Beach* (Manchester: Carcanet, 1990), pp. 299–337.

18. Ibid., p. 323.

19. Scruton insists that the communitarian ideal of thinkers like Walzer, Sandel, and Taylor offers no remedy to the emptiness of liberalism because these theorists fail to recognize that real community entails an affirmation of "sanctity, intolerance, exclusion, and a sense that life's meaning depends upon obedience, and also on vigilance against the enemy" (ibid., p. 310). Relative to this exacting standard, Scruton would surely say that my efforts to map out an alternative to the liberal idea of political membership really amount to just another version of liberalism.

20. Ibid., pp. 325, 318.

21. Parekh is the prime target in the Scruton essay cited in the preceding notes.

22. Bhikhu Parekh, "The Rushdie Affair: Research Agenda for Political Philosophy," *Political Studies* Vol. 38, 1990, p. 701. For a more balanced view of the reciprocal obligations of majority and minority cultures, see Parekh, "British Citizenship and Cultural Difference," in *Citizenship,* ed. Geoff Andrews (London: Lawrence & Wishart, 1991), pp. 183–204.

23. As is alluded to in my examples, this argument is coming to a boil in France in the political debates concerning assimilation of the Muslim North African population concentrated in the absolutely wretched suburbs circling most of the major cities, especially in the South. The F. N., like Scruton, argues that this is not a matter of racism, but of "national identity." The Socialist government, with Kofi Yamgnane as Secretary of State for Integration, attempted, I believe, to move towards something like what Habermas means by "constitutional patriotism." That is, one cannot be a proper French citizen without being able to accept, for instance, the equality of women, or without being able to serve in the French army in a war against Iraq, and so forth. For a good summary of these dilemmas, see *L'Express*, 31 Oct. 1991, pp. 74–88.

24. Does it make sense to apply the term "nationalism" to historical phenomena such as the process of Italian unification during the *Risorgimento* and the founding of Czechoslovakia under Masaryk? This would seem confusing insofar as we tend to think of nationalism today as a separatist force seeking to subdivide existing states according to national-ethnic criteria, whereas Italy under the leadership of Mazzini and Garibaldi and Czechoslovakia under the leadership of Masaryk built up political communities that joined together national subcommunities (Czechs and Slovaks in the case of Czechoslovakia; regional subgroups in the case of Italy). For the same reason, I would hesitate to speak of chauvinistic attitudes in America as "American nationalism," whereas the militancy of, for instance, Black Muslim groups in America would easily qualify as nationalistic. Perhaps what we require here is a distinction, corresponding to my national-civic/national-ethnic distinction, that distinguishes movements of national self-determination that gather together different groups in a more encompassing political entity and those that split up larger political entities along ethnic or religious lines. This would allow us to distinguish, for instance, the "synthesizing nationalism" of Czechoslovakia in 1918 from the divisive Czech and Slovak nationalisms we are witnessing today (and a similar process of deunification is afoot in contemporary Italy). Thus, one might opt for labels such as: a building-up or integrating nationalism vs. a demolishing or tearing-asunder nation-alism; however, as a point of terminology, I would prefer to reserve the term nationalism strictly for the latter. I am grateful to Clifford Orwin for pressing me to clarify this point.

25. See Jürgen Habermas, "Historical Consciousness and Post-Traditional Identity," in Habermas, *The New Conservatism*, ed. Shierry Weber Nicholsen (Cambridge, Mass: MIT Press, 1989), pp. 249–267.

26. For a somewhat similar laying-out of alternatives, see William Rogers Brubaker, "Introduction," in *Immigration and the Politics of Citizenship in Europe and North America*, ed. Brubaker (Lanham, Maryland: University Press of America, 1989), pp. 3–6. In saying that I find the multiculturalist alternative unsatisfactory, I don't mean to suggest that claims by cultural minorities for special treatment are always destructive of citizenship, or that they should never be accommodated. On the contrary, I am in full agreement with Kymlicka and Norman's conclusion (p. 309 below) that, given the great variance in historical, cultural, and political situations in multination states, it would not be realistic to expect any generalized answer to the question of how to reconcile common citizenship identity with more particularistic group identities. One must go from case to case and from country to country, and see what actually works in different situations. Federalism is obviously a major device for trying to accommodate cultural differences while preserving common citizenship.

27. These views are typically derived from what Charles Taylor rightly calls half-baked neo-Nietzschean subjectivism. *Multiculturalism and "The Politics of Recognition,"* ed. Amy Gutmann (Princeton: Princeton University Press, 1992), p. 70.

28. It is more than a little ironic that Nietzsche is generally cited as the patron saint of the post-modern movement, for Nietzsche anticipated by a hundred years this aspect of post-modernism—namely its "deconstruction" of a unitary culture—and bitterly criticized what he foresaw: see his discussion of the "style of decadence" in *The Case of Wagner*, section 7.

29. Salman Rushdie, *Imaginary Homelands* (London: Granta Books, 1991), p. 394: "*The Satanic Verses* celebrates hybridity. impurity, intermingling. . . . It rejoices in mongrelization. . . . *Mélange*, hotchpotch, a bit of this and a bit of that. . . is the great possibility that mass migration gives the world, and I have tried to embrace it. *The Satanic Verses* is for change-by-fusion, change-by-conjoining. It is a love-song to our mongrel selves." Cf. Edward Said (ibid., p. 182): "The whole notion of crossing over, of moving from one identity to another, is extremely important to me, being as I am—as we all are—a sort of hybrid."

30. This volume, pp. 47–48.

31. For a classic statement of this older vision of citizenship, see Sheldon S. Wolin, *Politics and Vision* (Boston: Little, Brown and Co., 1960),

pp. 9–11. In line with Wolin's delineation of the term "political," a society deserves to be thought of as a "polis" to the extent that it transcends groupism.

32. It is of decisive importance in this connection that one distinguish between countries like Israel and (contemporary) Germany, where citizenship laws are based on ethnic criteria, and countries like Canada and France, where citizenship laws avoid ethnic criteria. As is pointed out in a perceptive Toronto *Globe and Mail* editorial ("Behind Europe's fear of the foreigner," 21 June 1993, p. A10), there is a disturbing tendency, in France for example, in the direction of ethnically defined citizenship. For further discussion of this contrast between the French "state-centered" conception and the German "*Volk*-centered" conception, see Brubaker, "Introduction," pp. 7–9; and William Rogers Brubaker, "Immigration, Citizenship, and the Nation-State in France and Germany: A Comparative Historical Analysis," *International Sociology* Vol. 5, No. 4 (December 1990), pp. 379–407. See also Michael Ignatieff, *Blood and Belonging* (Toronto: Viking, 1993), pp. 3–10. I am much indebted to Nissim Rejwan for giving me a sharper angle on these questions, particularly on the issue of how nationalism contradicts the universalistic implications of the idea of citizenship.

33. Among the forms of social cleavage that may or may not coincide with national-ethnic cleavages, religion, of course, looms extremely large. One thinks, for instance, of recent efforts by Hindu extremists to subvert the tradition of secularism in post-colonial India. See Amartya Sen, "The Threats to Secular India," *The New York Review of Books*, 8 Apr. 1993, pp. 26–32.

34. I have tried to develop this reading of Rousseau in an essay entitled "Machiavelli, Hobbes, and Rousseau on Civil Religion," *The Review of Politics* Vol. 55, No. 4 (Fall, 1993), pp. 617–638. What I draw from Book 4, chapter 8 of Rousseau's *Social Contract* is the following schema:

liberalism = Christianity = anti-civic
nationalism = the "national religions" = parochial, inhuman
citizenship = the non-existent civil religion that would combine, impossibly, the universalism of Christianity and the civic character of the national religions.

35. Jean-Jacques Rousseau, *On the Social Contract*, ed. Roger D. Masters, trans. Judith R. Masters (New York: St. Martin's Press, 1978), p. 162.

36. Jean-Jacques Rousseau, *The First and Second Discourses*, ed. Roger D. Masters, trans. Roger D. and Judith R. Masters (New York: St. Martin's Press, 1964), p. 160.

37. It strikes me that the message of *The Satanic Verses* is in this respect exactly the same as the *Social Contract* (both books, on my reading, are committed to the dual teaching of the soullessness of cosmopolitanism and the inhumanity of tribalism), and it is interesting that in the twentieth-century case no differently than in the eighteenth-century case, the inner ambivalence of the author in relation to the contest between tribalism and cosmopolitanism does not spare his book the fate of being burned by members of his own tribe.

38. The same applies to Hegel's idea of citizenship as combining in a higher synthesis the substantiality of preliberal political community with liberalism's respect for universal humanity. Hegel, however, entertained the extravagant assumption that the historical evolution of the modern state somehow guaranteed the emergence of this synthesis. I fully share Hegel's aspiration for something more robust than liberal citizenship that does not involve relinquishing liberal principles, but I see nothing in the cultural and political experience of the last two centuries that warrants Hegel's confidence that the conditions for the realization of his civic ideal are already inscribed in the historical reality of the modern state.

39. I owe non-Canadians some words of explanation. Pierre Trudeau, Prime Minister of Canada between 1968 and 1984, left as his main legacy for the country a Charter of Rights and Freedoms that brought about a major shift away from Canada's tradition of parliamentary supremacy in the direction of a more American tradition of individual rights upheld by a Supreme Court. Trudeau and his followers fought strenuously, and so far successfully, against two major constitutional initiatives by the Mulroney government (the first, defeated in 1990; the second, defeated in 1992) that would have strengthened the prerogatives of collectivities. The argument of Trudeau and the Trudeauites is that these initiatives are a betrayal of the Charter's vision of the equal citizenship of rights-bearing individuals throughout the polity. Jacques Parizeau, current leader of the Parti Québécois, the nationalist-separatist party in Quebec, was equally opposed to the Mulroney constitutional initiatives. In his case, however, the grounds of opposition were not that too much was being conceded to the claims of collectivities, but rather that not enough (at least as concerns Quebec) was being conceded to collective aspirations.

40. It is a nice illustration of the ironies of Canadian citizenship that the leading spokesperson of "Anglo" liberalism in Canada is a French-Canadian!

41. In particular, my formula makes it seem as if nationalism were absent on the Czech side of the new border. As a corrective, it is worth noting that the new citizenship law adopted in the Czech Republic reposes on an ethnic classification that has the consequence that many Gypsies who had been citizens of Czechoslovakia find themselves stripped of Czech citizenship, notwithstanding the fact that they had been born on Czech soil; in this respect, the new law appears to follow the exclusivist German model rather than the inclusivist French model (see note 32 above).

42. I allude to this problem of why liberalism and nationalism offer unsatisfactory alternatives to each other in *What's the Matter With Liberalism?*, p. 123 and p. 110, note 33.

43. Lord Acton, *Essays on Freedom and Power* (Cleveland: Meridian Books, 1955), p. 160.

44. See Edward Said's defense of Palestinian nationalism in Rushdie, *Imaginary Homelands*, p. 183: one cherishes national particularity because "twentieth-century mass society has destroyed identity in so powerful a way." Cf. Alasdair MacIntyre, *Whose Justice? Which Rationality?* (Ind: University of Notre Dame Press, 1988), p. 388: "rootless cosmopolitanism. . . is the fate toward which modernity moves."

45. Rushdie, *Imaginary Homelands*, p. 175. It is striking that Said and Rushdie are so keen to unearth a distinctive Palestinian national identity, notwithstanding their remarks in celebration of hybridity and mongrelization cited elsewhere in this essay. They seem to allow themselves a little bit of irony here, but not so much irony as to upset their political purpose.

46. The seamy side of nationalism will be conceded by any nationalist who stops to reflect on *another* people's nationalism, rather than that of one's own people. By the same token, nationalists are more likely to acknowledge the extent to which the division of the human race into nations is governed by the contingent, the arbitrary, the accidental, when they consider their enemies. Note, for instance, how the moral arbitrariness of nations gets recognized in the opposing ideologies of two arch-nationalists: the pan-Arabism of Saddam Hussein, according to which the distinction between the Iraqi and the Kuwaiti nation is artificial; and the pan-Arabism of Ariel Sharon, according to which the distinction between the Jordanian and the Palestinian nation is artificial. If even diehard nationalists like these are able to realize, however perversely, the dependence upon paltry accidents of history of the boundaries between seemingly established nations, then perhaps there is some ground for hope that more moderate

nationalists will come to entertain similar insights into the contingency and evident arbitrariness of national differences.

47. For an excellent panorama of the various current debates, as well as a very helpful bibliography, see chapter 10 in this volume.

48. See, for example, Wilson Carey McWilliams, "Democracy and the Citizen: Community, Dignity, and the Crisis of Contemporary Politics in America," in *How Democratic Is The Constitution?*, ed. Robert A. Goldwin and William A. Schambra (Washington: American Enterprise Institute, 1980), pp. 79–101; and Sheldon Wolin, "What Revolutionary Action Means Today," in *Dimensions of Radical Democracy: Pluralism, Citizenship and Community*, ed. Chantal Mouffe (London & New York: Verso, 1992), pp. 240–253. For a good elaboration of a paradigmatically liberal idea of citizenship, see Judith N. Shklar, *American Citizenship: The Quest for Inclusion* (Cambridge, Mass.: Harvard University Press, 1991).

49. For some contemporary samples of the "high citizenship" view, see Hannah Arendt, *On Revolution* (New York: Viking Press, 1965); Quentin Skinner, "On Justice, the Common Good and the Priority of Liberty," in *Dimensions of Radical Democracy*, ed. Mouffe (London and New York: Verso, 1992), pp. 211–224; Charles Taylor, "Alternative Futures," in Taylor, *Reconciling the Solitudes*, ed. Guy Laforest (Montreal & Kingston: McGill-Queen's University Press, 1993), pp. 59–119. For critical responses to the republican tradition, see chapters 2, 3, 4, 5, 6, and 10 in this volume.

— 1 —

The Ideal of Citizenship
Since Classical Times

J. G. A. Pocock

When we speak of the "ideal" of "citizenship" since "classical" times, the last term refers to times that are "classical" in a double sense. In the first place, these times are "classical" in the sense that they are supposed to have for us the kind of authority that comes of having expressed an "ideal" in durable and canonical form—though in practice the authority is always conveyed in more ways than by its simple preservation in that form. In the second place, by "classical" times, we always refer to the ancient civilizations of the Mediterranean, in particular to Athens in the fifth and fourth centuries B.C. and to Rome from the third century B.C. to the first A.D. It is Athenians and Romans who are supposed to have articulated the "ideal of citizenship" for us, and their having done so is part of what makes them "classical." There is not merely a "classical" ideal of citizenship articulating what citizenship is; "citizenship" is itself a "classical ideal," one of the fundamental values that we claim is inherent in our "civilization" and its "tradition." I am puting these words in quotation marks not because I wish to discredit them, but because I wish to focus attention upon them; when this is done, however, they will turn out to be contestable and problematic.

The "citizen"—the Greek *polites* or Latin *civis*—is defined as a member of the Athenian *polis* or Roman *res publica*, a form of human association allegedly unique to these ancient Mediterranean peoples and by them transmitted to "Europe" and "the West." This claim to uniqueness can be criticized and relegated to the status of myth; even when this happens, however, the myth has a way of remaining unique as a determinant of "Western" identity—no other civilization has a myth like this. Unlike the great coordinated societies that arose in the river valleys of Mesopotamia, Egypt, or China, the *polis* was a small society, rather exploitatively than intimately related to its productive environment, and perhaps originally not much more than a stronghold of barbarian raiders. It could therefore focus its attention less on its presumed place in a cosmic order of growth and recurrence, and more on the heroic individualism of the relations obtaining between its human members; the origins of humanism are to that extent in barbarism. Perhaps this is why the foundation myths of the *polis* do not describe its separation from the great cosmic orders of Egypt or Mesopotamia, but its substitution of its own values for those of an archaic tribal society of blood feuds and kinship obligations. Solon and Kleisthenes, the legislators of Athens, substitute for an assembly of clansmen speaking as clan members on clan concerns an assembly of citizens whose members may speak on any matter concerning the *polis* (in Latin, on any *res publica*, a term which is transferred to denote the assembly and the society themselves). In the *Eumenides,* the last play in Aeschylus's *Oresteia,* another fundamental expression of foundation myth, Orestes comes on the scene as a blood-guilty tribesman and leaves it as a free citizen capable with his equals of judging and resolving his own guilt. It is, however, uncertain whether the blood-guilt has been altogether wiped out or remains concealed at the foundations of the city—there are Roman myths that express the same ambivalence—and the story is structured in such a way that women easily symbolize the primitive culture of blood, guilt, and kinship which the males, supposedly, are trying to surpass. But the men, as heroes, continue to act out the primitive values (and to blame the women for it).

This is a point that must be made strongly, and made all the time, but it does not remove the fact that, stated as an ideal, the community of citizens is one in which speech takes the place of blood, and acts of decision take the place of acts of vengeance. The "classical" account of citizenship as an Athenian "ideal" is to be found in Aristotle's *Politics,* a text written late enough in *polis* history—after the advent of the Platonic academy and the Macedonian Empire—to qualify as one of the meditations of the Owl of Minerva. In this great work, we are told that the citizen is one who both rules and is ruled. As intelligent and purposive beings we desire to direct that which can be directed toward some purpose; to do so is not just an operational good, but an expression of that which is best in us, namely the capacity to pursue operational goods. Therefore it is good to rule. But ruling becomes better in proportion as that which is ruled is itself better, namely, endowed with some capacity of its own for the intelligent pursuit of good. It is better to rule animals than things, slaves than animals, women than slaves, one's fellow citizens than the women, slaves, animals, and things contained in one's household. But what makes the citizen the highest order of being is his capacity to rule, and it follows that rule over one's equal is possible only where one's equal rules over one. Therefore the citizen rules and is ruled; citizens join each other in making decisions where each decider respects the authority of the others, and all join in obeying the decisions (now known as "laws") they have made.

This account of human equality excludes the greater part of the human species from access to it. Equality, it says, is something of which only a very few are capable, and we in our time know, at least, that equality has prerequisites and is not always easy to achieve. For Aristotle the prerequisites are not ours; the citizen must be a male of known genealogy, a patriarch, a warrior, and the master of the labor of others (normally slaves), and these prerequisites in fact outlasted the ideal of citizenship, as he expressed it, and persisted in Western culture for more than two millennia. Today we all attack them, but we haven't quite got rid of them yet, and this raises the uncomfortable question of whether they are accidental or in some way essential to the ideal of citizenship itself. Is it possible to eliminate race, class, and gender as prerequisites to the condition of ruling and being ruled, to participate as equals in the taking of public decisions, and leave the classical description of that condition in other respects unmodified? Feminist theorists have had a great deal to say on this question, and I should like to defer to them— and leave it to them to speak about it. At an early point in the exposition of the problem, one can see that they face a choice between citizenship as a condition to which women should have access, and subverting or deconstrucing the ideal itself as a device constructed in order to exclude them. To some extent this is a rhetorical or tactical choice, and therefore philosophically vulgar, but there are real conceptual difficulties behind it.

Aristotle's formulation depends upon a rigorous separation of public from private, of *polis* from *oikos*, of persons and actions from things. To qualify as a citizen, the individual must be the patriarch of a household or *oikos*, in which the labor of slaves and women satisfied his needs and left him free to engage in political relationships with his equals. But to engage in those relationships, the citizen must leave his household altogether behind, maintained by the labor of his slaves and women, but playing no further part in his concerns. The citizens would never dream of discussing their household affairs with one another, and only if things had gone very wrong indeed would it be necessary for them to take decisions in the assembly designed to ensure patriarchal control of the households. In the para-feminist satires of Aristophanes they have to do this, but they haven't the faintest idea how to set about it; there is no available discourse, because the situation is unthinkable. What they discuss and decide in the assembly is the affairs of the *polis* and not the *oikos*: affairs of war and commerce between the city and other cities, affairs of preeminence and emulation, authority and virtue, between the citizens themselves. To Aristotle and many others, politics (alias the activity of ruling and being ruled) is a good in itself, not the prerequisite of the public good but the public good or *res publica* correctly defined. What matters is the freedom to take part in public decisions, not the content of the decisions taken. This nonoperational or noninstrumental definition of politics has remained part of our definition of freedom ever since and explains the role of citizenship in it. Citizenship is not just a means to being free; it is the way of being free itself. Aristotle based his definition of citizenship on a very rigorous distinction between ends and means, which makes it an ideal in the strict sense that it entailed an escape from the *oikos*, the material infrastructure in which one was forever managing the instruments of action, into the *polis*, the ideal superstructure in which one took actions which were not means to ends but ends in themselves. Slaves would never escape from the material because they were destined to remain instruments, things managed by others; women would never escape from the *oikos* because they were destined to remain managers of the slaves and other things. Here is the central dilemma of emancipation: does one concentrate on making the escape or on denying that the escape needs to be made? Either way, one must reckon with those who affirm that it needs to be made by others, but that they have never needed to make it. The citizen and the freedman find it difficult to become equals.

If one wants to make citizenship available to those to whom it has been denied on the grounds that they are too much involved in the world of things—in material, productive, domestic, or reproductive relationships—one has to choose between emancipating them from these relationships and denying that these relationships are negative components in the definition of citizenship. If one chooses the latter course, one is in search of a new definition of citizenship, differing radically from the Greek definition articulated by Aristotle, a definition in which public and private are not rigorously separated and the barriers between them have become permeable or have disappeared altogether. In the latter case, one will have to decide whether the concept of the "public" has survived at all, whether it has merely become contingent and incidental, or has actually been denied any distinctive meaning. And if that is what has happened, the concept of citizenship may have disappeared as well. That is the predicament with which the "classical ideal of citizenship" confronts those who set out to criticize or modify it, and they have not always avoided the traps the predicament puts before them. In the next part of this paper, I shall consider how some alternative definitions of citizenship have become historically available, but before I do so, I want to emphasize that the classical ideal was and is a definition of the human person as a cognitive, active, moral, social, intellectual, and political being. To Aristotle, it did not seem that the human—being cognitive, active and purposive—could be fully human unless he ruled himself. It appeared that he could not do this unless he ruled things and others in the household, and joined with his equals to rule and be ruled in the city. While making it quite clear that this fully developed humanity was accessible only to a very few adult males, Aristotle made it no less clear that this was the only full development of humanity there was (subject only to the Platonic suggestion that the life of pure thought might be higher still than the life of pure action). He therefore declared that the human was *kata phusin zoon politikon*, a creature formed by nature to live a political life, and this, one of the great Western definitions of what it is to be human, is a formulation we are still strongly disposed to accept. We do instinctively, or by some inherited programming, believe that the individual denied decision in shaping her or his life is being denied treatment as a human, and that citizenship—meaning membership in some public and political frame of action—is necessary if we are to be granted decision and empowered to be human. Aristotle arrived at this point—and took us there with him—by supposing a scheme of values in which political action was a good in itself and not merely instrumental to goods beyond it. In taking part in such action the citizen attained value as a human being; he knew himself to be who and what he was; no other mode of action could permit him to be that and know that he was. Therefore his personality depended on his emancipation from the world of things and his entry into the world of politics, and when this emancipation was denied to others, they must decide whether to seek it for themselves or to deny its status as a prerequisite of humanity. If they took the latter course, they must produce an alternative definition of humanity or face the consequences of having none. *Kata phusin zoon politikon* set the stakes of discourse very high indeed.

I want to turn now to a second great Western definition of the political universe. This one is not aimed at definition of the citizen, and therefore, in Aristotle's sense, it is not political at all. But it so profoundly affects our understanding of the citizen that it has to be considered part of the concept's history. This is the formula, ascribed to the Roman jurist Gaius, according to which the universe as defined by jurisprudence is divisible into "persons, actions, and things" (*res*). (Gaius lived about five centuries after the time of Aristotle, and the formula was probably well-known when he made use of it.) Here we move from the ideal to the real, even though many of the *res* defined by the jurist are far more ideal than material, and we move from the citizen as a political being to the citizen as a legal being, existing in a world of persons, actions, and things regulated by law. The intrusive concept here is that of "things." Aristotle's citizens were persons acting on one another, so that their active life was a life immediately and heroically moral. It would not be true to say that they were unconcerned with things, since the *polis* possessed and administered such things as walls, lands, trade, and so forth, and there were practical decisions to be taken about them. But the citizens did not act upon each other through the medium of things, and did not in the first instance define one another as the possessors and administrators of things. We saw that things had been left behind in the *oikos*, and that, though one must possess them in order to leave them behind, the *polis* was a kind of ongoing potlatch in which citizens emancipated themselves from their possessions in order to meet face-to-face in a political life that was an end in itself. But for the Roman jurist it was altogether different; persons acted upon things, and most of their actions were directed at taking or maintaining possession; it was through these actions, and through the things or possessions which were the subjects of the actions, that they encountered one another and entered into relationships which might require regulation. The world of things, or *res*, claimed the status of "reality"; it was the medium in which human beings lived and through which they formed, regulated, and articulated their relations with each other. The person was defined and represented through his actions upon things; in the course of time, the term "property" came to mean, first, the defining characteristic of a human or other being, second, the relation which a person had with a thing, and third, the thing defined as the possession of some person. From being *kata phusin zoon politikon*, the human individual came to be by nature a proprietor or possessor of things; it is in jurisprudence, long before the rise and supremacy of the market, that we should locate the origins of possessive individualism.

The individual thus became a citizen—and the word "citizen" diverged increasingly from its Aristotelian significance—through the possession of things and the practice of jurisprudence. His actions were in the first instance directed at things and at other persons through the medium of things; in the second instance, they were actions he took, or others took in respect of him, at law—acts of authorization, appropriation, conveyance, acts of litigation, prosecution, justification. His relation to things was regulated by law, and his actions were performed in respect either of things or of the law regulating actions. A "citizen" came to mean someone free to

act by law, free to ask and expect the law's protection, a citizen of
such and such a legal community of such and such a legal standing
in that community. A famous narrative case is that of St. Paul
announcing himself a Roman citizen. Paul not only asserts that as
a citizen he is immune from arbitrary punishment but he also goes
on to remind the officer threatening the punishment that he is a
citizen by birth and the officer only by purchase and therefore of
lower prestige and authority. Citizenship has become a legal status,
carrying with it rights to certain things—perhaps possessions,
perhaps immunities, perhaps expectations—available in many kinds
and degrees, available or unavailable to many kinds of persons for
many kinds of reasons. There is still much about it that is ideal,
but it has become part of the domain of contingent reality, a category
of status in the world of persons, actions, and things. One can say
in the world of St. Paul that citizenship is a right to certain things,
and say far more than by saying the same in the world according
to Aristotle.

We now ask: in what sense does "citizen" remain a political term
after it has become a legal or juristic concept? An Aristotelian citizen,
ruling and being ruled, took part in the making or determining of
the laws by which he was governed. There had been a time when
civis Romanus had similarly denoted one who participated in the
self-governing assemblies of republican Rome. But Paul—who is not
a Roman, has never seen Rome, and will find no assembly of the
citizens if he ever gets there—means something quite different. By
claiming to be a Roman citizen, he means that of the various patterns
of legally defined rights and immunities available to subjects of a
complex empire made up of many communities, he enjoys access
to the most uniform and highly privileged there is. Had he been
only a citizen of Tarsus, the officer might have ordered him to be
flogged, especially as they were not in Tarsus at the time. But he
is a Roman citizen and can claim rights and immunities outside the
officer's jurisdiction. The ideal of citizenship has come to denote
a legal status, which is not quite the same thing as a political status
and which will, in due course, modify the meaning of the term
"political" itself. Over many centuries, the *legalis homo* will come
to denote one who can sue and be sued in certain courts, and it

will have to be decided whether this is or is not the same as the *zoon politikon*, ruling and being ruled in an Aristotelian *polis*.

The status of "citizen" now denotes membership in a community of shared or common law, which may or may not be identical with a territorial community. In Paul's case it is not; the status of "Roman citizen" is one of several extended by Roman imperial authority to privileged groups throughout the empire (who enjoy it, wherever they may be, while living and moving—empires can be highly mobile societies—alongside others who enjoy only local and municipal privileges in communities more localized and territorial in terms of the laws that define them). In much later centuries, these municipal communities become known by the medieval French term *bourg*, and one's right of membership in them, one's right of appeal to the privilege and protection of municipal law, comes to be known as one's *bourgeoisie*. In virtue of one of those rhetorical devices that extend meaning from the part to the whole, the universal community of legal privilege to which St. Paul laid claim, and his right of membership within it, came to be described as his *bourgeoisie Romaine*, the municipal authority of that city having become imperial. But *"bourgeois"* and *"bourgeoisie"* came to denote membership in a municipal—rather than an imperial or political—community. While the *bourgeois* might sue and be sued, it was not clear that he ruled and was ruled, even when his *bourg* might claim to be free and sovereign. In consequence, although many cities and *civitates* had been reduced to the municipal status of *bourgs* within empires and states, and the words *"bourgeois"* and "citizen" were used interchangeably as a result, there was always room for doubt whether they conveyed the same meanings—whether the *bourgeois* really enjoyed, should enjoy, or wanted to enjoy the absolute liberty to rule and be ruled asserted by the ideal of citizenship in its classical or Aristotelian sense.

It was the notion of law that profoundly altered the meaning of the political. As Paul and Gaius both knew, law denoted something imperial, universal, and multiform; there were many ends of law, some of which applied everywhere and some of which did not. As soon, therefore, as one employed the term "citizen" to denote the member of a community defined by law, there might be as many definitions of "citizen" as there were kinds of law. There was a community of Roman citizens like Paul, who might claim the same status wherever they went in the empire; there were numerous communities of those whose citizenship was only municipal and did not apply where municipal authority could not be appealed to; there was half the population according to gender and about half according to the distinction between slave and free who were not citizens at all and could not take the initiative in claiming the protection of the law even if it was offered them. And there was the notion—a new "classical ideal"—of a universal community to which all humans belonged as subject to the law of nature. But whether one was a "citizen" of the community defined by the law of nature was a question that strained the resources even of metaphor. Certainly one did not "rule" in it, if by "rule" was meant determining what the law of the community should be; there was no assembly of all mankind, and the very notion of a universal law meant that one could be a citizen only municipally, determining what the local, particular, and municipal application of the law of nature should be. There had by this time appeared the figure, or ideal type, of the philosopher who, as the word was used as a classical ideal, claimed that the cognition of natural law was an intellectual activity, and that by a separation between contemplation and action, theory and practice, the philosopher had acquired in his ideal world the absolute freedom of determination once sought by the citizen in his *polis*. There are those who think the history of political thought has no meaning outside the history of this claim by the philosopher, but my commission in this lecture is to pursue the history of the concept of the citizen.

The advent of jurisprudence moved the concept of the "citizen" from the *zoon politikon* toward the *legalis homo*, and from the *civis* or *polites* toward the *bourgeois* or *burger*. It further brought about some equation of the "citizen" with the "subject," for in defining him as the member of a community of law, it emphasized that he was, in more senses than one, the subject of those laws that defined his community and of the rulers and magistrates empowered to enforce them. It would do litttle violence to our use of language to suppose that St. Paul claimed to be a Roman "subject" since by doing so he could claim protection and privilege as well as offering allegiance and obedience. This is why the last action he performs as *civis*

Romanus is to exercise his right of appealing to Caesar, after which the local magistrates are obliged to send him to Rome to be judged by Caesar, and we don't know exactly what Caesar did with him when he got there; Caesar's jurisdiction certainly extended to judgment of life or death. All this would be in the minds of Lord Palmerston and his parliamentary hearers when he proclaimed that any British subject might say with Paul *"civis Romanus sum."* In terms of protection and allegiance, right and authority, "subject" and "citizen" might be interchangeable terms, and when my passport declares me to be a United Kingdom "citizen" as well as a British "subject," I know that it is offering me rights and protections within the United Kingdom which may be denied to other "British subjects," and I am not altogether reassured, even though I am being privileged, by the implied separation between "subject" and "citizen," which once meant the same thing.

What is the difference between a classical "citizen" and an imperial or modern "subject?" The former ruled and was ruled, which meant among other things that he was a participant in determining the laws by which he was to be bound. The latter could appeal to Caesar; that is, he could go into court and invoke a law that granted him rights, immunities, privileges, and even authority, and that could not ordinarily be denied him once he had established his right to invoke it. But he might have no hand whatever in making that law or in determining what it was to be. It can be replied that this is too formal a way of putting it; the law functions in such a way that it is determined in the process of adjudication, and litigants, witnesses, compurgators, pleaders, and so forth play a variety of parts in the process of determining it. The *legalis homo* is not necessarily a subject in the rigorously passive sense. But the growth of jurisprudence decentres and may marginalize the assembly of citizens by the enormous diversity of answers it brings to the questions of where and by whom law is made, and how far it is made—how far determined and how far discovered. It may be found in the order of nature, the revealed will of God, the pleasure of the prince, the judgment of the magistrate, the decree of the assembly, or the customs and usages formed in the processes of social living themselves; and in this majestic hierarchy of lawgivers, the assembly of citizens, meeting face-to-face in the utter freedom to determine what and who they shall be, can only be one and may sink into entire insignificance. *Legalis homo* is perpetually in search of the authority that may underlie determinations of the law; the need to close off this search within the human world may induce him to locate sovereignty whenever it seems to have come to rest, in prince or people, and there are circumstances in which sovereignty may be lodged in the assembly of the citizens, so that the individual as citizen comes again to be what he was in the classical ideal, a coauthor of the law to which he is subject. But there are so many other possible locations of sovereignty, and so many ways of determining and discovering law other than by the sovereign's decree, that even when the subject is a member of the sovereign, he is unlikely to forget Charles I's dictum that "a subject and a sovereign are clean different things" and may ask whether he is the same person when ruling that he was when being ruled. This is the question repeatedly asked by Jean-Jacques Rousseau, the last great philosopher of early modern politics, and it reminds us that even from the world of Paul and Gaius—let alone from the world of Jean-Jacques—the road back to the heroic simplicities of the *polis* may be too long to be traversed. Yet the meaning of "the ideal of citizenship since classical times" is that we constantly need to explore this road back, even if we cannot travel it, and it is important to understand why we have this need.

It is no less important to represent the substitution of the Gaian formula for the Aristotelian as a highly successful, and in many ways beneficial, revolt of the real—and even the material—against the ideal and against the classical ideal of citizenship. The Greek citizen, stepping from the *oikos* into the *polis*, stepped out of the world of things into a world of purely personal interactions, a world of deeds and words, speech and war. The Roman citizen, subject to both law and prince, was constantly reminded by the Gaian formula that he lived in a world of things, as well as of persons and actions. And since the word for things is *res*, the world of things has ever since asserted its claim to be "the real world." The formula insistently returned his attention to his *oikos*, to the things and persons he possessed and in whom the law gave him property—the adjudication of which made him a citizen in the legal sense of the term. Possession, rather than the emancipation from possession, became the formal center of his citizenship, and the problem of freedom became increasingly a problem of property: that of seeing how women could become proprietors and slaves cease to be property. This was the step by which personality itself—not merely the ideal of personal freedom—acquired a material infrastructure. The rhetoric of materialism is as old as the rhetoric of law and property, and history embarked on the long journey from being the narrative of actions performed by persons to being, at the same time, the archaeology of changes in the infrastructure of things, the precondition of both action and personality. Property, from the same point, embarked on its long career in the metaphysics of social, historical, and political reality, the essential link through which personality became real through interacting with the world of things and law became the regulation of interaction and reality. The citizen, redefined as a legal rather than a political being, found himself connected to a world of things which he possessed and rights to things which the law would also treat as his possessions. He could define himself as a citizen (or *bourgeois*) of a community of laws defining his rights to things, and could go so far as to believe in the global universe as such a community, in which the laws of nature defined his natural rights and made him, as it were, a citizen of nature. The enormous importance of possessive individualism was that it made possession and right the constituent links between personality and reality, in which framework action became increasingly *actio legis*, the forms of action, action according to law. The universe of natural jurisprudence was a universe of due process.

The Gaian universe had only one defect, which was that though it was capable of being idealized, it could never be ideal. That is, it could never satisfy the hunger of individuals in the Hellenic tradition to be free of the world of things, free to interact with other persons as free as themselves in a community of pure action and personal freedom, in a political community good in itself and an end in itself. The citizen claimed this freedom through action, the philosopher through contemplation, and having been once articulated as an ideal, it simply cannot be eradicated from the ideals of a Greek-derived civilization. The Gaian formula has persistently opposed the real to the ideal; that is, it has insisted that we live in a world of things, that our actions are for the most part performed upon things, and come to be interactions with other persons only through the dense medium, the material texture, of things upon which our actions constitute "reality." How far that "reality" is an order objectively existing is another question: the point here is that it constantly mediates, deflects, and conditions the personalities we seek to assert in thought and action. There is such an intolerable diversity of things on which we act, and of interactions between the things and the actions we perform upon them, that we can exist as persons, and encounter other persons with whom to interact, only by submitting to the innumerable deflections, fragmentations, specializations, and redefinitions of personality which action in the world of things imposes upon us. In the Gaian universe we are all foxes, never lions or hedgehogs. But since we also live in a Homeric and a Platonic universe, we desire to be all three of these symbolic creatures at the same time.

Consequently, we can simplify the history of the concept of citizenship in Western political thought by representing it as an unfinished dialogue between the Aristotelian and the Gaian formulae, between the ideal and the real, between persons interacting with persons and persons interacting through things. Both formulae have left us a divided legacy. Aristotle and the ancients have left us believing that it is only in the interaction with others to shape our lives in political decisions that we are free, human, and ends in ourselves. But, at the same time, they remind us that in the relation of ruling and being ruled we are simultaneously ends in ourselves and means to the ends of others; it is a relationship of using and being used, and there is a question whether any ethos of community, friendship, or love quite overcomes that, even among citizens—let alone between those who are citizens and those, like slaves or women in the ancient world, who are not. Gaius, the jurists, and, as we shall see the moderns tell us that we know and understand better, and communicate better with one another, once we accept the discipline of things as well as persons, of admitting that we live by interacting with a world of things that we possess, transfer, and produce, and in which we recognize others as having rights of property and labor that make us into persons. In this formula we live at a slight distance from others and even from ourselves, separated by the medium of things on which we act and so make ourselves into persons; we act only indirectly on one another and see selves as created in what is termed "reality," but thus we escape the intolerable strain of interacting directly with persons whom we must consider, as they consider us, both ends in selves and means to the self-creation of others. But the discipline of reality leaves undispelled the danger of a dictatorship of things; in ceasing to regard others as merely things to be used to our own ends, may we not become things to our selves, acknowledging that we are never fully persons and that our selves remain contingent upon dear old reality? To this the jurists, and those political philosophers we have come to term "liberals," have proposed the solution of regarding the person as the bearer of what are called "rights." These are modes of interaction between the person and the world of things, and with other persons through the medium of things; persons recognize one another as human, and so recognize themselves as human, through recognizing one another's rights in a universe of shared law—as Paul, the Roman officer, and even Caesar may be thought of as doing in the biblical story. Very impressive efforts have been made, by means both revolutionary and constitutional, to convert that legal universe into a political universe, thus enlarging the rights-bearer or *legalis homo* into a citizen in some sense both Aristotelian and Gaian, political and legal, ancient and modern. This is where we encounter the liberal or modern ideal of citizenship, in maintaining which we believe ourselves to be engaged; it remains possible to ask how successful it is being in making us persons, or selves.

The Gaian formula became the formula for a liberal politics and a liberal ideal of citizenship during the early modern and modern historical periods and in the following way. The world of persons, actions, and things was imagined operating in a primitive condition, with no settled laws to give it structure. In this condition, the individual was supposed to develop relations with things through the actions he performed upon them, which relations made the things pertain in a peculiar sense to his personality, while making him a person defined by his relations with the things. The term "property" came to be used in a double sense, meaning that the things came to be both objects possessed by the person and attributes of the proprietor's personality. From a very early time it was possible to ask whether this was a sufficient account of personality; was it possible to describe the individual as a moral being simply by describing the sum of his possessive relationships? But once other beings came to recognize these relationships as enjoyed by the individual, it became possible to recognize them as his "property" and him as a "person" constituted by them, and so to define them as his "rights." By describing all this as going on in the so-called state of nature—in a world of persons, actions, and things not yet organized as politics—it was possible to describe the person as a product of "reality," as creating himself by interacting with things and recognizing others as acquiring moral being through the same interactions. The individual became a person through acquiring rights and recognizing their acquisition by others, and this process occurred in a material world, one in which things were the objects of actions and persons the subjects of their own actions. In this way, the person appropriated the material world, or world of "nature," and carried his interactions with it into a legal and political world, constituted by his recognition of the rights of others and the magistrate's recognition of his obligation to administer the law that regulated the relations between possessive individuals. If government were a matter of law, and law a matter of property, then the relations between persons, actions, and things had been organized as political, real, and material.

I am emphasizing the material component in all this because I am aiming to organize the history of the ideal of citizenship around the Gaian introduction of the concept of "things." Materialism as a tool of social thought is much older than Marxism—as old as the Gaian formula, which is older than Gaius himself, and it is part of the destructive arrogance of Marxism that it has laid claim to a monopoly upon materialism. In the liberal or proto-liberal process I have been describing, the person defined himself as proprietor before he claimed to be a citizen, and thus set up a world of relations with things and persons which he did not leave behind in an Aristotelian *oikos* when he entered politics and became a citizen, but, on the contrary, carried with him into politics as the precondition of his citizenship. This move raised many problems: how far could politics be described as the maintenance of a prepolitical and natural set of relationships? Was not the person claiming that he existed by nature before he became a citizen, and so had a natural and (so to speak) private existence and personality to which his citizenship was merely contingent? Was there a natural history of property and society existing prior to the civil history of politics? All such questions emphasized that politics had become secondary to, and defined by, the social history of property, and that the individual existed, became a person, and endeavored to remain one in that history—the history of persons, action, and things— far more than in the world of ruling and being ruled, which the Aristotelian formula defined as a world in which citizens met to decide (as Plato once put it) "no trivial question, but how a man should live." One tremendous strength that the Gaian, jurisic, and liberal ideal of citizenship possesses is that it enables us to define an indefinite series of interactions between persons and things, which may be restated as rights, used to define new persons as citizens, and carried over into the world of liberal politics; we break down the patriarchal narrowness which separated the *oikos* from the *polis*, and empower all manner of social beings to claim rights and legal citizenship, irrespective of gender, class, race, and perhaps even humanity. In so doing, however, we necessarily make citizenship a legal fiction, brought about by the invention of persons and the decision to attribute rights and personality to them. At this point we hear the voice of the classical citizen—now fully as likely to be female as male—proclaiming unequivocally that she or he is a person, self-proclaimed as such by joining with her or his equals to rule and be ruled and decide to be individuals, and at this point we have encountered the limitations of a world in which we must consent to be fictions in order that we may be free. The classical ideal—which may now be joined in alliance with the classical liberal—has identified and begun its quarrel with the post-modern.

This has come about since about 1700, when the juristic ideal of citizenship seemed to have attained theoretical completeness; the nature of property—of the person's interaction with the world of things—began to change and to be seen as changing. It had been known as "real property," the possession of an inheritable tenure in land, and this in turn was based on a process of appropriation very closely associated with arable cultivation. Humans appropriated the earth, and in so doing became persons and citizens, because they ploughed it and exchanced its fruits; the only alternative claim, made by such as the English Diggers, was that they had been created in a spiritual communion with the land because they were the incarnate children of God. But so dominant was the ideology of the plough that hunter-gatherer societies—like the Inuit and Indians of North America or the *tangata whenua* and aborigines of the South Pacific—were very easily considered "savages" and denied legal citizenship or even human personality, simply because they did not plough and were therefore thought not to appropriate. Just as these encounters were taking place, however (we can find them in Locke), it had increasingly to be recognized that the power of the state and the personality of the individual were basing themselves on what was, most interestingly, termed "personal," as distinct from "real" property: that is on interaction with things that were moveable and exchangeable and—as *res* had always had the capacity to be— fictitious, or created in the interaction between persons: property in commodities, cash, credit, and capital. It was Locke who observed that territorial government became necessary only when media of exchange made it possible for persons to interact with others at a distance; Edward Gibbon observed that the savage was confined to a prepersonal existence by his lack of money and letters as well as his lack of the plough. The linguistically remarkable fact about "personal" property was that it involved the person through his actions in the world of things far more efficaciously and powerfully than merely "real" property had ever done; he now acted upon things that were themselves dynamic and made his actions and his personality far more dynamic than ever before. And yet so many of the things on and through which he acted were fictions—were the media of action rather than things acted on—that it became increasingly a question whether the personality and the citizenship with which they provided him were not themselves fictitious and consequently not "real." Could a person be a citizen if he was unreal even to himself?

These were the historical circumstances in which the modern to post-modern ideal of citizenship took shape: the ideal of the citizen as a social being, involved in an indefinite series of social actions—actions by persons upon things which set up relationships now exceeding the limits set by possession and appropriation. These citizens are able to make claims upon others and upon the civic process itself—claims that may all, at least in principle, be reducible to the language of rights. Citizenship therefore becomes a practice of rights, of pursuing one's own rights and assuming the rights of others within the legal, political, social, and even cultural communities that have been formed for purposes of this kind. There are problems here of membership (*bourgeoisie*), allegiance, and even sovereignty, and these come to exist in two ways. In the first place, an adjudicative community may demand final authority and closed identity if it is to function properly—the buck has to stop somewhere—and may require the citizen to acknowledge that he or she is a subject, whose allegiance is finally given to some community as sovereign authority. In the second place, among the citizen's objectives is the freedom, autonomy, authority and power to define herself or himself as a person, which in this context means as a citizen of a community, and there is a bipolar danger to be confronted at this point. A community or a sovereign that demands the whole of one's allegiance may be foreclosing one's freedom of choice to be this or that kind of person; that was the early modern and modern danger. A plurality of communities or sovereignties that take turns in demanding one's allegiance, while conceding that each and every allocation of allegiance is partial, contingent, and provisional, is denying one the freedom to make a final commitment which determines one's identity, and that is plainly the post-modern danger. I recall reading, a couple of months ago, an article in the *Economist* forecasting that Canada might become the first post-modern democracy, and wondering whether this was an encouraging prospect. It is one thing to decide that being a Canadian—or, like me, a New Zealander—offers one an open range of identities, and that freedom consists in retaining one's mobility in choosing between them. It is quite another when the sovereign or quasi-sovereign powers of this world get together to inform one that there is no choice of an identity, no commitment of an allegiance, no determination of one's citizenship or personality that they regard as other than provisional (or may not require one at any moment to unmake). Under post-modern conditions we do confront these alliances of unmakers, deconstructors, and decenterers, and our citizenship may have to be our means of telling them where they get off. The predicament may be the result of our having immersed ourselves in the world of persons, actions, and things, when the production of things has become exponential and uncontrollable and is constantly redefining the actions and the persons using them. And if the things being produced are in fact not material objects, but fictions and images, we have entered that post-modern and post-structuralist world in which the languages, constantly producing themselves, are more real than the persons speaking them. We may have to resist this, and say that we have decided and declared who we are, that our words have gone forth and cannot be recalled, unspoken, or deconstructed. To say this is an act of citizenship, or rather an act affirming citizenship. But to affirm citizenship without a sufficient consensus as to the republic of which we are to be citizens can be a very dangerous thing to do. To find the Red Guards or their successors on my doorstep, affirming that I am henceforth a citizen of their republic is to find myself not liberated but appropriated.

I am using the imagery of revolution—at a moment when revolutionary action everywhere is directed at the demolition of revolutionary regimes—because we are looking back over a two-century period at the outset of which the ideal of citizenship became a revolutionary ideal. About 1700, as mentioned above, citizenship in the Gaian universe began to look like involvement in a constantly changing, expanding, and diversifying process of commercial growth, and there instantly arose a criticism that emphasized the danger that the citizen might not be able to maintain his freedom in this process, because his personality would become distracted and fragmented. This criticism engaged, consciously and specifically, in a restatement of the classical Greco-Roman ideal; it wanted the citizen to retain the possession of arms instead of making them over to the state, and it wanted him to maintain the antique virtue (meaning the active consciousness of the self as citizen) of the Athenians, Spartans, and Romans. To this the reply was made, in an age of increasing historical sophistication, that the classical ideal was archaic—that it implied a heroic warrior society, a patriarchal household, a subjection of women, and a slave economy, that its ideal of personality was inhuman and barbaric, because it neglected all the enrichments of personality brought to the individual by a religion of universal love and an economy of universal exchange. The citizen, involved by the growth of commerce in an explosively growing universe of persons, actions, and things, could affirm his enriched personality by claiming rights he or she had never before possessed and by appointing representatives to protect and govern him or her in ways never before possible. It is from this period that we date the centrality of the notion that the defining characteristic of the citizen is his or her capacity to be represented, and that there is no reason why she should not have a representative (and be one) as well as him. Faced with all this and much more besides, however, the critics of commercial modernity continued pertinaciously to ask how and whether the citizen could maintain unity of personality if constantly making over the essential attributes of his citizenship to be managed on his behalf by someone else. And they responded to the great discovery of representative democracy by asking how, if my citizenship was my personality, I could possibly appoint someone else to be me for me? It was all very well to say that I could always recall my representative and appoint another; the question remained unanswered how much of myself I had retained in making myself over to these characters, and certainly there are moments in the course of an American presidential campaign when one wonders what personality has to do with it. Are these things? Are these actions? Are these persons?

The debate continued through the eighteenth century, and one could say that it continues still. Because of this duality of values—the capacity of the classical ideal to persist under the modern conditions so deeply opposed to it—the great revolution in France was at one and the same time a declaration of the Rights of Man, an attempt to devise a Gaian formula to give legal personality to the human race, and an affirmation of active citizenship and its classical virtue, in which Parisians took arms and went out to spill the blood of the impure, affirming themselves to be the free masters of their destinies and determinants of their selves. They took to the streets as Muscovites were doing while I was writing this lecture (with the difference that Parisians showed a certain carefree innocence about what spilling the blood of the impure could lead to, whereas Muscovites know so much about it that they are understandably reluctant to begin again). Several significantly titled recent studies—Carol Blum's *Rousseau and the Republic of Virtue,* Simon Schama's *Citizens*—have investigated once more the connections between virtue and terror, the circumstances in which the ideal of citizenship becomes an instrument of collective homicide, and though this is not the whole of the truth about the French or any other revolution, there has been quite enough of it to merit invesigation. The answer given by these and other authors seems to be that once my citizenship becomes the affirmation of the purity and integrity of my self, any adversary I may have becomes the adversary of citizenship, purity, and integrity themselves, whom I must destroy if I am to remain myself. And I find it easy to attribute a malignant lack of purity to whole categories of human beings—hence the grisly succession of puritanical holocausts perpetrated from Robespierre to Pol Pot. To this diagnosis, Edmund Burke, at the beginning of the revolutionary story, added the observation that it was what happened when the energies of the human mind escaped from the restraints of property. However unsatisfying we may find Burke's description of "property," he was making a Gaian point. If persons forgot that they were living in a world of things—which imposed a material discipline that was the foundation of moral personality—then persons encountered persons face-to-face. The only instruments, the only obstacles, that my self-affirming action encountered consisted of other persons, whom I must use or destroy as the imperatives of virtue commanded. This kind of action was the only kind available when, as Burke put it, nothing ruled except the mind of desperate men. Burke, in this respect a conservative materialist, was uttering one of the great Gaian attacks upon the classical ideal; it was better to live in a world of things than to be governed by the ideal of personal action.

But we think of materialism as a dialectical and revolutionary force; I am contending that it does not have to be that, but it certainly has been. On the long road from Robespierre to Pol Pot, the citizen acting in a political community merged into the revolutionary acing in a historical process, but claiming to exert there the same capacity to join with others in making their world and themselves that we found in the classical ideal. This historization of citizenship has been the history of the ideal of revolution, and most of us find good reason to hope that its history is coming to an end; as we all know, it went disastrously and genocidally wrong, and since Burke himself it has been a valuable half-truth to say that it went wrong from the beginning. It failed on both the Aristotelian and the Gaian counts; it was very bad at understanding the relations between ruling and being ruled that constitute politics and citizenship, and there was much that was amiss with its understanding of the relations between persons, actions, and things that constitute both jurisprudence and history. Since the Roman lawyers themselves, the relation between persons and things had typically been the relation of possession or of property. Marx and his predecessors endeavored to substitute the relation of production, and set the capacity to labor at the center of the human paradigm, where Aristotle had set the capacity to rule. The worker, making and being made, took the place of the citizen ruling and being ruled. The person, by his actions, produced things and produced himself, thus creating his world instead of merely appropriating it. This was clearly a noble ideal, however appallingly it became corrupted by errors not unlike those Burke denounced in the Revolutionaries (and however much we may wish to say that it mistook the nature of the productive process as badly as that of the political). While it lasted, it offered the human creature a vision of being the author of human history, and of forming communities of worker citizens engaged in the production of history, but it does not seem to have lasted longer than the industrial technology that associated human labor with the operation of machines. While the politics of socialist revolution were destroying themselves through a series of appalling misconceptions about the relations between persons, high-technology capitalism—with its usual devilish cunning—was destroying their basic premise by the single step of substituting information for labor. The myth of the proletariat, and the reality of social-democratic politics with a role for organized labor in them, began a rapid disappearance, and we found ourselves in a postindustrial and post-modern world in which more and more of us were consumers of information and fewer and fewer of us producers or possessors of anything, including our own identities. When a world of persons, actions, and things becomes a world of persons, actions, and linguistic or electronic constructs that have no authors, it clearly becomes much easier for the things—grown much more powerful because they are no longer real—to multiply and take charge, controlling, and determining persons and actions that no longer control, determine, or even produce them. Under these conditions of the information explosion, we have—since we are still under the imperatives of the classical ideal—to find means of affirming that we are citizens: that is, of affirming that we are persons and associating with other persons to have voice and action in the making of our worlds. Whether the subordination of the sovereign community of citizens to the international operation of post-industrial market forces has been a good or a bad first step in the architecture of a post-modern politics remains to be seen.

— 2 —

The Myth of Citizenship

Michael Ignatieff

In its noble meaning, the word myth refers to some ancient story which, in allegorical form, tells us a truth about the universe and how we are in it. Since ancient times, for example, the myth of Oedipus has told human beings disturbing truths about the hidden nature of our desires for our mothers and fathers. In this sense of the word, myth is a bearer of truth in disguised form. But the word myth is also shadowed by a more ironical meaning. In modern times we use the word as a synonym for everything that is fanciful, dubious, inflated, and untrue. In this sense we think of myths as an inheritance from the past that deserves a dip in the acid bath of our scepticism.

Citizenship is a myth in both the noble and the ironical sense. On the one hand the Western political imagination remains haunted by the ideal of citizenship enunciated in Aristotle's *Politics*. What is haunting, specifically, is the ideal of a public realm in which through participation the citizen transcends the limits of his private interest and becomes, in his deliberation with others, what Aristotle said man[1] truly was—a political animal. The myth of citizenship holds that political life is the means by which men realize the human good. On the other hand, to the modern Western political tradition, inaugurated by Hobbes and Locke, citizenship has seemed a fanciful conception of man and his political nature. Man in such a conception is a bundle of passions and interests which he satisfies chiefly in market relations and private sociability: the political or public realm is a necessary evil—the institutional arrangements necessary to protect and enhance private freedom. It is these two conflicting images: citizenship as noble myth, citizenship as fanciful lie and two political paradigms—the republican and the liberal— that I want to examine here.

I am not concerned here to trace the history of citizenship since ancient times. Thanks to the work of some great historians—John Pocock, Quentin Skinner to name just two—the way stations of this history have become ever clearer in the past twenty years: Aristotle's *Politics*, the constitution of Athens; the Roman republics; the early Italian city states of the thirteenth century; Calvin's Geneva; the Commonwealth ideology of the English civil war; and the republicanism of the Enlightenment, culminating in the Declaration of Independence and the Declaration of the Rights of Man; finally, the republican despotism of the Committee of Public Safety. In each of these moments, what it is to be a citizen is at the center of political discussion.

My own work as a historian concerned the period in late eighteenth-century England and Scotland when a republican discourse on virtue and citizenship encountered the nascent discourse of political economy: economic man confronts the citizen. I have argued that one of the intentions governing Adam Smith's *Wealth of Nations* was a root and branch critique of the economic and social assumptions underlying the Rousseauian ideal of the self-sufficient, virtuous city state republic.[2] What this work brought home to me was the tension between the republican discourse on citizenship and liberal political theory of market man. The one defends a political, the other an economic definition of man, the one an active—participatory—conception of freedom, the other a passive—acquisitive—definition of freedom; the one speaks of society as a *polis*; the other of society as a market-based association of competitive individuals. This tension between man the citizen and economic man divides our spirits and loyalties to this day: we live as market men, we wish we lived as citizens.

I do not want to recapitulate my own work here or to use the work of others to retrace the history of citizenship in detail. Instead I want to do what no historian with any sense of professional prudence should attempt: I want to develop what Max Weber would have called an "ideal type" of citizenship and to use that ideal type to cast some light on the practice of citizenship today. The point of the exercise is to work both ways at once: to criticize the reality of contemporary citizenship from the standpoint of myth and to criticize the myth from the standpoint of reality. From this exercise,

I hope we will end up understanding a little more precisely what kind of citizenship is possible in a modern world, or to put it another way, what elements of the ancient myth we should hold on to and what elements were either dubious in the original or are simply inapplicable in modern conditions. When I speak of modern conditions, I mean the tiny portion of the globe in which advanced liberal democracy exists, in which human beings have the valuable and often taken for granted privilege of being free to determine what kind of citizen they would like to be.

What is the point of such an exercise? Briefly this. These essential tensions between conceptions of men as civic actors or as economic ones reerupt again and again within our tradition. We are living through such a period today. In the past twenty years there has been a sustained attack on the civic contract of postwar liberal democratic society. I refer to the neoconservative revolution in political thinking, a revolution in thought which, among other things, has helped bring Mr. Reagan and Mrs. Thatcher to power, and has rearranged most of our mental furniture about the proper balance between state and market. I want to argue that this revolution has been above all an attack on citizenship as a coercive bargain: citizenship is seen as a commitment to others which does not give "value for money"; in place of civic relations between strangers, it is proposed to substitute market relations because these enable a person not only to choose the extent and degree of his commitment to others but also to put a price on this commitment relative to other expenditures of time and money.

When seen as a critique of citizenship, the neoconservative revolution can be understood in larger terms than as a class-interested or selfish assault on the postwar welfare state. Its roots go deeper: its challenge cannot be met unless we see it as an expression of the deep-seated contradictions between citizenship and economic life as we live it in a market society. It is this contradiction, both analytically and historically, that I want to explore.

Let me begin by putting together an ideal type of the citizen as it comes to us, first of all, from Aristotle. A citizen, said Aristotle, is one who is fit to both govern and obey, fit both to make the laws and to observe them. Citizenship thus implies both an active and a passive mode: participation through office holding and election in the governance of the state; and obedience to the laws made by other citizens. Civic virtue, the cultural disposition apposite to citizenship was thus two-fold: a willingness to step forward and assume the burdens of public office; and second, a willingness to subordinate private interest to the requirement of public obedience. What Aristotle called the "right temper" of a citizen was thus a disposition to put public good ahead of private interest. Crucial to this vision is a conception of the public being a higher truer arena than the private. Aristotle did not deny that there were many worthy private avocations, especially contemplation, but he did insist specifically that the realm of the *oeconomia*—the household realm in which the material necessities of daily life were reproduced— was a lesser realm than the public. For it was in the public that man exercised his highest capacities as a social animal.

Who then was fit to be a citizen? Since Aristotle assumed that political discussion was an exercise in rational choice of the public good, he also assumed that the only persons fit for such an exercise were those capable of rational choice. And the only ones capable of rational choice were those who were free. Dependent creatures could not be citizens: slaves, those who worked for wages, women and children who were both subject to the authority of the domestic *oeconomia* were excluded from citizenship. Adult male property owners were the only persons vested with civic personality.

From its inception, therefore, citizenship was an exclusionary category, justifying the coercive rule of the included over the excluded. As Michael Walzer has pointed out, the rule of citizens over noncitizens, of members over strangers, is probably the most common form of tyranny in human history. Among citizens, however, a rough equality of fortunes was always considered necessary since inequality of property among citizens would give the rich the means to suborn the interests of the less wealthy and corrupt the state. But how was such rough equality to be maintained? By sumptuary legislation against luxury? By confiscatory taxation? At what point would such enforced equality abolish the freedom the *polis* was intended to defend? Throughout its life, civic discourse struggles with the contradiction between economic processes ceaselessly generating inequality, and political processes requiring equality among citizens.

From its inception, the myth of citizenship implied the following crucial chain of associations: political choice requires independence of mind; independence of mind presupposes material and social independence; citizenship therefore inheres only in those capable of material, social, and intellectual independence. By a paradox which underlay refusal of citizenship rights to working people and women from ancient Athens to the dawn of the twentieth century, property holding, far from being a proof of interest, was taken to be the material precondition for disinterestedness. The civic monopoly of adult male property holders was justified on the grounds that their independence acted as a guarantee of the rights of those under their tutelage and in their employ. Citizenship in the republican tradition thus is undergirded throughout its ancient and modern history by patriarchialism. As such, a civic paradigm was bound to come into eventual conflict with a rights-based paradigm of political community. There is a clear contradiction between the restrictive property-based citizenship implied in the classical republican model and the universal adult citizenship that follows necessarily from any conception of human beings as equal rights-based creatures. Yet in the thought of founding figures of the liberal tradition like Locke, rights-based conceptions of political inclusion ceded place to property-based conceptions of inclusion, and the exclusive definition of citizenship prevailed until clamor from out-of-doors—popular campaigns, first for working men's suffrage, then for female suffrage—made the contradiction within liberal theory between universal rights and restricted citizenship impossible to sustain.

To our eyes, and rightly so, republican citizenship is disgraced by its patriarchalist underpinnings, yet these underpinnings were something more than the defense of aristocratic privilege. They proceeded from a particular view of the intellectual, social, and economic preconditions for disinterested, that is, good judgment in politics. Property owners had leisure and education; they were free from a narrow inscription within the division of labor—they did not have their noses to any particular grindstone—and could thus raise their eyes up to the higher questions of political art. Moreover, since the property that classical citizenship implied was property in land, rather than in moveable goods or stock, property holding automatically vested its owner with an interest in the territory of the nation state. By virtue of landed property, therefore, a citizen was automatically a patriot.

There are two additional features of the myth of citizenship which need to be pointed out: to use modern and therefore anachronistic parlance, its antibureaucratic and its antiimperial features. The civic paradigm assumed a constant rotation of office and looked askance at the consolidation of any form of permanent administrative cadre set apart from the citizenry. The civic paradigm also stood against the creation of a standing army of paid professionals. Such an army of paid hirelings would prove a weapon in the hands of any tribune of the people bent on suppressing republican liberty. Moreover, once a citizen devolved his obligation to defend the republic onto a paid professional, his own patriotic virtue would wither away. The civic model opposed the creation of a separate army and a separate bureaucratic cadre on the grounds that specialization bred interests at variance with the general interest of citizens. In the folklore of Roman republicanism, the civic hero was Cincinnatus, the farmer who left his plough to lead the republic out of danger and then returned to the humble soil as soon as the job was done. The civic myth opposed not only the creation of a permanent political class, but the social division of labor which sets the state above and against civil society. In its ideal, self-rule means just that: citizens, known to each other, rule over each other in turn. Yet, from its very inception, such a myth of self-rule was a fiction at variance with the facts. Aristotle himself remarks that there are few democracies in which true rotation of office occurs: "moved by the profits of office and the handling of public property men want to hold office continuously" (*Politics*, Book 3). Into the discourse on citizenship there had to be inserted a discourse on corruption, on how self-governing citizens could be led astray by the profits of office and the lure of power into setting themselves up as permanent office holders, and on some occasions, despots. The civic myth is thus a myth of the fall in politics: how virtuous self-rule is corrupted and transformed into despotism by human cupidity. Citizenship implied a tragic and often nostalgic sense of lost human possibility. Civic life was a ceaseless struggle to preserve the human good—the *polis*—from the forces within human nature bent on its deformation into tyranny.

This tradition of principled opposition to a demarcation between ruler and ruled, leader and led, helps to explain why the civic tradition was antiritualistic, that is, hostile to the pomp of power, to the self-inflating rituals used by leaders to raise themselves above the common herd. The civic model came to admit the necessity of executive power within republics but it took pains to insist that a leader should always remain only a *primus inter pares*. Republicanism's fusion with Protestantism in the Genevan city state and in the American colonies only heightened this suspicion of ritual display in the exercise of power, a ritual associated with corrupt monarchies and bloated churches. Washington and Jefferson were republican ideals because they adopted the plain, simple, and unadorned style becoming a republican leader.

One essential path to civic ruin, as far as the civic paradigm was concerned, was the temptation to empire. Civic discourse was always antiimperial. Civic discourse believed the optimum size of polity should be small: the city state, where political relations could remain face-to-face relations. Imperial expansion violated these conditions and required bureaucratic administration and executive despotism. Moreover, citizens could not consistently rule barbarians: citizenship properly applied only to adult male property holders who shared the language and values of the state—it could not be extended to those who did not share the premises of the *polis*. Hence, barbarians could only be ruled by force rather than consent, and the use of force abroad was not compatible with the maintenance of democracy at home. In very different historical circumstances: from the late republican discourse of Cicero, to the civic discourse of the early eighteenth-century British Commonwealthman, the incompatibility of citizenship and imperialism was always stressed.

Let me pause here and summarize the paradigm of citizenship as I have described it so far: an antibureaucratic or antiimperial ideal of self-rule by adult male property owners, equal among themselves, sustained by an economy of noncitizens. In Rousseau's *Social Contract*, this vision of polity receives its fullest eighteenth-century expression. It is at just such a moment, as political theory enters the modern age, that citizenship is then exposed as a fanciful myth, out of touch with the realities of market society.

In the eighteenth century there was a vital debate about the material conditions of political disinterestedness or virtue in the British polity. The debate centered on the question of whether holders of mercantile or moveable property could be true, disinterested citizens. The rural squirearchy of early eighteenth-century England, in whom this neo-republican ideology of citizenship was particularly vested, looked askance at the emergence of a new type of economic man, the stock-jobber, financier, international merchant and nabob, all of the new men created by Britain's expansion as an imperial economic power. Could such men be loyal citizens if their interests were international, if their property were not tied to the land? Given that most of their fortunes were built in alliance with the state as empire builder, could they be expected to be disinterested in deliberation over public affairs? These debates, vividly recreated for us by John Pocock, show an ancient ideal of citizenship struggling to come to terms with a new type of economic man.

In the discourse—political economy—which challenged the civic paradigm, the classical civic condescension towards the economic and private was subjected to withering scorn. As Adam Smith and David Hume insisted, far from being the lesser realm of rude mechanics, slaves, and artisans, the *oeconomia*—the private realm of providing food and shelter, necessities and luxuries for people—was the essential realm of life; even more so, a society was just to the degree that its poorest members had an adequate standard of living. By such a standard, they argued, modern commercial, or as we would say capitalist society had nothing to reproach itself in any comparison with the virtuous but materially backward republics of the past. It was the modern division of labor which made such a standard of living possible, not only the subdivision of tasks within industry, which enabled dramatic improvements in the productivity of labor, but also the social division of labor between the state and civil society. The very aspects of modernity, which classic republicans regarded as a dangerous departure from the ideal of an unspecialized civic democracy: a strong executive, backed up by a bureaucracy and a standing army, Smith praised as essential to the achievement of society's essential goal: an adequate standard of living for the very poor. A democracy of property-owning citizens who shared office in rotation might be free, Smith conceded, but it was bound to be unequal and poor. A society that allowed government and the holding of public office to become a specialized function, that , in other words, encouraged the demarcation between state and civic society, was bound to be both more productive and more capable of satisfying the needs of its people.

For Smith and Hume, the state is essentially an instrumental creation, crucial to the adjudication and containment of self-interest in the private and market sphere. The public sphere is not the arena in which citizens realize their natures by transcending their self-interest. Indeed, it makes no sense to speak of human beings as having an essential nature or ultimate purpose which can be attributed to their various activities. Human beings are creatures of the passions, desires, and interests that they have: the task of politics is to find the political form that enables them to satisfy these passions and interests at the least cost in liberty and regulation. Democracy is not a value in itself in such a theory, although liberty is. The liberty which is the *sine qua non* of market society is passive liberty; the right to enjoy and acccumulate property, to be safe from arbitrary arrest, to be free to express one's opinions and to worship as, or if, one pleases. The active liberty valued in the civic paradigm— the freedom to make the laws one lives by, to participate in the making and ordering of the polity—was regarded as valuable but secondary. Hume said that if he had to choose between living in a despotism under the rule of law—one which allowed him freedom to advance his affairs in private—and a democracy which gave him rights of citizenship but could not guarantee the security of his property or the freedom of his private life, he would choose to live in a despotism. This is to make the analytical point that market society requires the rule of law to guarantee security of contract, but it does not require democracy. Economic man *may* be a citizen but he need not be. Indeed, the possibility emerges that as long as a state leaves a private individual in the possession of his property and his legal rights, that individual need have no business in politics whatever.

The relation between private freedom and democracy may be contingent and many people in modern society live the contingency of that relationship. That is to say, they conceive of participation in the elective process as a vestigial duty, rather like going to church. It really has nothing to do with them, and as long as they are left alone, they are happy to leave politics to others. Apathy or disinterest of this sort is one of the great privileges of the tiny fraction of the world which calls itself "democratic." In most of the world, people are not free to pick or choose their relation to the political. In societies like Argentina in the late 1970s, citizenship was abolished altogether; in others, like Mao's China under the Red Guards, citizenship was enforced to the exclusion of all private rights.

Hume could envisage—and the Committee of Public Safety of the French Revolution certainly validated his prediction—a radical deformation of the civic tradition in which the communitarian bias of the civic discourse, its subordination of the private realm to public duty, would legitimize real tyranny. Majoritarian tyranny in all its modern forms—from Jacobin democracy through modern totalitarianism—has always exploited the public spiritedness associated with the word citizen: in such regimes, the "good citizen" is the one who denounces and informs on his neighbors, the one who sets aside *bourgeois* moral scruple and submits his will to what the authorities deem to be the public good. Germans who stood by while their Jewish neighbors were deported were "good citizens." Aristotle had not envisaged a situation in which a good citizen was not also a good man.

We can read these eighteenth-century debates now as matters of archival curiosity or we can try to formulate them in modern form. This classical discourse on citizenship, however dated, however disgraced its premises may now seem, still retains the power to enable us to pose still valid questions of modern citizenship: what are the conditions of political disinterestedness? what exactly ties our material interests to the interests of our country? do the harried conditions of modern life—our inscription in a narrow division of labor and our restricted leisure—disable our political judgment? If, as we rightly think, we cannot let our politics beome the sport of a monied aristocracy, who would fit the criterion of ancient civic-mindedness, how will we, ordinary harried citizens that we are, approximate to these ancient virtues? Or is the ancient paradigm asking too much of us?

If we put our faith in a majoritarian democracy based on universal citizenship in preference to an aristocratic democracy based on a minority franchise, it is because we have ceased to believe in the natural disinterestedness of aristocracies and because we believe that in the exercise of mass suffrage, the prejudices and interests of minorities cancel out each other in the will of a majority. The trouble is, of course, that majorities make mistakes: democracies safeguard themselves against these mistakes by the requirement of regular elections and by the entrenchment of rights of minorities which protect individuals from the zealous tyranny of majority rule. In other words, entrenched rights and democratic constitutions are held to compensate for the potential lack of disinterested virtue in electoral majorities.

In the republican civic paradigm, the virtue of citizens is held to be the ultimate guarantee of good government. In the literal politics that sought to make its peace with economic man and with the realities of market society, good constitutions, checks and balances are held to matter more than virtue. The idea that virtuous institutions are an instance of history's cunning in redeeming unvirtuous men is an essential part of the thinking that went into the framing of the American Constitution. This Constitution is the most successful fusion of republican and liberal traditions and attempts to make peace between them. Many traditional republican features are in evidence: the suspicion of standing armies, the entrenchment of the right to bear arms; yet the ascription of sovereignty to "we the people" is qualified both by entrenchment in a written constitution of rights that "we the people" are not allowed to abuse; and by the creation of checks and balances between executive, legislative and judicial branches.

The question of whether civic virtue in the citizens or a firm structure of countervailing powers is the more effective guarantee of democratic freedoms is recurrently put to the test. For example, one is entitled to wonder whether, if the conduct of two recent American Presidents—Nixon and Reagan—had been put to the test of a plebiscite, they would not have been vindicated or forgiven by the American people. Were their behavior in Watergate or Irangate to have been put to a plebiscite, it would have been judged a matter of personal honesty or the lack of it, matters a judging public might leave to easy forgiveness or general indifference. Fortunately, their conduct involved infringements of the powers of Congress, and for this reason their censure could be achieved by institutional rather than popular means. The great nineteenth-century commentator on these eighteenth-century debates was of course the young Marx. Much of his early writing in 1843 and 1844, particularly on the Jewish Question, can be read as his reckoning with the civic discourse on citizenship and the discourse of political economy. For him political economy's anatomy of real life in civil society—economic man in competition with others in a war of interests—had shown up the mythic quality of the civic ideal. Modern man was divided between his identity as *bourgeois* and as *citoyen*; the former was his real identity, the latter a false, mythic identity. In the market, he lived as an unequal competitor; in the *polis* he was supposed to be a rights-bearing equal. His identity as a citizen was entirely legal and therefore imaginary (and thus ineffective) as a motive.

While subjecting the myth of citizenship to devastating scrutiny Marx remained the tradition's greatest nineteenth-century exponent. He held true to an Aristotelian ideal of man, freed from material necessity, and therefore equipped with the leisure and judgment to realize his own nature—his *species being*—in concert with others. Socialist man was supposed to reconcile the contradiction between *bourgeois* and *citoyen*. Socialist production would create the equal and universal conditions of affluence and leisure which would allow men to realize the Aristotelian ideal and overcome the split between private and public. Aristotle saw this as the true mark of the citizen. In this sense, Marxism is the culmination of the civic ideal and socialism is the greatest attempt to render the ideal of citizenship applicable in modern economic conditions.

If this is the case, why, in almost all communist societies which hold themselves heirs of Marxist ideals, has socialist citizenship proved incompatible either with democracy or with private rights? Isaiah Berlin's famous answer in "Two Concepts of Liberty" is that, of the two available conceptions of liberty—"freedom from" versus "freedom to"—Marxism showed a disastrous preference for the latter over the former. What Marx disdainfully called "bourgeois civil rights"—"freedom from"—were held to be subservient to the higher task of creating socialist man, *freeing* him *to* realize his inner nature as a communal being. If this is the case, the fault lies not only in Marxism, but in the original civic ideal which—unless balanced by the cautious constitutionalism of institutional checks and balances and natural rights as in the American Constitution—favors civic community at the expense of private right. If citizenship is a myth, therefore, it has proven a dangerous one whenever civic duty is not balanced by a strong dose of private rights.

If Marxian socialism is one *terminus ad quem* of the civil ideal which shows up some of its promise and some of its danger, it is not the only one. What about the fate of strictly bourgeois republicanism, the attempt to marry ancient concepts of citizenship to a market economy?

We have already seen that the patriarchal elements of the ancient discourse contradicted the liberal ideal of equal human rights: accordingly, the political history of the nineteenth century can be interpreted as the attempt by working people and women to force this contradiction into the open and resolve it in favor of an essentially new doctrine, in which citizenship was held to be a right of all adult individuals irrespective of their property. That achieved, however, the empty formality of citizenship in an unequal market society became more and more evident. If that eminent nineteenth-century bourgeois Anatole France could admit that bourgeois equality amounted to nothing more than the equal right of rich and poor to sleep under a bridge, then the contradiction between formal and real equality in his society was apparent even to the bourgeoisie. Marx's indictment of bourgeois citizenship—that it confers formal legal equality upon citizens without conferring upon them the social and economic equality necessary for the exercise of the right—is surely correct; and, once again, much of the history of citizenship since the nineteenth century can be understood as the attempt to reduce the contradiction between real inequality and formal equality in the civic contract of modern society. This is a struggle, it must be said again, led from below—from the working class and feminist organizations—and from above—by liberal philanthropic circles who were repelled, for reasons of Christian principle, by the contradiction between the formal and the real. It was in struggling against this contradiction that an essentially individualistic market society generated what A. V. Dicey called the "collectivist solution." Despite the libertarian and antiétatist principles of much nineteenth-century statecraft, bourgeois society created the modern interventionist state essentially to reduce an intolerable moral contradiction between the promise of citizenship and the reality of a market economy.

Out of this struggle emerged the modern welfare state. Following T. H. Marshall and others, I would interpret the history of the welfare state as a struggle to undergird formal legal rights with entitlements to social and economic security so that citizenship could become a real as opposed to a purely formal experience. Given the inertial tendency of market processes to generate unequal outcomes, the state is called upon by its own populace to extend entitlements to keep the contradiction between real inequality and formal inequality from growing too large.

As such, modern politics made a crucial marriage between the liberal and civic ideals, thus hoping to have the best of both worlds. From liberalism came the idea that the state exists to enable individuals to be "free from"; from the civic tradition came the ideal of "free to." By using common resources to create common entitlements, the formal freedom promised by liberalism was to be undergirded by the real freedom. Thus we have a polity formally neutral on what constitutes the good life, yet committed to providing the collective necessities requisite for the attainment of that good life, however individuals conceive of it.

To view the history in this way is to insist that the size and weight of the modern state bureaucracy is not some ghastly collectivist mistake foisted upon us by bureaucrats bent on the expansion of their prerogatives or by liberal politicians bent on making other people pay for their expensive experiments in social betterment. That is how the history of the welfare state is seen by its contemporary right-wing critics, but that, I would argue, is not how it was. What happened, surely, was an attempt to use state power to make sure that the market economy's natural tendencies would not be allowed to vitiate the ideal of a community of equal citizens. That attempt was sustained by important social forces: the trades unions and the liberal professions together with those elements of the business class who understood that a just civic bargain was the essential precondition of economic efficiency. Keynesianism sought to marry equity and efficiency by using public expenditure to reduce the severity of the natural business cycle.

The names of William Beveridge and John Maynard Keynes are not usually associated with the history of citizenship but they have a crucial place in defining the terms of the civic bargain that prevailed from 1945 to the 1970s. In this new conception of citizenship, the citizen could count, as a matter of right, to be protected against illness, old age, and unemployment out of a common fund to which he has himself contributed. Welfare benefits were universal; the new civic bargain was not between "haves" and "have nots" on the basis of need. Taxation was thus explicitly conceived as the instrument for building civic solidarity among strangers. Civic solidarity was built upon the presumption that the more a citizen received from the state the more easily he would connect his private interest to the public.

The Keynesian ascendancy, from 1945 to 1973, masked the long-term contradiction between the market and citizenship. As soon as western economies entered their storm of troubles in the 1970s, this contradiction began to reassert itself. What at first seemed a crisis of inflation, of adjusting everywhere to higher raw material costs and of restraining excess demand soon revealed itself as a crisis of transition from an industrial to a postindustrial economy. Keynesianism and welfarism depended upon a heavily centralized and often nationalized industrial economy built around huge extractive and manufacturing industries—steel, coal, petrochemicals, automobiles—which benefited from state-capitalist partnership. Now these foundations were crumbling: the social welfare costs of adjusting to permanently high levels of unemployment eroded private profitability and put all of the apparatus of the postwar welfare state under permanent strain; the whole apparatus of employment security put into place in the Keynesian partnership between unions, management and the state began to prove an obstacle to the restructuring of the labor market in the late 1970s. The political constituencies tied to the nationalized industries and public sector employment—the unions, local communities, and their political elites—spent most of the decade resisting economic restructuring: denationalization, the watchword of politics in the early 1980s, is an attempt to break the power of these obstructive collectivities and to force through modernization on lines that follow a purely economic rather than civic or public logic. Security had been the watchword of the Keynesian/Beveridgian pact: security in employment, housing, illness, and old age. Now mobility is the watchword of a postindustrial economy rather than security: jobs emerge and disappear, move from one process to another, from one region to another—skill not seniority counts. The logic of postindustrial growth seems to work against both nationalization and traditional welfarist conceptions of employment security. The emerging pattern is towards smaller units of production adapted to rapid fluctuations in level and patterns of demand. These units may be owned by multinationals but their management and recruitment are left to local employers. Nationalizations work in industries with a stable demand tied to the delivery of some essential and essentially stable public utility. They will not work with small companies in a life and death relation to the international market.

Alongside economic crisis, there was the experience of learning from the welfare state's successes and failures. First of all, extending citizenship rights to welfare did not increase social solidarity: it did not engender a stronger general commitment to the public interest. Instead, once the state was defined as the provider of last resort, the new civic culture unleashed expectations which both exposed a vast amount of unmet demand for social services and created new and unlimited demands once these initial demands were met. For example, instead of taking pride in public hospitals as a common civic asset, most people only noted how inadequate many public hospitals were in comparison to private provision. Small but significant numbers of dependents exploited the welfare system and this attracted disproportionate outrage because exploitation of the welfare system was seen as a violation of the tacit civic contract. It was seen as bad citizenship—a more serious matter than mere fraud. Likewise, the rising real rates of criminality since 1945 seemed to contradict the expectation that if everyone were given a real stake in society through the welfare system, they would behave towards others as mature citizens. This simply did not happen. Right-wing critics of the welfare society could point to both crime and welfare fraud as instances to show that the supposed civic bargain was nothing more than a rip-off.

The impact of the welfare state on social solidarity is paradoxical. When, for example, social workers take over the caring functions formerly discharged by family members, there is both a gain and a loss: the dependent individuals may be better cared for in some instances and family members, particularly women, will be freer to enter the labour market; but a sense of family obligation may be weakened and community solidarity may suffer. The welfare state did increase collective solidarity in certain ways: in societies with a public health service, we all accept an obligation to contribute to each other's health care costs—indeed this is very much the core of the social democratic civic ideal. At the same time the welfare state allowed the emergence of new styles of dependency and new lines of moral exculpation. "It's the state's job, not mine" becomes everybody's first line of excuse when confronted with vandalism, neglect of civic property or, more seriously, abuse of children next door. In public housing especially, the maxim, "everybody's property is nobody's property" goes some way to explaining the all too frequent downward spiral of neglect.

If the idea of citizenship is in crisis today, it is precisely because experience has not validated the postwar civic ideal that public goods would extend civic solidarity. It becomes less surprising (when the history is read in this way) to understand why of the two elements that went into the making of the postwar consensus—the liberal insistence on freedom and the civic insistence on public goods—it should be the liberal which is now seeking to detach itself from its civic integument. The two were always in potential conflict and have been so since the dawn of the market era: any emphasis on freedom as the primary goal of a market society must be in eventual contradiction with a view which envisages society as a polity of risk-sharing citizens. As long as the market is functioning adequately, these contradictions can be contained. When economic crisis forces restructuring, the costs of citizenship and of public provision begin to seem too high and citizenship itself comes to be seen as a coercive bargain.

The focal point of this crisis of citizenship is of course taxation. People begin to ask why they are paying more for declining levels of public service; or they ask why they are paying publicly for a service they would prefer to contract for privately. Where competing private services exist in education and health care, individuals with wealth begin to clamor for the right to "opt out" of public provision: to send their children to private schools, to have their operations in private hospitals. The logic of a politics which aims at reducing taxation in order to give private individuals more disposable income to spend as they please on a range of private rather than public services becomes irresistible. Yet it is clear that citizenship, not to mention equality, suffers.

Citizenship reposes in not too strict an accounting of what the bargain is worth. Childless couples pay through their taxes for the education of other people's children; young working people help to pay for the retirement and sickness costs of the aged; those who work help support those out of work; those who take good care of their children often end up paying for the mistakes made by those who don't take good care of theirs. This impersonal civic altruism is further undergirded by the insurance principle: we pay into a common fund in order to draw on it ourselves and as long as we get adequate public services when we need them, we don't mind paying for free riders.

Universality of benefits provides the essential legitimacy of the civic pact: it is not a pact, between "haves" and "have nots," but among equal partners in a civic enterprise, each of whom can count on the baby bonus, unemployment insurance and the old age pension as a matter of right. But the civic bargain is bound to come under strain if the growth machine of the modern economy slows down and thus reduces the disposable income available for the civic sphere, and if the quality of goods delivered begins to decline. We all then begin to live through that characteristic double consciousness of the urban middle class: not wanting to opt out of public education or public health but feeling that the longer we stay in for the sake of civic principle the more our private interests suffer. Ultimately any of us will take our children out of a crumbling inner-city school rather than persevere with civic mindedness simply for the sake of principle.

If I have spoken of modern citizenship in terms of passive entitlements to welfare, this is because the active elements of

citizenship—running for public office, voting, political organizing—
were underemphasized in the Beveridgian welfare state. A welfare
state generated an enormous bureaucracy only partially accountable
to elected officials. Instead of confirming a citizen's membership in
a common enterprise, the experience of any form of public assistance
was all too often a lesson in bureaucratic arbitrariness or ineptitude.
Citizenship was thus a bureaucratic rather than a democratic reality;
and as such was weakly implanted in the political culture, vulnerable
to the first plausible attack from the right on social democratic red
tape. It was never obvious in fact how exactly to make the welfare
bureaucracy more accountable without reproducing more
committees and review bodies. One of the important ironies about
citizenship is that no one wants to be a citizen all the time. Socialism,
as Oscar Wilde said, is all right, but it takes too many evenings.
Participatory democracy—the slogan of citizenship in the 1960s—
foundered on its inability to propose any solution to the problem
of democratic control over the state bureaucracy other than more
meetings. This laid the welfare state open to the argument that its
problem is the state's monopoly over the services it delivers. Remove
this monopoly, charge market prices for welfare and social services
of all kinds and the state will then have to become accountable and
responsive to consumer demand. The enormous moral prestige of
markets derives chiefly from the failure of the civic bargain behind
welfare to live up to its democratic promise. Markets have to respond
to customer demand; bureaucracies seemingly do not. It is a
symptom of the crisis of citizenship in the 1980s that most political
rhetoric, whether of left or right, addresses the electorate not as
citizens but as taxpayers or as consumers. It is as if the market were
determining the very language of political community.

The reassertion of the market model can be understood as the
outcome of a class struggle between labor and capital over the
percentage of economic surplus that should go to wages, public
expenditure and capital or profit. Certainly a class analysis will take
us part of the way: reasserting the rights of capital, increasing the
profitability of companies and breaking the hold of public sector
unions were undoubtedly central to the conservative parties which
came to power in so many Western democracies in the 1980s. But
as usual, class analyses will take one only so far. Equally important

is what might be called an "epistemological" factor: markets have proved better predictors of the future than government planning. The inability of government to anticipate let alone plan for post-industrial conversion brought back to the fore the market model's oldest claim to plausibility: as a signalling device of emergent trends. Market signals are more accurate and more responsive predictors than government-backed planning based on social science indicators.

Yet there was a further specifically political attraction in the market model besides its predictive plausibility. One of the crucial functions of the market solution—denationalization, privatization—has been to take distributional conflicts out of the political arena. When a company is privatized, its decisions about plant location, investment and levels of employment, are supposed to be guided by market rather than political considerations. Ridding companies of "political interference" means, in effect, reducing the influence of unions and electoral considerations on company behavior. If service in a newly privatized company remains bad, the government is off the hook, while the heat is on the company. The market solution is thus an attempt to take economic decisions out of the political arena. This is fully intended, of course. "Overpoliticization" is a key term of neoconservative argument. It implies that in many areas—from the economy to the private sphere of family life—a host of issues were being made subject to legislative interference in ways that were inimical to liberty or efficiency or both. Given the intensity of union-management conflict over the share between capital and labor in the public sector during the 1970s, the political attractions of privatization appear obvious: the government simply ceases to be the court of last resort in such battles. Likewise in the field of welfare. Neoconservatives argue that since the public debate about how much income should be spent on welfare is interminable and endless, it would be more efficient and less constrictive of the choices of individuals if they were left free to contract privately for such health care services and educational services as they chose. Democratic allocation of these services, they argue, is bound to infringe the rights of minorities who want to spend either more or less than the democratically agreed mean.

It should be clear that the market solution is an attack on citizenship and democracy. The consequence may be a diminution of that area of collective life—the economy—which ought to be subject to the collective will of citizens.

It is here in its definition of politics that neoconservatism becomes incoherent. Neoconservatives limit the state's powers and, therefore, the domain of collective political discussion to the provision of external defense and internal law and order. Every other feature of the welfare state tends to be regarded as a regrettable pragmatic concession of principle to the debauched tastes of the electorate: welfare benefits may not be justifiable in principle but abolition of welfare is impossible in practice, both for political reasons and for fear of the law and order consequences. But this stance in effect contests the revealed preferences of the electorate for effective social security protection. Yet these preferences are not to be taken as a sign of an electorate debauched by state handouts but rather as evidence of the degree to which in an interdependent mass-society, private welfare is intimately linked to public provision and cannot be otherwise. The modern welfare state is not sustained by a culture of altruism but by public awareness of the acute interdependence of public and private utilities. Because they fail to grasp this interdependence, neoconservative governments are increasingly confronted by the contradiction between their rhetoric and their performance, between telling their supporters they will get government off the backs of the people and the plain fact that government expenditure is either stable or rising as a percentage of gross national product. Indeed, in Britain, the privatization of public assets, far from reducing the level of state expenditure within the economy, has simply enabled the state to maintain or increase welfare services while slightly lowering general taxation.

There is also an interesting tension between conservative enthusiasm for the market and their distaste for the culture of the market place: its pandering to the taste of the lowest common denominator, the vulgarity, violence, and sexuality that seem to be what sells in a market culture. Out of this tension is born a contradictory cultural policy: the privatization of public broadcasting networks or the relaxation of broadcasting licensing requirements in order to improve the efficiency of the media market, coupled with the moral browbeating of broadcasters on the issue of violence in the media and strongly moralistic stances on the content of both the criminal law and the school curriculum. Conservatives are unhappy with a culture that appears to relativize value or that appears to stand for nothing beyond the general permission to be free. But to say this is a tension in their thought is merely to say that their thought stands astride an enduring tension between the market and the polity on both the economic and cultural plane. Those who want a culture to stand for something beyond generalized permissiveness know in the end that that "something" cannot be left to the market or to private morality. It must receive legitimation by the polity, by citizens collectively deciding this is what we stand for.

What this amounts to is that the necessity for citizenship is inextinguishable. One can be agnostic on the question of whether man is or is not, by nature, a political being, whether citizenship is or is not a human need. But it seems indubitable that, in the Western tradition, he has sought to reconcile two competing political ways: maximum freedom in the private sphere coupled with collective deliberation over the content of justice and the shape of moral value. If men are citizens, it is because they cannot avoid the constantly renewed and ever changing dimensions of this choice. The pendulum of choice may swing and we are, indeed, in a strong market phase. It is strictly impossible, however, for this phase to endure forever because the choices that have been made are too fraught with contradiction to remain unchallenged.

What, then, are we to expect when the pendulum begins to shift away from the liberal market phase towards a renewal of the civic phase? We cannot expect a restoration of the *status ante quo,* a return to the post-war welfare state consensus. In the postindustrial economy, it is hard to envisage government once again in the commanding heights of industry, simply because the acceleration of economic change makes it imprudent for government to manage areas where risks are more safely left to private managers. Government will stay out of the economy, in other words, for reasons of political prudence: in order to reduce the political costs of failure and misjudgment. In the sphere of what is now the welfare state, one can easily envisage that citizens on rising real incomes will want to spend more of their disposable income on private welfare services—health care, education, pensions—and that state resources will be increasingly concentrated on ensuring adequate provision for those in need. This implies a new contract of citizenship no longer based on universality of coverage and contribution, but one more explicitly based on obligations between those who "have" and those who "have not." There is the risk that those in need will be stigmatized by dependency and maintained at the lowest levels consistent with social decency. They are treated this way now and it is to be feared their condition will deteriorate once the welfare state ceases to be a collective social asset and becomes instead what it once was in the Poor Law era, a set of social provisions exclusively for those in need. A new social contract is only saleable politically if the middle class receive sufficient reductions in tax to offset their foregone benefits and if administration to those in need is seen to be a credit, an honor to the whole community, a sign of its civic spirit. The crucial point here is that the demand for equality of opportunity, for common starting conditions, is something more than a passing political fad or contingent political allegiance of the social democratic and socialist tradition. As we have seen, the belief that a *polis* cannot either be a community or a democracy unless there is rough equality of opportunity among its citizens is constitutive of our oldest and most distinguished political inheritance. As such, the demand for equality simply will not go away, because it is coequal with the even more basic demand of human beings that they live in a community. To paraphrase John Kenneth Galbraith, no one, to my knowledge, has ever proposed the squirrel wheel as an adequate model of human society.

Yet it is also clear that the very notion of community is changing and becoming ever more global in its reach. There is a new politics about in the world since 1945 which takes the universal human subject as its subject and the doctrine of universal human rights as its chief demand. In such a politics, dramatically instanced in organizations like Amnesty International, the responsibilities of the citizen are held to cede before the obligation to be a human being. When a man is being tortured in another jurisdiction, I can no longer regard our difference of citizenship as grounds to leave it to someone else to protest. Likewise in the politics of environmental protection, the field of political intervention is now global, since the threats to that habitat are now global. Pollution from one country's steel and automobile industries becomes acid rain in another country. When the rain forests in Brazil are felled, the lungs of the whole world come under threat. Weapons made in one nation's laboratory can end human life on the planet. If we are becoming citizens of the world, it is because the threats to our lives and livelihoods no longer stop at the frontier of the nation state. It is perhaps here that the ancient myth of citizenship serves us least well in its explicit distinction between citizens and barbarians, between those who rule and those who are ruled. As Canadians know, citizens of other countries are now wading ashore claiming our protection against oppression in countries we have never heard of. We may try to use our citizenship laws to deny them right of entry, but there is simply no escape from the impingement of their problems upon us because these problems have become ours too. In more practical terms, this means, I think, that our national citizenship and our national government are important to us chiefly to the degree that they become the instruments by which we exert our influence in the international community of nations. We are the first human beings ever to see the planet Earth from outer space, the first to grasp the fragility of its environment and the total interdependence of our fates. Our conception of citizenship will have to adjust to that knowledge; it will have to become a myth, an ideal, adequate to the way we live now. The paradox of a global economy is that the nation state becomes *more* not *less* important as our instrument for defending our interests and solving our problems in the international sphere. Any tendency to balkanize spheres or to concede self-determination to provincial interests puts us in a dilemma. We want a strong local government to be responsive to our local needs and we need a strong federal government to speak for us in the global sphere.[3]

Notes

1. "Man,"in the context of this article, refers to man and woman.

2. *The Needs of Strangers* (New York: Viking, 1984). See chapter 4, "The Market and the Republic."

3. This chapter is a substantially revised version of a lecture given at Queen's University on 22 September 1987. The lecture was given in the annual "Corry" series, which was established to commemorate the former Queen's Principal.

— 3 —

Who Needs a Theory of Citizenship?

George Armstrong Kelly

A short while ago C. B. Macpherson wrote a crisp and lively paper entitled "Do We Need a Theory of the State?" By theory he intended "great theory" in the style of Bodin, Hobbes, Hegel, Green, and Bosanquet (i.e., connecting human nature with the state's ideal values), and not simply a coherent account of empirical political processes, further qualified as "pluralist-elitist-equilibrium theory."[1] His answer was that liberals of both the normative (e.g., Nozick and Rawls) and empirical (e.g., Lasswell or Dahl) schools either do not need such a theory or cannot obtain it from essentially economistic premises about man, but that social democrats and Marxists do, and that the former may be able to develop one by paying close attention to the contemporary debates of Marxist theoreticians.[2]

Since I do not share certain of Professor Macpherson's presuppositions regarding the actual or ideal political orders, I shall not pursue his rationale in exploring "citizenship." But I am indebted to him and to others for reopening the question of the state, because I doubt whether a reasoned analysis of the concept of citizenship can make very much sense without it, even though we must realistically allow that the citizen's activity is pluralistic and not exclusively state-oriented.

Today's problematic nature of citizenship (in the democracies, and especially the United States) is in part linked to the demise of the concept of the state in the twentieth century, the very time when the powers of the empirical state were growing inordinately. That demise was related to a sequence of factors that are in no sense joined propositionally: (1) A revulsion against the notion of "state" emerged from the brutalization of peoples by state action in World

Wars I and II and in the demonic practices of totalitarianism. (2) "State" was further stigmatized by linkage with a superannuated idealism of the nation's corporate will, which now either passed into the equally mystical notion of "society"—sometimes an idealized world order—or was dispelled by empirical analysis and the decompositional method. (3) Marxist theory, increasingly influential, tended to reduce the state to an epiphenomenon of economic domination and class struggle. (4) Liberal theory, which had traditionally preached a minimal and consensual state with formal-legal anchorage, tended more and more to identify the state with the coercive power of regimes and to confuse it with the realm of unfreedom. (5) In the United States, whose new modes of political science would achieve hegemony by midcentury, the national experience had stressed a diffused notion of political community overweighed by the activity of voluntary associations and private profit-making corporations. (6) That political science, as it abandoned institutional analysis for behavioral analysis in the presumed interest of greater realism and empirical specificity, strove to eliminate the notion of state altogether, substituting such concepts as "group," "political system," and "political process," and allying its manner of analysis with parallel developments in psychology and sociology.[3] (7) That same political science also tended to see the functions and jurisdictions of the state (or whatever other term was used) as the arena of countervailing social and economic forces—at most, as a regulator of pluralism without independent majesty; at the minimum, as a "black box" where they resolved their periodically shifting claims.[4]

Two chief impulses were at work: one was to attack the state as inhospitable to human values, whether these were of a higher or an ordinary sort; the other was to render it analytically innocuous for political science. In both cases there was an attempt to achieve "demythification" in the service of a curious rationality by which free men could be conceived and studied as objects of science.

Many of the same influences that produced the banishment of the state both as a source of veneration and as an object of inquiry remain potent today. Even within political philosophy itself, welfare liberals like Rawls, minimalists like Hayek and Nozick, conservatives like Oakeshott, and communitarians like Nisbet are all either vocally or tacitly skeptical of the state's right or capacity to inaugurate justice, embody the common interest, or promote freedom.

But it is no clearer today than it was a generation ago whether Leviathan is (or ought to be) analytically null or whether it is the *bête infernale*. A paradox of its continuing existence and extension of function is well expressed by Giovanni Sartori:

> Though the state expands, political processes can no longer be contained within, or brought under, its institutions. Consequently, the concept of state gives way to the broader and more flexible idea of the political system....This leads to a dilution of the concept of politics which comes very close to vaporizing it [i.e., politics] out of existence.[5]

Can it be possible that the expansion of the state—an entity declared nugatory as early as Bentley—destroys its own concept and comes close to "vaporizing" the concept of politics itself? If we do without the concept, how are we to judge the realities? The relentlessly behavioralist concept of politics—*who gets what, when, how*—does not, of course, need any corresponding notion of the state, for it might as easily apply to a family, a faction, a firm, or a farm. But our conventional concept of politics—the public business—unless totally unmasked and deprived of substance, does require the regulative notion of a state, not just because it is there, but because men must be guided in how they use it. There was surely a concept as well as a structure of the state at a time when political involvement was reserved to ascriptive minorities. This may be true as well in an age when the empirical state, incredibly distended and entangled in its social jurisdictions, discourages unflinching qualities of political vision as well as the analyst's ability to account for its precise boundaries and accepted criteria of legitimation. Indeed, the so-called legitimation crisis and the postliberal intensification of the "administration of things" also seem to combine in blurring our conception of the proper sphere of the citizen.

No one can doubt that the empirical state persists today and is perceived as such by its indwellers. "Modernized" Westerners deplore the state's cost, waste, and corruption; seek security beneath its umbrella; and scramble for its uneven distributions. State expenditures in the modern Western democracies now approach or exceed 40 percent of the gross national product.[6] The inhabitants of "people's republics" know all too well what a state is and what it can do. Four score of Third World countries are more or less precariously trying to build and maintain states, which are sometimes the only integrating factor of their elusive commonality. "Welfare state" is a term embedded in ordinary language. Despite the relative military or economic impotence of certain countries, neither world opinion nor international organizations nor multinational corporations have rendered the state's armature a fiction or caused any basic collapse of the state's value as a vehicle of common law. Instances of violence superficially perceived as revolutionary (i.e., directed toward the overthrow of the state and its powers) often turn out, on closer examination, to be representational conflicts (i.e., directed toward the regime) over the distribution of material or moral goods that the state is in a position to grant, but not without the pain of change.[7] Western Marxists are suddenly discovered debating the issue of the "relative autonomy of the state."[8] And I would judge that a return to the "theory of the state," however tentative, betokens not just a weariness with the trivialities of empiricism but also a disillusion with the disguised idealism that was supposed to lead beyond the nation-state.

What, then, would be a satisfactory normative description of the state? My cursory remarks will be vulnerable to criticisms on all flanks. Nevertheless, they must be hazarded. I begin with Georges Burdeau's observation that "the state is...the form by which the group finds its unity in submission to law."[9] This means, in brief, that the state is not a nation; neither is it an express form of regime, nor "the people," nor a gestalt of the agents of government. It also means that the state is the embodiment, although not necessarily the source, of law (the mysterious word *sovereignty* is often shipwrecked on this issue). At its core, the state is a juridical ensemble that enables men—especially strangers—to live together in relative peace, intelligible concord, and with reasonable expectations of one another's performances. This necessarily implies coercion and punishment, but it implies much more. In Avineri's brilliant gloss on Hegel, the state is both *instrumental* and *immanent*.[10] It is instrumental because it secures the peace that permits persons a higher vision as expressed through their talents and particularity.

It is immanent because it is the general form by which man's aspiration is reconciled with his actuality in the secular sphere.

Thus, the state is neither merely juridical, nor is it simply an alien apparatus correcting man's social vices, although it must sometimes be called on to protect some from others or even from themselves. As I have written elsewhere:

> The state is a network of exchanged benefits and beliefs, a reciprocity between rulers and citizens based on laws and procedures amenable to the maintenance of community. These procedures are expressive of the widest range of mutual initiative and compliance that the members can regularly practice, and they depend on a consensus that asserts individual freedoms while accepting such constraints [or sacrifices] as are necessary to the cohesion and self-respect of the whole.... Self-defense, self-determination, welfare, public virtue, and the advancement of culture comprise some of its major values, to the degree that these reflect a common interest. The organization of the state's powers is directed toward these ends. Obviously, "welfare," "virtue," and "culture" will often collide in collective life. The state must buffer and temporarily settle these collisions."[11]

It must also renew itself for new bufferings during the quasi-eternity that politics may be expected to last.

In brief, the normative state has pacification, adjudication, and guidance functions. Its purpose is not to fulfill instantly the wants and needs of its citizenry (however organized in tribes, "estates," groups, or parties) but rather best to express the values that are its own in a lawful way. This entails, historically and globally, that the parliamentary or democratic regime is not the only legitimate form of state, although it denies the legitimacy of countless regimes (modern states would seem to have to be constitutional, that is, with the distinguishing features of garantism, pluralism, and the division of powers). It implies that the state requires the capacity for wisdom, arbitration, and authority. *Wisdom* is a function of the talent and integrity of the state's agents, the propriety of its institutions, and the gathered strength of its political traditions. *Arbitration* depends on a sensitive balancing of values, rights, and interests by the appropriate parts of the state machinery (especially judicial and administrative). *Authority*, whose failure in the modern world was so eloquently dissected by Hannah Arendt,[12] "depends on an acquiescence in certain forms and uses of power; but it does not inhere totally in persons or even in role-playing persons as a general role. It is an intersubjective sensing of patterns of conformity built on social and public confidence."[13] The task of state-building and state-maintenance is to act so as to approach these conditions. Conversely, it will be the task of citizens to contribute to the enterprise by debating their interests and values in order to cultivate a common viewpoint, by judgment and surveillance of the state's agents, by adaptation to consensual rules and procedures, by forming reservoirs of new capacities, and by practicing a reciprocity of respect. A state's *dignity* is articulated through its agents and magistrates; its *legitimacy* is confirmed or consented to by its citizens, that is, all those who hold rights within it and receive its protection.

Several points are to be noted about this vignette. First, it is not metaphysical. Second, it is suitable to a number of constitutional arrangements that will undoubtedly vary according to a state's territorial or demographic size, social structure, culture, technology, and other factors. Third, it makes no privileged assumptions about human nature: although it enjoins virtue and public-spiritedness and connects these with knowledge, it does not claim these must be achieved by the manipulation of some fixed set of moral propensities, only that they are encouraged by the regular practice of trust and reciprocity. Fourth, it assigns a special role to the art of politics, refusing to reduce this sphere either to a psychology of power or to a reflection of the prevailing economic order. Finally, it exposes the practical failing of most empirical states—either because their personnel are corrupt, or they are excessively partisan, or their reactions are guided by short-sighted expediency.

I fully recognize that my description is not compatible with a minimalist state; but I feel that historical reality itself has prejudiced the credibility and effectiveness of such a state, however seductively it may be reborn in philosophy. I recognize, too, that in my normative discourse I have sidestepped the nasty actualities of the power state— both the Machiavellian assumption that it is the brute truth of politics and the apocalyptic diagnosis that it can be overcome through a social-structural revolution guided by science. My belief here is that my own scheme—which I have described elsewhere as the neutral state (meaning *positively* neutral, not merely permissive)—is regulatively logical and possible, neither mired in the *libido dominandi* nor dissolved by some quantum leap in brotherhood and equality born from the terrible triumph of the "wretched of the earth." It is, above all, the kind of state in which citizenship is rendered possible.

Is this state, in the language of a continuously fertile discussion, *nomocratic* or *telocratic* (i.e., rule-governed or purpose-governed)? These distinctions, as we shall see ahead, are important to the rationale of the democratic state in the twentieth century. "Nomocracy," writes de Jouvenel,

> is the supremacy of law; telocracy is the supremacy of purpose. Modern institutions [i.e., Western] were developed around the central concept of law. Individual security is assured if the citizens are not exposed to arbitrary acts of the government, but only to the application of the law, which they know....The guarantees of such a regime are precious. But institutions of a judicial type are not [designed] for action.[14]

By contrast,

> What distinguishes contemporary government is its vocation for rapid social and economic progress....Once government activity has a relatively precise goal, the regime's inspiration is *telocratic* and political forms necessarily reflect this.[15]

The tenor of these remarks discloses de Jouvenel's distaste for telocracy, that is, for governmental promotion of so-called social rights and welfare activities. In slightly different language we can find similar reproofs in the writings of Lippmann, Hayek, Nozick, and Oakeshott.[16] Yet it is abundantly clear that in practice, if not always in rhetoric, most contemporary Western governments have operated with telocratic assumptions. And it is certain that explicit telocracy has had its share of defenders. For example, as Andrew Shonfield writes: "The efficient and humane modern state is 'telocratic,' taking an increasingly long view of its purposes."[17] Surely this is also asserted by François Mitterrand when he sees human freedom depending on "the reform of economic structures and relations of production" as determined by "the science or scientific approach to existing economic and social facts, at a given moment and in a given place."[18]

It is important to notice a certain slippage in the levels of analysis in this debate. De Jouvenel would appear to refer his dichotomy to the actions of a government or a regime and not, as I have defined it, the state. Hayek, who finds the notion of a state inadmissible (except in international relations),[19] bases his defense of the "Great Society" on the nomocratic "conception of the common welfare or of the public good," further defined as a "catallaxy."[20] Oakeshott denies all telocratic license to the general purpose or sovereign organization of a political community, while granting it to subordinate special-purpose associations, using the medieval distinction of *societas* and *universitas*.[21] However, as we have seen, Shonfield writes "state" explicitly. And Georges Burdeau argues likewise, implicitly, when he speaks approvingly of "law [having] an active function in the arrangement of social relations. . . [being] no longer a reflection or an echo, but a creative power. . . ."[22] This is of course what Lippmann, like Hayek, condemns: "When legislatures and electorates are asked to settle not more or less specific issues of justice, but the purposes, plans, and management of a social order in the future, they have no rational criteria for their opinions."[23]

The position taken here, which follows from my normative definition of the state, is that the state cannot, in any ordinary sense, be telocratic, although it has the responsibility of managing telocratic initiatives that are (and frequently were, if we brush away ideology) the periodic practice of liberal governments or regimes.[24] The state cannot be telocratic and remain neutral: this is the price that eternal justice must pay to mundane order. What the state must do (and the reference here is not only to its pacificatory and adjudicative functions, but to its guidance function as well) is to cushion and resolve telocratic thrusts that collide, threatening the integrity of the unit or the legitimate rights and well-being of its parts, and confusing the reasonable expectations of the members of the body politic. Historically, when public morale and political restraint were defective in achieving this result, the burden was best borne by an independent judiciary. Yet an intelligent citizenry can also play a role in not pushing hostile claims to the breaking point or endowing special interests with the halo of presumptive rights. And we should acknowledge that substantial telocratic projects inaugurated by a government may thwart the alternance of power that is held to be a *sine qua non* of the practice of Western democracy.

We are above all concerned with the species of state that arose in parts of modern Western Europe, the United States, and certain former British dominions, usually described as "the democratic state." This kind of state has been in evolutionary process along different national lines since the turn of the nineteenth century, with yet deeper roots in a more distant past. Applauded by many progressive thinkers prior to World War I as the consummation of political wisdom, liberty, and "civility," both in practice and as goal, it received some rather harsh buffetings in the twentieth century. The prophesied polity of nineteenth-century liberals was transformed: from a state of political rights to a state of social intervention; from a state of individualist to pluralist (or even corporatist) conception; from a formal-legal to a quasi-administrative state. Questions of leadership, organization, participation, and welfare became highly problematic. Competitive markets ceded partially to oligopolies or to the discontinuous planning of the mixed economy. Still, the credo of the democratic state remained cherished in the core countries, even though there were increasing doubts about exporting the system. That credo and those doubts, from which we can take our point of departure, are well expressed in three propsitions by A. D. Lindsay:

> Government strictly understood is necessarily confined to the few. The people cannot govern but they may control. . . .The democratic problem is the control of the organization of power by the ordinary person. . . .Modern conditions have made this problem much more difficult than it has ever been.[25]

Or, put another way, the problem has been to achieve the desired consequences of an "arbitral view of state function," including these important conditions:

The state must not be allowed to fall into the hands of men concerned only for the interest of a limited group. It must be sensitive to all, without succumbing to any one or to any limited coalition of interests. . . . [Moreover], the problem is not only that of preserving the state from selfish domination. Because "the public interest" is not a matter of fact but of moral valuation, there may well be two opinions about the rightness of any given decision. The state will remain at peace only if the government's policy is morally intelligible at least to the more powerful interests that it affects.[26]

If the foregoing is valid, it then becomes a part of the task of citizenship (however its rights and responsibilities are directly exercised or delegated) to control if not govern; to control somehow through the exertions and in the interest of the ordinary man; to control against selfish or partial domination of the state; and to contribute to the moral intelligibility of state action. These conditions modify and restrict, but do not contradict, what I have previously said about the normative state. Moreover, it is quite obvious that they are not being effectively achieved by the empirical states of the Western countries, especially the United States.

Some linguistic research will be useful in grasping the concept of citizenship. In English at least, *citizenship* (derived, of course, from *city* and *civitas*) has a number of interesting cognates, among which are *civic* and *civil* and their substantives *civism* and *civility*. Sparing the reader the tedium of the dictionary (in this case, Webster's *Second International*), I shall attempt to summarize the results of my exploration:

1. *Civic* and *civil*, responding to particular resonances, both make reference to citizenship, the relations of citizens, and the common public life. In the case of *civic*, we may say that the tone is more affirmative, even patriotic, as when we refer to "civic virtue" or "civic duty." *Civil* is more passive and, conceivably, less political: "civil rights" or "civil life," but also "civil behavior" or "a civil answer."

2. *Civic* and *civil* are both connected to life in cities, to the *citadin* as well as the *citoyen*. The latter term implies culture and refinement ("civilization"), as opposed to rusticity and barbarism.

3. *Civil* has the additional meanings of "civilian," "polite," "orderly," and "legally entitled to obtain private justice." Its derivative

civility carries all these same connotations, with special emphasis on the attainment of a decent level of culture and social behavior.

4. *Citizenship* applies to a free city-dweller (a *bourgeois*) or to the member of a state who exchanges political allegiance for the right to certain privileges and protections (the dictionary's "right to a privilege" as opposed to "right," *tout court*, is a notion fraught with some ambiguity). Some modern writers would cut this short by saying that citizenship is "the right to act in the public realm." But this leaves us with the burning question: What precisely is the public realm?

Adepts in political theory and ideology will recognize that the identification between *civic* and *city* (i.e., city-state), as in the academic locution "civic humanism," originally an aristocratic ideal, deserves further stress.[27] They will also know that, in the wake of the Scottish political economists, Hegel, and Marx, the term *civil* has been used specifically to indicate the commercial or bourgeois society that launched the Industrial Revolution—a society of "contract," or economic connections, embedded in, or perhaps dominating, but in some significant way exclusive from, the state. Indeed, the word *civil*, first used as emphatically distinct from *ecclesiastical* in the seventeenth century, became a kind of counterpoint to *political* in the nineteenth, until relieved of this burden by an extension of the word *social* (connected with the rise of sociology). Impacted in these attempts to cope with new phenomena or to reorder the received wisdom in new ways lies some of the cryptography of the notion of modern citizenship.

There is a basic cleavage between civic and civil. In our common terms of today, the civil is more oriented toward private individualism and the civic toward public solidarity. Cato is civic; Henry Ford is civil. Of course these simple symbols scarcely exhaust the issue. Granted some license of metaphor, I submit that we can profitably use the dualism to explore some of the quandaries of citizenship. I must stipulate that I understand the concepts civic and civil in two ways: (1) They are expressive of more or less historical situations in which certain social and political imperatives have occurred; and (2) they dwell, with more or less vitality, within the complex concept of citizenship itself, externally as a means of defining it, internally as a level of consciousness or principle of action in the life-world of the modern citizen.

Requirements of space compel me to abbreviate my descriptions of these models enormously.[28] The task is further complicated because both civic and civil are apparently divisible in two: I call them Civic I and Civic II, Civil I and Civil II. Although these neutral-sounding labels pack no adjectival wallop and are unfortunately reminiscent of the well-interred categories of Charles Reich, I prefer them to terms that might resonate more, for two reasons. First, I would like to maintain the ambivalence between their phenomenological and historical properties. Second, I feel that more concrete terms would mostly ring hollow or skew the descriptions ideologically, for example, "solidaristic," "messianic," "constitutionalist," "welfarist," and the like. I intend something more and something less than such notions, but I must apologize in advance for this poverty of imagination. Each model does have an extensive set of descriptive variables; each will recur disproportionately in the notion of citizenship, depending on person, role, situation, perceptions, and ideological milieu. The civic dimensions are more aggressive and participatory, stressing obligations; the civil are more passive and *zweckrational*, stressing security and rights. Some of this same sense is conveyed in Isaiah Berlin's famous dichotomy of positive liberty (freedom as self-realization) and negative liberty (freedom as absence of coercion).[29] We live today in an overwhelmingly "civil" condition of political consciousness, although aspects of the "civic" are latent within it: Almond and Verba's "civic culture" is more accurately a "civil culture."

Civic I is best introduced by the phrase *dulce et decorum est pro patria mori*. It is the attitude of the small and solidary *polis*-type unit, the self-aware citizenry where politics and faith are mobilized in a common task and members feel conscientiously responsible for the destiny of the community.[30] Institutions such as education and the family subserve or at least do not conflict with the civic enterprise. The community is confident in its foundations, defensive in its posture: the roles of the captaincy and the magistracy are virtually interchangeable.

Civic II stands to Civic I somewhat in the same way as romantic stands to classic. Most specifically, the consciousness may be attached to the rise of nationalism in the nineteenth century.[31] As opposed to Civic I, the ethos is more creative than protective, stressing liberation rather than defense. Prophetic leadership is more in evidence; the canvas of *Gemeinschaft* is far broader;[32] political arousal is more hierarchically achieved. The militancy of Leipzig or Budapest (or the Sierra Madre) is not the militancy of Marathon. In cases of success, patriotic self-awareness is often linked to the nation (a heightened notion of kindred and culture) and deceived by the day-to-day platitudes of state politics.

Civil I is a condition of mind where the heroic is exchanged for the secure; where the political is exploited to free men not from the enemy, but from the arbitrary ruler or from each other, and where "rights" are formalized and institutions constructed to guarantee this outcome. This impulse creates a "civil society," commercially competitive and detached from the most stringent demands of citizenship; a tolerant society of plural religious truths; a formal-legal society aspiring, in view of the above, to the rule of laws and not of men; and, finally a society of "civility" where, as in a great city, bonds can be forged with strangers across social distances through settled rules of conduct and with hardly a whiff of *Gemeinschaft*—a vast agora where strangers meet.[33] In Civil I, "politics" is basically a protection for the "social"; but though the two are distinct, the social forces manage to weigh on politics in both direct and deviant ways. This ethos is fundamentally the nomocracy of de Jouvenel and Hayek. Paradoxically, it reinvents citizenship—up to a point—through the granting and exercise (over time) of civil and political rights and by the representative electoral process. In Civil I, politics is legitimized not only by the dogmas of the economic system but also by the conviction that the constitutional state is expanding.

Civil II, many of whose features have affected citizenship in the last generation, is both an extension of Civil I and a break from it: it is an extension because in many essentials it carries forward the goal of democracy and attempts, willy-nilly, to preserve certain features of Civil I like representation and the rule of law; it is a break because it has also been a response to crisis conditions endemic in war, economic depression, and a later prosperity that the nomocratic order could not manage, and also because it has involved a basic redefinition of the relations between public and private and among state, society, and economy.[34] Moreover, the state now actually structures conditions necessary to the reproduction of private capital. Generally speaking, Civil II has widened access to the political process, but it has also tended to denature politics into less of a vocation or species of vision and into more of an overloaded mediating system of demands and satisfactions. Could the advance toward a telocratic order inaugurate a more forceful and organized democratic citizenship, a *démocratie gouvernante* in Burdeau's phrase, or would it stimulate the powers of bureaucracy and technocracy?[35] The complete returns are not yet in, but they would not appear to favor a highly meaningful civism or even much civility. They would not appear to control against the selfish or partial domination of the state or enhance the moral intelligibility of state action. As a voluntarily retiring U.S. Congressman has put it: "I think the American public has been right all along in their bemusement, indifference, and downright animus. We haven't done our job in educating people. The country has no goal, no sense of direction, no vision. Congress is a bureaucracy. We have government by manager and engineer."[36]

A great deal has been left out of these encapsulations. Moreover, I have made no attempt to discuss specific national experiences, which vary considerably, from Sweden to New Zealand. But it now comes time to ask, What is the impact of this on the bewildered notion of citizenship? I should recall here that the citizen (especially as he self-consciously examines his role) does not dwell pristinely in the world of Civil II or, more accurately, with a foot planted there and another in Civil I. Obviously he is in part allegiant to the nation, to which he has given a part of his *amour-propre*.[37] He knows that his country is precious to him, and that some have been called on to die for it; he may also love his city with a passion that is far from just "civil"; he may harbor notions of national greatness in his heart. He may, conversely, practice his version of citizenship through active, even criminal, opposition to state institutions that he considers unjust. Further, citizenship may signify passive entitlement, security, and the enjoyment of "rights," whether or not exercised. Or it may mean participation in altruistic but essentially nonpolitical associations like playgrounds or hospitals. It may vanish bleakly in the death of the public soul. Is the contemporary citizen confident of his status or bearing? One of our ablest political theorists thinks not: "The state has simply outgrown the human reach and understanding of its citizens. It is not necessarily monstrous, divided, or subjugated, but its citizens are alienated and powerless. They experience a kind of moral uneasiness."[38] That the state has grown and become obscure is undeniable. Yet it has, to a considerable degree, grown in support of public demand—that is, the demands of citizens. If they bear the weight of anxiety, they must also bear a part of the blame, for citizens have allowed themselves to become clients of a bureaucracy and have, probably unwittingly, allowed non-responsible and sometimes unresponsive officials to become their masters. Moreover, although it is an important one, the expansion of the empirical state has not been the sole factor in the crisis of citizenship.

It is not possible in this essay to canvass all the current problems, but I would like to mention a few that seem to have particular bearing in the so-called welfare era:

1. As the state expands there is, at the same time, an unbalanced expansion of some of the most uncivic features of "civil" society. In the ideological space of Civil I—however much it has been despised as elitist and bourgeois—a more or less flexible and shifting balance was maintained between the guidance and adjudication mechanisms of the state. This contributed to the persistence of nomocratic legitimacy. It is not specifically Civil I that caused the catastrophes of the twentieth century (although its technology certainly did), but the evil confluence of Civil I and Civic II, when the robust economic ideology and political cosmopolitanism of the former inspired the cultural, often messianic explosions of the latter. However, a value that Civil I brought forward abundantly was what Benjamin Constant called "modern liberty," akin to our notion of negative liberty. Modern liberty was not, in the first instance, participatory, for politics was being superseded by commerce in promoting the renown of the city. It was an instrument of protecting man's free enjoyment of his lawful private activity against the invasion of others, including the state. Constant saw that the danger of modern liberty lay in the fact that it could too easily lead to an excessive preoccupation with private well-being and too great a

renunciation of the burdens of citizenship,[39] for citizenship tended to become mobilized only when enough people believed their rights, security, and property were threatened. Response depended on a sort of utilitarian calculus and protected "civility," that is, the semiautonomous activities of civil society.[40] In Civil II this same ethos remains to a very great degree: citizenship is mobilized at the point of threat (at least in time of peace) around interests or issues that remain in some sense private, or at least restricted to special groups (rarely extensive to fundamental rights). The irony is, of course, that many of our adepts in modern liberty are now petitioners to a state that allocates hard goods and not just judicial remedies, to a politics that penetrates society with distributions. In such circumstances the practice of modern liberty becomes an aspect of consumerism.

2. In Civil II, where the complexities of social corporatism have revised the content of individualism, previous definitions of public and private have changed, and this in a number of senses. Of course, in its original meaning public referred to what went on in the street, open to public view, outside the intimacy of the family. Later, our vocabulary appropriated an ambiguous notion of "public affairs," sometimes seen as relating to the affairs of state, but sometimes to other matters of wide interest; correspondingly one spoke of a "private sphere" that included large sections of the (free enterprise) economy and, at the very least, the activity of voluntary associations. The notion of public and private sectors is still with us. But the terms are again in flux, as we perceive in the moral sphere. In effect, Civil II appears to present us with at least four frames of reference: the strictly private, where what we do is our own business (now considerably retracted in the economy but extended in moral affairs); the social, where people commune or participate, but the state has little or no influence; the socio-public, including a vast range of institutions—industries, universities, foundations, etc.—where the partnership, stewardship or penetration of the state is prominent; and the official or strictly public, which comprises matters or functions distinctly assigned to government. Citizenship has been conceptually disoriented because of its problematic extension in the third of these milieux. Often, the citizen operates there without obvious guidelines, with divided loyalties, with unexpected consequences, and with, as Walzer puts it, "moral uneasiness." Confusions

of the public, the social, and the private bewilder the goals of the citizen, just as they obscure his rights and duties. The dynamic of the state is to expand the public realm; the propensity of the citizen is to get lost in it.

3. In a well-known formulation made a generation ago by T. H. Marshall, the concept of citizenship was analytically divided into three parts:

> The civil element is composed of the rights necessary for individual freedom—liberty of the person, freedom of speech, thought, and faith, the right to own property and to conclude valid contracts, and the right to justice. . . . By the political element I mean the right to participate in the exercise of political power, as a member of a body invested with political authority or as an elector of the members of such a body. . . . By the social element I mean the whole range from the right to a modicum of economic welfare and security to the right to share to the full in the social heritage and to live the life of a civilized being according to the standards prevailing in the society.[41]

Broadly speaking, Marshall assigns civil rights to the eighteenth century, political rights to the nineteenth, and social rights to the twentieth. This seems to follow a certain logic of democratization issuing from the Enlightenment and undauntedly approaching fulfillment despite the terrible tempests of the past seventy years, a movement from what John Dewey once called the "Great Society" toward the "Great Community."[42] For our purposes, we can say that the first two stages belong to Civil I and the last chiefly to Civil II.

Marshall's thesis is open to certain doubts, not simply because "conspiratorial elites" endemic in Civil I have delayed the consummation of a full and satisfying citizenship, but also because of its own ambiguities. Marshall seems too readily to associate citizenship, at all levels, with the acquisition of rights. No one will question that rights are an enablement to the practice of citizenship. But it is far from clear (especially under the rubric of modern liberty) what responsibilities are to be associated with those rights. This is especially difficult to judge when, as opposed to the earlier rights that were clearly connected with the state in respect to control and moral intelligibility, the social rights of Civil II appear to be indefinitely expansible. In the words of a recent writer, "Some Americans...hold as *rights* what only the luckiest human beings in history have managed to attain, usually in struggle, suffering, and defeat."[43] Does the receipt of a right—especially in the redistributive welfare sense—actually activate or redefine the scope of citizenship? For Marshall, "the right to share to the full in the social heritage" evidently assumes that the rights-holder will make a contribution to that heritage. But is this necessarily true? Marshall speaks of "a direct sense of community membership based on a loyalty to a civilization which is a common possession...a loyalty of free men endowed with rights and protected by a common law."[44] If this is so, what is that sense of civilization? Or is it instead possible that the acquisition of social rights can promote what Habermas calls "civil privatism,"[45] accentuating divisions between the social and the political and "massifying" the phenomena observed in Civil I? With the swelling of bureaucracies, might this not encourage a new category of "negative citizenship," that is, persons tied to the state for their livelihood and protection, in the manner of clients, but basically uninvolved in public issues and public business? And might this not debase the civil gains (given the increased importance of administrative as opposed to judicial procedures) or the political gains (insofar as "government" and "opposition" become less coherent and lose the power of public interest-aggregation to the closed politics of a self-perpetuating administration)?

4. Some mention must be made of the capacities and energies of the citizen. His capacities are clearly hindered when traditional modes of access to government are blocked not only by the size and unfamiliarity of the public space but also by the breakdown of the representative process and the party system and by his increasing inability to fathom the rationale of public policy or understand the law. In Europe at the end of World War II, it was widely believed (especially by a resurgent Left and a democratized Catholicism) that mass parties, possessing the technical means and the functional virtuosity for assembling the fragmented parts of the general will and bringing them constantly to bear on government action, could manage the adversary social claims of Civil II. This hope has been pretty well dashed by corporate bargaining and *"partitocrazia."* Just as in the malfunctioning system of Weimar

Germany, the parties had aggregated interests within the regime, out of sight of the public, rather than as a prelude to public choice, they now also began to sacrifice this opaque initiative to the bureaucracy. In the United States and certain other countries whose parties were scarcely "massified," the evolution has been different, but no less baneful to citizenship. The personalization of politics (partly through the media clichés) has produced the idiocies of image-making. Potential party cadres have often been assimilated to the bureaucracy. And despite the vast increase of employees in the public sector, it cannot be said that any heightened consciousness of citizenship accompanied the phenomenon.

As for energies, it must be remembered that not only is a person's public time and commitment limited, but that the small portion of it bestowed on the contemporary commonwealth can be reallocated to other enterprises: intensely private group relations, salvationary religions, aestheticism, physical culture, barbarism, and so on. Politics is no exclusive passion that cannot be replaced. The technological sterility and bureaucracy—and the unintelligibility—of modern government seem unlikely to discourage these other options,[46] but their callousness may also promote the abrupt and spasmodic reentry of smoldering energy to the political process.

5. The citizen also faces a theoretical problem. In contemporary life he is what Walzer correctly identifies as a "pluralist citizen."[47] This not only means that he is confused by his ventures into what I earlier called the socio-public realm, but a number of other things as well. It refers to the condition that Almond and Verba praise in *The Civic Culture*, that multiple memberships in nonofficial, voluntary groups encourage civic interest and are reservoirs of citizenship.[48] A century and a half ago Hegel theorized the "corporations of civil society" in this fashion.[49] And for Tocqueville, "those associations that are formed in civil life without reference to political objects" substituted for aristocratic leadership in a democratic country; without them, "civilization itself would be endangered."[50] This reservoir theory is both attractive and plausible.[51] But there is a darker side to pluralist citizenship. The groups *may* be explicitly political. Their members may "actually [be] making claims against the state, and then they *may be* obligated to disobey its laws. . . [becoming] disobedient citizens and, in critical cases,

traitors."[52] The poignant questions of private judgment and loyalty infest pluralist citizenship. Can a citizen also be a traitor? Probably not, in any normal way, although we should not infer from this that moral claims can never supersede the state's commands. But there are two strategies for coping with this problem. One is Walzer's neo-Lockean argument that separates *society* ("pact of association") from the *state* ("trust of government") and further submits that there are cases where men owe a higher allegiance to society, being *alien* from obligations to the state.[53] I cannot do justice here to Walzer's sophisticated reasoning, but it seems to me that his assessment of loyalty moves precariously between such focuses as one's individual conscience (or the promises one has made), a primary group of stated purpose to which one is joined, the best interest of the national society, and society understood as humanity. At one extreme, subjectivism; at the other, a hypostatization of will and interest at least as mysterious as that of the state. Other writers in the liberal tradition have even avoided Walzer's careful reference to the state. For example, John Dewey, who wrote, "The moment we utter the words 'the State,' a score of intellectual ghosts rise to obscure our vision,"[54] appears to have believed intensely in the value of citizenship, in a citizenry publicly active and alert to scientific problem-solving, without much respect for its focus, at least until he endorsed New Deal interventionism in *Liberalism and State Action* (1936).

I think Walzer and many other liberals or radical liberals confuse the state with the regime. Above all, we should not take a Donatist view of the administration of the public sacraments. My own position is that the citizen (fully granting his plural activities) is bound in loyalty to the state, although it is the normative, rather than the empirical, state to which he owes his allegiance in the last resort. That state will be highly cognizant of the implications of plural loyalties (despite the damage that, as we have seen, can be wrought by mobilized single-issue pressure groups).[55] But it cannot tolerate the formalized principle of disobedience, for the appeal may be to a solipsistic, capricious, or destructive source. Since the gravest injustices of the empirical state are usually attributable to the regime, the citizen's appeal will, in effect, be from the regime to the state. Walzer's citizens can be protected—and even the right to rebellion can be asserted—by a more intelligible process than the liberal myth of how men choose to enter or leave political life: by pooling their "rights" or picking them back out of the bundle.

6. It is nevertheless indisputable that in Civil II the notion of citizenship has been buffeted by a crisis of allegiance, in both theory and practice. Whether or not one agrees with Habermas's specific analysis of the "legitimation crisis," many of his observations are acute. As he writes: "The ultimate motive for readiness to follow is the citizen's conviction that he could be discursively convinced in case of doubt," and "Traditions important for legitimation cannot be regenerated administratively."[56] This is surely correct. I am not so convinced that the replacement of "administered capitalism" by true socialism would solve the issue, for I know of no socialism that would axiomatically transform the "structurally depoliticized public realm" in a benign way. Yet the questions of control and moral intelligibility must be answered.

Questions of legitimation were also raised in Civil I (not least in the strongholds of the "social movement"), but, not fortuitously, the liberal-constitutional system handled them quite skillfully on two grounds: the procedural ground that laws made to be obeyed could nevertheless be changed by the political process; and the idealistic ground that democracy was being progressively implemented. Civil II has a deeper problem with legitimacy. First, it is not so easy to give an uncontested description of the system that is held to be legitimate: it is overburdened with transactions, and its structures and functions, not to mention its institutions, are less coherent. Second, in a period when the acquisition of social rights is paramount, these rights may be multiple or preferential; any derogation of a supposed social right may be conceived as a reason for withholding loyalty. Political "communicative competence" can only be restored when the state and its "notion" are intelligible to those in its jurisdiction, when its laws and the expectation of justice are clarified, and when its values are rebalanced.

No attempt has been made here to construct a theory of citizenship, for it cannot be done under present conditions. I have instead tried to assort and clarify the principal confusions of citizenship in the empirical context of the modern democratic state. I have also endorsed the need to rethink the state in its normative proportions and have given my views about how we might start. That contemporary states are far from the norm I have little doubt. Nor do I doubt that citizenship lacks both true civility and civic commitment. My own guess is that citizenship will be frozen in these dilemmas until or unless the empirical state changes its ways. If it should be asked, "Who needs a theory of citizenship?" my answer would be, "The state." But there must first be a theory of the state to inform the citizen.

Notes

1. C. B. Macpherson, "Do We Need a Theory of the State?" *Archives européennes de Sociologie,* 18 (2) (1977): 223–224.

2. Ibid., 226–230.

3. See Alexander Passerin d'Entrèves, *The Notion of the State* (New York: Oxford University Press, 1967), pp. 59–65.

4. See especially Theodore J. Lowi, *The End of Liberalism* (New York: W. W. Norton, 1969), pp. 310–313, for a concise indictment of pluralism and interest-group liberalism.

5. Giovanni Sartori, "What is Politics?" *Political Theory* (February 1973): 20.

6. See Bob Rowthorn, "Late Capitalism," *New Left Review,* 98 (July-August 1976): 71–73.

7. I borrowed the term "representational violence" from Martin Needler, *Political Development in Latin America: Instability, Violence, and Evolutionary Change* (New York: Random House, 1968), p. 47, and used it in a somewhat different fashion in my *Hegel's Retreat from Eleusis: Studies in Political Thought* (Princeton: Princeton University Press, 1978), pp. 207–208.

8. See Claus Offe, "Political Authority and Class Structures—An Analysis of late Capitalist Societies," *International Journal of Sociology,* 2 (1) (1972): 70ff; and Ralph Miliband, *Marxism and Politics* (New York: Oxford University Press, 1977), pp. 66ff, especially p. 83: "Different forms of state have different degrees of autonomy or independence (the terms are used interchangeably here) from all classes, including the dominant class."

9. Georges Burdeau, *Traité de Science politique*, vol. 2: *L'État* (Paris: Librairie Générale de Droit et de Jurisprudence, 1949), p. 145.

10. Shlomo Avineri, *Hegel's Theory of the Modern State* (New York: Cambridge University Press, 1972), p. 101.

11. Kelly, *Hegel's Retreat*, pp. 100–101.

12. Hannah Arendt, "What Is Authority?" in *Between Past and Future* (New York: Viking Press, 1961), pp. 91–141.

13. G. A. Kelly, "Politics, Violence, and Human Nature," *NOMOS XVII: Human Nature in Politics* (New York: New York University Press, 1977), p. 132.

14. Bertrand de Jouvenel, "Sur l'évolution des formes du gouvernement," *Du Principat* (Paris: Hachette, 1972), pp. 77–78.

15. Ibid., p. 79.

16. Walter Lippmann, *An Inquiry into the Principles of a Good Society* (Boston: Little, Brown, 1937); F. A. Hayek, *Law, Legislation and Liberty*, vol. 1: *Rules and Order* (London: Routledge and Kegan Paul, 1973), vol. 2: *The Mirage of Social Justice* (London: Routledge and Kegan Paul, 1976); Robert Nozick, *Anarchy, State, and Utopia* (New York: Basic Books, 1974); Michael Oakeshott, *On Human Conduct* (New York: Oxford University Press, 1975).

17. Andrew Shonfield, *Modern Capitalism* (New York: Oxford University Press, 1965), p. 419.

18. François Mitterrand, *Politique* (Paris: Fayard, 1977), pp. 516, 524.

19. Hayek, *Rules and Order*, p. 48.

20. F. A. Hayek, "The Principles of a Liberal Social Order," in *Studies in Philosophy, Politics and Economics* (Chicago: Chicago University Press, 1967), p. 164.

21. Oakeshott, *On Human Conduct*, especially pp. 199–206.

22. Georges Burdeau, *Traité*, vol. 6: *La démocratie gouvernante: son assise sociale et sa philosophie politique* (Paris: Librairie Générale de Droit et de Jurisprudence, 1956), p. 358.

23. Lippmann, *Good Society*, p. 294.

24. The state is of course telocratic in the sense that it promotes the values mentioned earlier (which are clearly separable from procedural justice). But it promotes these values negatively through adjudication and the maintenance of concord.

25. A. D. Lindsay, *The Modern Democratic State* (New York: Oxford University Press, 1962, 1943), pp. 25–26.

26. S. I. Benn and R. S. Peters, *The Principles of Political Thought: Social Foundations of the Democratic State* (New York: Collier Books, 1964), p. 324.

27. Cf. J. G. A. Pocock, *The Machiavellian Moment* (Princeton University Press, Princeton: 1976).

28. More detailed descriptions of these models are given in my unpublished paper, "The Civic and Civil Models of Public Behavior," from which certain parts of this essay are adapted.

29. Isaiah Berlin, "Two Concepts of Liberty," in *Four Essays on Liberty* (New York: Oxford University Press, 1969), pp. 118–172.

30. There is a complexity of the relationship between politics and faith in Civic I that cannot be encompassed by the notion that they are undifferentiated; see on this, Roland Robertson, *The Sociological Interpretation of Religion* (New York: Schocken Books, 1972), p. 84. My definition of Civic I is drawn wide enough to accommodate instances of Judaism and Christianity as well as "Olympian religion." Rousseau's "civil religion" (*Social Contract*, IV, viii) is intended as an artificial support for the waning of the relationship.

31. But not limited to the nineteenth century: the *prise de conscience* of Islam or of the Muscovite Empire, as well as developments in the Third World of today, could fit the picture.

32. See Ferdinand Tönnies, *Community and Society* (New York: Harper & Row, 1963), pp. 43–44, for the spiritual "leap" to conditions of ideal community transcending the criteria of neighborhood and immediate familiarity.

33. See on this, Richard Sennett, *The Fall of Public Man* (New York: Cambridge University Press, 1974), p. 264.

34. A classic treatment is Karl Polanyi's *The Great Transformation* (Boston: Beacon Press, 1957).

35. There is a tendency to confuse "bureaucracy" and "technocracy." Conceivably, a truly glacial technocratic administration might (at what cost?) avoid having to deal with the time-consuming interest-group politics of Civil II that encourages the growth of bureaucracy.

36. Rep. Michael Harrington (D-Mass.), quoted in *The Boston Globe*, 5 November 1978.

37. See J.-J. Rousseau, *Economic politique*, in *The Political Writings*, ed. C. E. Vaughan, 2 vols. (New York: John Wiley, 1962), i, p. 256.

38. Michael Walzer, *Obligations: Essays on Disobedience, War, and Citizenship* (New York: Simon and Schuster, 1971), p. 204.

39. Benjamin Constant, "De la liberté des anciens comparée avec celle des modernes," in *Oeuvres politiques*, ed. C. Louandre (Paris: 1874), p. 283.

40. For a theory denying even a minimal spontaneity of common response, see Mancur Olson, Jr., *The Logic of Collective Action* (Cambridge, Mass: Harvard University Press, 1971), especially pp. 125–131 and *pass.*

41. T. H. Marshall, "Citizenship and Social Class," in *Class, Citizenship and Social Development* (New York: Harper & Row, 1965), pp. 78ff.

42. John Dewey, *The Public and Its Problems* (Chicago: Swallow Press, 1954), pp. 154–157.

43. Michael Novak, *Choosing Our King* (New York: Macmillan, 1974), p. 280.

44. Marshall, "Citizenship," p. 101.

45. Jürgen Habermas, *Legitimation Crisis* (London: Heinemann, 1976), p. 75.

46. Indeed, the moral pluralism and individual life-styles of Civil II legitimize them as safety valves.

47. Walzer, *Obligations*, p. 227f.

48. Gabriel Almond and Sidney E. Verba, *The Civic Culture* (Princeton: Princeton University Press, 1963), pp. 323ff.

49. G. W. F. Hegel, *The Philosophy of Right*, trans. T. M. Knox (Oxford: Oxford University Press, 1967), paras, 250, 253, pp. 152–153.

50. Alexis de Tocqueville, *Democracy in America*, trans. Henry Reeve, 2 vols. (New York: Vintage Books, 1945), 2, pp. 114–115.

51. Being trained for politics in this fashion obviously does not mean the education of the young in school: cf. Arendt, *Between Past and Future*, p. 177.

52. Walzer, *Obligations*, p. 227.

53. See especially Walzer's thoughtful essay "The Obligation to Disobey," ibid., pp. 3–23.

54. Dewey, *The Public and Its Problems*, p. 8. There is an interesting parallel in Dewey's assertion of the validity of the religious in the absence of religion: see *A Common Faith* (New Haven: Yale University Press, 1934), especially, p. 28.

55. This worry is expressed in the article "Disarray and Inefficiencies in American Government Generate Wide Concern," *The New York Times*, 12 November 1978.

56. Habermas, *Legitimation Crisis*, pp. 43. 47.

— 4 —

Citizenship and Authority: A Chastened View of Citizenship

Richard E. Flathman

My purpose in this essay is to present and defend what I think of as a chastened view of citizenship. "Chastened" means subdued or tempered as compared with some alternative understanding that is more enthusiastic, celebratory, or evangelical in tone and character. Because this essay is addressed primarily to professional political scientists, and because the most influential recent discussions of citizenship in the political science literature could hardly be called celebratory, characterization of my view as chastened needs immediate explanation. Chastened as opposed to what?

We can make a (rough) beginning by adverting to the familiar distinction between empirical and normative theories. Much recent writing about citizenship—for example, the works of Schumpeter, Downs, Lipset, Berelson and his associates, Dahl, Sartori[1]—adopts something like the following stance: the "classical" ideal of citizenship, deriving from such daunting personages as Pericles, Aristotle, and Rousseau, elevates citizenship to the highest moral and political standing. Citizens are free, equal, and engaged with one another in pursuing matters of high and distinctively human import. Citizenship is the distinctive human activity and the distinctively important feature of a political society. Whatever the merits of this ideal from a normative perspective (most of the recent writers just mentioned, one surmises, do not rate them very highly), the ideal is unachievable in and hence irrelevant to political life and practice in the modern nation-state. The continuous, intense, morally uplifting interactions that the ideal presumes can obtain, if at all, only in and among subgroups within the large, complex, and impersonal societies of the modern world. Attempts to achieve and sustain such interactions at the level of the political society are distracting and destabilizing. Accordingly, political scientists must resolutely set the classical ideal aside and investigate the realities of and realistic possibilities for citizenship in the political societies of our day. The empirically grounded descriptions and prescriptions that result, uninspiring though they may be, will have the greater merits of accuracy and realism.

These "empirical" accounts and theories of democracy and citizenship are not chastened in the sense I intend here. Rather than temper or refine the classical theories against which they are (in part) reactions, they abandon the normative objectives and commitments characteristic of the latter. They are less a chastened species of an explicitly normative genus than a covertly moralistic species of an allegedly empirical or scientific genus.

The prevalence of these notionally scientific theories of citizenship has (along with numerous other factors) spurred a revival of insistently normative theorizing that takes its bearings from the classical theories of Aristotle and Rousseau. Writers such as Arendt, Barber, Pateman, Thompson, and Walzer[2] have insisted that the fundamentally normative questions raised by the classical theories cannot be disposed of by showing that the practice of those contemporary societies conventionally labeled democratic do not comport with any of the versions of the classical ideal. If practice does not satisfy ideal, we must conclude not that ideal should be scrapped but that practice is unsatisfactory and should be changed. Several of the recent revivalists of the classical ideal, moreover, insist that the ideal is much more compatible with, could be much more fully realized in and by, contemporary societies than "scientific" critics of that ideal contend.[3]

It is by comparison with the classical ideal and its recent revivals and restatements that the view presented here is chastened. Insofar as the "normative-empirical" distinction can be sustained, I agree that the normative issues raised by the classical view cannot be settled by adducing some set of alleged facts about modern societies. If (1) there were such a thing as a set of ideal-neutral factual observations, or such a thing as an "empirical theory" that was independent of ideals, if (2) those facts or that empirical theory were discrepant from the classical ideal, but (3) the ideal were nevertheless normatively superior, then our task would be to attempt to alter the facts. It would fall to us to act politically and morally to try to bring the facts and hence the empirical theory into conformity with the ideal. Or at least it would fall to us to lament the discrepancy between the two. As my sometime colleague Ralph Lerner used to say, we may be swept down the stream, but we are not therefore obliged to shout hosannas to the gods of the river.

Of course clauses (1) and (2) in the previous paragraph are patently counterfactual. Leaving aside general questions in the philosophies of meaning, theory construction, and scientific method, no reader of studies and theories of democracy such as Berelson's, Lipset's, or Sartori's can fail to see that those works are imbued by moral and political values and preferences sharply at variance with those that inform the thought of Aristotle and Rousseau. More fundamentally, no student of the moral and political practices over which these theories claim to generalize can fail to see that the participants in those practices accept and act upon a set of beliefs and values which, while residually influenced by the classical ideal of citizenship, include understandings and orientations difficult to accommodate to the classical ideal.[4] The notion that we could study and theorize about democracy and citizenship without addressing the normative issues raised by the classical ideal is no better than a more or less willful misunderstanding.

The present view, then, is intended to be chastened in the sense that it seeks to temper the moral and political ideal of citizenship that comes down to us from the deepest thinkers on the subject. It addresses the question of whether the third of the above subjunctive clauses is counterfactual; whether the beliefs and values that constitute that ideal deserve our reflected allegiance. It is intended, moreover, to be chastened, not antagonistic. The initial, the immediate, moral appeal of the Aristotelian and, on some readings, Rousseauean variants of the classical ideal seems to me undeniable. There is even reason to doubt whether a self-respecting human being could justifiably accommodate to a politically organized society that is not committed to and that does not substantially realize the values and objectives of this ideal of citizenship. To put this point another way, it is not surprising that many of those who have rejected the Aristotelian view have been led to a strongly antipolitical stance. Even the most scrupulously chastened—as opposed, again, to antagonistic—view of the ideal of high citizenship tends toward a political withdrawalism, the fully developed expression of which is now philosophical anarchism.[5] One way to state the question that will concern me is to ask whether this tendency can be arrested; whether a stable, ratiocinatively defensible position can be established between a politics of high citizenship and a non- or antipolitical stance. I suggest possibilities along this line. But we should note that to put the matter this way is to assume that anarchism or other extreme versions of withdrawalism are not choiceworthy and hence that the classical ideal of citizenship must be tempered, not rejected or abandoned. I am not able to defend this assumption systematically in this essay, but I try to say something concerning it.

As indicated by the title of this essay, I address these questions by attending to the relationship between citizenship and authority. A step toward doing so can be taken by recalling a well-established position—namely, Plato's—which is distinct from both the high citizenship argument of Aristotle and withdrawalist views such as those of the Stoics, Pascal, and nineteenth- and twentieth-century anarchists. No one would accuse Plato of amoral scientism in his thinking about politics. For Plato, active, vigorous political arrangements and processes are indispensable to the well-being of all but the most superior members of the human race. Yet for all save those superior few (who take on an active political role as a painful duty), human beings should be subjects not citizens. Their well-being will be achieved by submitting to the moral-cum-political authority of the philosopher-kings. A political society that accords anything like citizenship to any very large segment of its populace is unjust in itself and will of certainty produce severe instability and moral degeneration. The choice is not between a politics of high citizenship and withdrawal from political society; it is between a political order that fosters moral excellence through the proper distribution and exercise of authority and a moral and political disorder in which the many are encouraged to meddle in matters beyond their ken.

In its insistently anticitizenship Platonic version, this understanding is no more a serious contender for the intellectual allegiance of the twentieth-century political mind than is philosophical anarchism. Few among us would accept Plato's identification of justice with a society employing a division of labor in which significant moral and political decision making is the all but exclusive prerogative of a narrow elite. As attenuated as citizenship has become in even those societies of our time with some justification for their self-designations as democratic, not many of their members would exchange the values of citizenship for the stability, order, economic efficiency, or other desiderata said to be the yield of all but entire subordination to—what Plato was prepared to call—political authority.

The Platonic view is nevertheless important for my present purposes. This is so generically because it presents insistently normative arguments against citizenship; it is important specifically because the arguments it presents invoke authority and subordination to authority as essential elements in a proper moral and political order. It is made to appear that the moral values and objectives of political society are to be achieved not by interaction among citizens but by the subordination of subjects to those who are deservedly in possession of public authority. We are to think about political society and its moral characteristics and objectives not in an undifferentiated manner as if all members or participants contribute to those objectives in the same ways, but in terms of highly organized specializations of function and insistently hierarchical patterns of superiority, subordination, and deference.

From Aristotle on, much of the argumentation for high citizenship has been in reaction to the Platonic understanding. Sharing the objectives of moral excellence in human life, and sharing the conviction that an organized political society is at least a necessary condition of such excellence, proponents of such citizenship have tried to show that the excellence can be achieved—perhaps can only be achieved—in a politics of citizenship as distinct from and opposed to a politics of authority on the Platonic model. By defining citizens as persons who are equal in the sense that they share in offices and who rule and are ruled in turn,[6] and by celebrating political societies characterized by citizenship in this sense, Aristotle at least appears to have banished (what Plato had taught him to regard as) authority to the private realm. He believed that Plato was correct that the naturally, the necessarily, superior should rule over the naturally inferior. Masters should rule over slaves, parents should rule over children, husbands over wives. But politics occurs in the realm of freedom not of necessity; at its best, political life takes place among persons who have no claim to Platonic authority over one another. When Rousseau said that in a proper political society "every person while uniting himself with all...obeys only himself and remains as free as before,"[7] he restated, in radically democratized form, this same understanding, this same opposition between a politics of citizenship and a politics of authority.

Whatever we may think of its epistemological foundations, Plato's position depends on an untenable, indeed an incoherent, conception of authority. The notion he seeks to articulate is of authority in the sense of someone who is *an* authority concerning a subject matter, for example, Corwin as *an* authority on the United States Constitution or Samuel Beer as *an* authority on British politics. Plato is correct that this notion presupposes a sharply drawn inequality between those who are authorities and those who are not. Corwin is *an* authority concerning constitutional law because he knows more about that subject matter than most others who are interested in it. But because the latter must be able to recognize the superiority of Corwin's knowledge, at least some among them must know a good deal about it. Authority, even of the kind Plato sought to delineate, involves a relationship not just with the subject matter on which one is *an* authority but between the person (a) who is *an* authority and those other persons (b) for whom (a) has that standing. Keen to establish the unqualified superiority of philosopher-kings, Plato made it impossible for them to attain or sustain authority as opposed to power or domination.[8]

The foregoing criticism of Plato's understanding of authority is important in my attempt to find stable conceptual and normative ground between the ideal of high citizenship and political withdrawalism. My more immediate concern is with an incoherence into which, by the wrongheaded brilliance of his formulations, Plato induced the partisans of high citizenship who reacted against him. If Plato had been correct that authority and citizenship are incompatible, then a politics of citizenship would have to exclude authority. But this is an impossibility. Citizenship, I argue, presupposes authority. Those "offices" in which the Aristotelian citizen shares are established by rules (for example, the rules of a constitution) which are themselves invested with authority and which invest the offices and their officeholders with that same property. That "ruling and being ruled in turn" that defines the Aristotelian citizen would be incomprehensible apart from laws and commands that, once adopted, are binding on rulers and ruled alike because invested with authority accepted by both. However the array of offices may have been decided on, through whatever process it may have been invested with authority, a citizen dissatisfied with it must accommodate to that array unless and until it has been changed by established procedures—by procedures themselves invested with authority. In the same way, a citizen discontent with a law or command must obey it until those whose turn it is to rule— which of course may include the dissenter—have seen fit to repeal or alter it. In both cases the "must" in question is an obligation of citizenship, one that is supported by sanctions that may include the loss of the status of citizen itself. In the absence of such authority, the notion of citizenship has the echoing political emptiness of the phrase "citizen of the world."

As these remarks indicate, it would be overstating the case to assert that proponents of high citizenship propose, implicitly or explicitly, to eliminate public authority altogether. However we resolve the controversy about the presence or absence of the concept of authority in Aristotle, he is not only aware but insistent that citizens *rule* one another.[9] Nor can there be any doubt that the decisions of the Sovereign of Rousseau's *Social Contract* bind all citizens until those decisions have been changed; or, for that matter, that the decisions of what he calls "government" bind the citizenry until such time as the latter have acted as Sovereign to override those decisions. Something akin to authority is and must be at work in at least these respects.

An adequate treatment of these matters will require some refinements concerning the concept of authority. Leaving these refinements to later sections, it remains the case that my discussion thus far commits no worse than an exaggeration. The politics of high citizenship is intended to be sharply contrasted with a politics of authority. Interactions among citizens are distinctive just in that they are interactions among equals; they are among persons who have no binding authority over one another in respect to the subject matters of their interactions as citizens. And it is this interaction itself that is distinctively valuable. Familiar sociological language may help us here. There is a kind of recognition that citizenship is a status or office defined by rules that are invested with authority. But the more powerful tendency is to think of it as a role rather than as a status. There are proprieties and improprieties in the performance of the role; indeed it is through the identification of those proprieties, through delineation of the notion of citizenship, that theorists of high citizenship give expression to some of their deepest values. These proprieties, however, are to be defined less by legal rules invested with authority than by customs and conventions that develop in the course of the interactions and by moral principles derived from thinking about the objectives and purposes distinctive to the role itself. Salient among those objectives and purposes is the aim of fostering interaction as little inhibited as possible by authority. The thought seems to be that success in pursuing this objective will reduce authority (over and among citizens) to the minimal possible proportions.

No one suspicious of or wary about authority will be insensitive to the appeal of this understanding. Even if one is skeptical (as I have been and remain) concerning the project of seeking a moral transformation of human beings through a politics of high citizenship, one can appreciate the ways in which active citizenship can improve the quality of the decisions reached and can limit the excesses to which political authority—and its all but invariable handmaiden, political power—has shown itself to be prone. But if I am correct that citizenship is itself inseparable from authority, if a commitment to citizenship is itself a commitment to some species of political authority as a feature of one's political arrangements, then the very considerations that lead one to value citizenship are also reasons for tempering one's enthusiasm for it. If authority is objectionable, and if citizenship does not come without authority, then citizenship cannot be an unalloyed good.

Such at least is the thought I explore in these pages. I propose to reexamine the ideal of high citizenship in light of the relationship between that ideal and a political phenomenon, authority, about which proponents of the ideal have themselves been ambivalent if not skeptical. This program requires closer attention to authority than is usual in the literature concerning citizenship;[10] it requires an attempt to articulate and to assess the complex relationships among the suppositions, elements, and implications of both authority and citizenship.

Types of Authority

There are two main types of authority and two basic kinds of argumentation supporting a place for authority in a political association.[11] The first type has been called by a variety of names, including "substantive" and "personal" authority. It is perhaps most clearly exemplified by a person who is *an* authority on a subject matter such as a body of knowledge or an activity. Arguments for authority of this kind in politics are presented in Plato's thought, in Thomism and some other moral and political doctrines substantially influenced by religious dogma, in Marxism, and by sociological theories of a strongly functionalist bent. I have elsewhere called political theories that are primarily about and that argue for authority of this kind "substantive-purpose" (S-P) theories. The second main type is often called "positional" or "formal" authority. Authority of this kind is most familiar to us as vested in an office and thereby accruing to the holders of that office. Persons who hold such an office are therefore *in* authority; that is, they are invested with authority to make certain decisions whether they are *an* authority on the subject matters that the decisions concern. Max Weber's discussion of "rational-legal" as opposed to "charismatic" and "traditional" authority is one of the most influential treatments of formal authority.[12] Forceful arguments for it are to be found in Thomas Hobbes, in the tradition of the rule of law as opposed to men (especially in the theory of the so-called *Rechtsstaat*), and most recently and powerfully in the writings of Michael Oakeshott.[13] I refer to theories of this type as formal-procedural (F-P) theories.

Substantive Authority

Arguments for personal or substantive authority typically have a large factual dimension. They involve propositions of the form "It is the case that..." and frequently "By nature..." or "In the nature of things..." It is the case that Charles Goren knows more about the game of bridge than most other people. In the nature of things, there are classes of human beings who are fitted for reflection and for rule, others for military service, for household or menial work, and for being ruled. These propositions, which in principle are supportable by evidence about what is indeed the case, establish (claim to establish) differences or inequalities that are the basis of the distinction between those who possess authority and those who do not. These inequalities are a distinctive feature, perhaps the distinctive feature, of authority of this type. The truth of some such propositions is therefore a necessary condition of authority of this kind being justified, and the belief that some proposition of this kind is true is a necessary condition of any person actually achieving the standing of *an* authority concerning any particular subject matter or activity.

The existence or believed existence of such a factual inequality, however, is not a sufficient condition for either the existence or the justified existence of personal authority. I might concede that there are philosophers who know more about morals and politics than I do and yet insist that personal authority has no proper place in political life. Perhaps making and learning from mistakes is regarded as integral to the pleasure of the game of bridge. Perhaps I think that a politics in which decisions are made by authority destroys or derogates from the dignity or autonomy of those who accept that arrangement. As already indicated, to be *an* authority is to stand in a distinctive relationship not just with a subject matter or activity but with other persons who are interested or involved in it. The latter must recognize, accept, accede to, that relationship. And a justification for authority of this type must take account of the significance of that relationship for those who are party to it. It is interesting to note that even Plato accepts a version of this understanding. He seems to think that the superior wisdom and goodness of philosophers is itself sufficient to justify, though not of course to establish or sustain, the political subordination of nonphilosophers. In the peculiar ontological-cum-deontological manner in which he uses the term *justice*, such subordination is just in itself and needs no further justification. (Of course he also believes that the subordination is to the advantage of the nonphilosophers.) But the task of ruling is worse than merely uncongenial or distasteful to the philosophers; it is unnatural in that it forces them to return to the cave of appearance and opinion. Thus, there is an ontological wrong involved in requiring philosophers to be kings, a wrong that cannot be justified by the sheer superiority of the philosophers. Accordingly, both Plato and his opponents must supplement their claim that there is in fact inequality with further arguments for basing authority on it.[14]

A great many such arguments have been offered. Of those with which I am familar, all are instrumental in character. Some end will be attained, some good will be achieved, some value served, by including relationships in terms of personal authority among the arrangements and practices of the society or group. That good or value—among political writers justice, stability, order, efficiency, and community have been among the favorites—is of sufficient importance to justify what would otherwise be objectionable aspects of authority relations. In short, a tradeoff is proposed. The philosopher-kings give up some of the elevation and nobility of a life in communion with the good in order to contribute to the justice and well-being of all of the members of their society (or perhaps they give up some of the nobility that they wish for in exchange for a measure of protection against the demos); free, autonomous persons give up some of their freedom and autonomy in order to obtain material well-being, substantive justice, security, or stability.

Owing to this combination of characteristics, the argument for substantive authority can be attacked by objecting to either its factual or its instrumental premise. The classical exponents of the ideal of high citizenship, who have without exception opposed any very large role for personal authority among citizens, have done so primarily by attacking the factual premise. As we have seen, Aristotle accepts Plato's view that some human beings are by nature fit to rule, some only fit to be ruled. But he diminishes the qualities or characteristics necessary in order to be fit for rule, thereby enlarging, as against Plato, the number of those who fall into that category.

By the same move, he largely rejects Plato's view that personal or substantive authority has a proper place in political life. Political life occurs among citizens; all citizens are equal in the sense of being eligible for or fit to rule; therefore no citizen is entitled to personal authority over any other citizen. In a society featuring the politics of high citizenship, personal authority is largely if not entirely banished to the private realms in which the requisite inequality obtains. Rousseau's theory of citizenship involves an analogous move. He does not, however, so much lower the requirements for participation in rule as change their content from the primarily cognitive capacities and attainments insisted on by Plato to moral or dispositional characteristics. And he contends not that all in fact possess those characteristics but that participation in a properly ordered political society will itself develop the characteristics in all (adult males) who engage in it. (Substantive authority does retain what might be called a "protopolitical role" in the vital activities of that Platonic figure who haunts the *Social Contract*, the Legislator who establishes—and sustains?—Rousseau's ideal political society.)

These moves by theorists of high citizenship, however, produced difficulties of a high order of theoretical complexity and practical significance. These difficulties may have contributed importantly to the emergence of formal or positional authority in politics, and in any case realization of them did much to foster the development of F-P theories of authority. But neither the practice nor the theory of formal authority resolved the difficulties, and they continue to beset both thought and action concerning citizenship and authority. I will first identify the difficulties as they present themselves in Aristotle's uncertain movements toward a formal-procedural theory of authority and then look at some of the more salient moments in the later history of attempts to deal with them.

In rejecting, as regards politics, the premise of a natural inequality that justifies the rule of some citizens over others, Aristotle's theory of high citizenship abandons what seems then to have been the only accepted foundation for political authority.[15] But this leaves Aristotle in a difficult position. On his understanding of politics, including the politics of high citizenship, political life does involve ruling and being ruled. But as already suggested here, it is difficult if not impossible to invoke these notions without also invoking, however implicitly, some mode or kind of authority. Holding that tyranny is rule exclusively in the interest of the ruler, Aristotle does not make the modern equation between rule without authority and tyranny.[16] Yet ruling and being ruled have to be distinguished from other forms of superiority and subordination, dominance and submission. Drawing this distinction requires a theory of the nature and basis of authority. In other words, Aristotle has left himself with political authority for which he lacks a satisfactory basis or justification.

Formal Authority

Insofar as he recognizes and tries to resolve this difficulty Aristotle does so by foreseeing, albeit dimly, the possibility of a formal concept of authority and by foreshadowing later F-P arguments for its instrumental value. As in all F-P theories, his argument begins with the premise that equality (in relevant respects) obtains among those party to the authority relationship. Citizens are equal to one another in the sense that each of them possesses those qualities and characteristics requisite to participation in the ruling of the *polis*. In terms I have already used, citizens are equal in that each of them participates in the offices of the *polis* and thereby "rules and is ruled in turn." These famous formulae anticipate the later understanding that persons otherwise equal to one another could nevertheless be *in* authority over one another by virtue of having acceded to an office invested with formal authority. Acceding to such an office did not assume, and consistent with the premise of natural equality, could not be allowed to have created, personal superiority of the kinds that yield standing as *an* authority. Rather, justifications for the authority had to respect the foundational assumption of the equality of citizens.

A certain discomfort with this situation on Aristotle's part may already be intimated by the formula that citizens rule and are ruled in turn. True, Aristotle suggests that this arrangement itself contributes to the *telos* of political life. Learning to be ruled is said to be part of learning to rule.[17] But even if we allow him this somewhat unspecified notion, it remains unclear why the process of learning to be ruled cannot be completed at a relatively early age, thereby allowing all mature citizens to rule themselves continuously rather than intermittently.[18] If politics is conceived of as an activity through which development toward the fully and distinctively human end is achieved, any limitations on full participation qualify the ideal in unacceptable ways. Insofar as reliance on offices of authority creates divisions of labor or specializations of function, those excluded, however temporarily, from some tasks must thereby be deprived of some of the distinctive benefits of political life. Thus, when Aristotle says that citizens rule and are ruled in turn, it looks as if he is trying to give the most favorable appearance to an arrangement that he knows to be discrepant from the ideal he is advancing.

It was of course Rousseau who sought to remedy this defect in the ideal of high citizenship. His emphatic rejection of representation[19] is, among other things, a rejection of the notion of a distinct office or set of offices invested with the authority to act on behalf of—that is, to rule over—those not occupying that office or those offices. All citizens must participate equally and continuously in all of the actions of the Sovereign. But there is a further difficulty in reconciling offices invested with formal authority with the ideal of high citizenship. I have noted Aristotle's acceptance of Plato's view that politics have the high moral purpose of making it possible for citizens to achieve a morally excellent life.[20] Of course Aristotle thinks of morals and politics as practical not theoretical sciences, indicating thereby his rejection of Plato's view that incorrigible or undeniable truths can be attained concerning the good life.[21] He nevertheless holds firmly to the conviction that morals and politics allow better as opposed to worse understandings, superior as opposed to inferior judgments and conduct. And while he dismisses the view that there are infallible philosopher-kings, he believes with equal firmness that there are some who are morally and politically wiser, who consistently (dispositionally) choose and act in a morally and politically superior manner.[22] Because the class "morally and politically wiser" does not coincide with the class "citizens,"[23] the arrangement by which all citizens rule and are ruled in turn seems to guarantee periods in which the morally and politically less wise will rule over those who are wiser than they.

Awareness of this difficulty may inform Aristotle's discussions of the good man versus the good citizen and the practical versus the contemplative life,[24] discussions that with hindsight might even be read as anticipating the reflections of political withdrawalists such as Montaigne and Pascal. The truly superior person, the person capable of the fully contemplative life, will *not* participate in politics. At the end of this essay, I suggest a quite different interpretation of these among Aristotle's discussions, one that may help in arriving at a defensible conception of citizenship and political participation. However this may be, there is undeniably a tension (one we will encounter again) between the procedural aspects of Aristotle's theory of high citizenship and its substantive or moral purposes. This tension compounds and deepens the more general difficulty of reconciling authority and high citizenship. In addition to limiting participation itself, it appears that including offices of formal authority within the arrangements of a *polis* will allow the morally less wise to rule over the morally wiser. Insofar as it is the objective of high citizenship to achieve the morally good life among the members of a society, it is not easy to see how this arrangement can be justified.

I consider Aristotle's responses to these objections below. But first I want to note a kind of justification that, while almost certainly not intended by Aristotle, might be read into his discussion. The formula "rule and ruled in turn" suggests at least that offices of authority circulate among citizens over time, perhaps even that all citizens occupy one or more among the array of offices at any given moment in time. We have to qualify somewhat the ideal of fully and continuously equal participation in political life, but we attempt to do so fairly or equitably. The sense of the fairness of the arrangement, moreover, might be augmented somewhat by the following consideration: perhaps Able disapproves of Baker's decisions during the latter's tenure in office. But because Able can look forward to her own turn as holder of that office, it is unreasonable for her to object to the arrangement. Perhaps Able can reverse Baker's decisions or undo the effects of Baker's actions. Even if such steps are impracticable, Able can take comfort, perhaps even satisfaction, in the thought that Baker will like Able's rule no better than Able liked Baker's. The outcome of this arrangement may not otherwise be very edifying, but the reciprocity it involves makes it fair and to that degree justified.

These last thoughts are not in the idiom characteristic of Aristotle the theorist of high citizenship. (Of course high citizenship is not Aristotle's sole moral or political concern and its vocabulary is not his exclusive moral and political diction—a caveat that must be entered with respect to this entire discussion.) Read in the perspective of later discussions of citizenship and authority, they do evoke familiar images and set by now conventional reflections in motion. Acceptance of offices of formal authority does qualify and require compromises concerning the attributes and objectives distinctive of citizenship. But because the same qualifications are required of all citizens, because the qualifications are distributed fairly or justly and maintained reciprocally among the entire citizenry, it is reasonable for each citizen to agree to them.

Authority as Authorization

To understand the notion of reasonable agreement to a just arrangement of offices of authority we must consider a subtype of authority relations not obviously classifiable as either substantive or formal. This subtype is represented by the concept "authorization." In the simplest case, I authorize you to act on my behalf, to be my agent, to represent me. This arrangement may involve elements of personal or substantive authority. I may authorize you to represent me in part because I believe that you are *an* authority concerning the matters with which you will deal in acting on my behalf. Once again, however, we need more than the premise of inequality. My belief that you deserve standing as *an* authority is neither a necessary nor a sufficient condition of the relationship in question. I may give authorization to a person who lacks standing as *an* authority and I may withhold it from a person who deserves that standing. At the same time, the arrangment involves some of the elements of formal authority. You do not occupy an office in the sense of a position in a hierarchy that may remain constant through changes in officeholders, and thus far your "jurisdiction" is limited to me. But my authorization itself permits you, within the scope of the authority I have accorded you, to bind me to what may be a considerable array of performances. If I dislike the content of your actions, I may withdraw my authorization. But my assessment of the merits of those of your actions that are within the authority I have accorded you is, at least often, irrelevant to my obligation to perform as you have committed me to do.

In the simple case I am discussing, your authority and the authority relation between us are less a feature of a collectivity than a personal, even a private relationship. This feature of the arrangement, especially the fact that your authority results directly from, is limited by, and terminates with the withdrawal of my authorization, may do much to make it attractive to me. Clearly I have more control over the arrangement than is available to me in the more collective, institutionalized arrangements characteristic of political authority. If political authority could be founded on such authorizations, the qualifications effected against the ideal of equal citizenship would be justified not merely by the fact that they apply equitably but by the further fact that they would arise from and depend on each party's decision or choice.

Before developing the significance of these considerations for the concerns of this essay, it will be well to put them in perspective by noting that authorizations commonly acquire important social, public, and even legal characteristics that constrain the conduct of those who are party to them. In some cases, they become practices in the sense exemplified by law and medicine. If I engage a lawyer to represent me, our relationship takes its character not merely from my authorization but from the customs and conventions, and indeed the legal rules, that surround and to some extent govern the conduct of lawyers and their relationships with clients. Although my lawyer as such does not hold an office with a specified authority and jurisdiction, she does occupy a social status and does play a socially and in part legally defined role. The norms and rules that define and govern her status and role place restrictions and requirements on her relationships with me and her actions on my behalf. Thus, despite the fact that my lawyer's authority depends on my authorization, I cannot hope to have entire control over her authority in relation to me.

The attractions of authority relations based on authorizations have nevertheless been considerable. Because each such relationship requires an authorization from the person or persons over whom the authority will be held and exercised, the arrangement appears to accord a measure of respect to the basic equality that is fundamental to the ideal of high citizenship. Regardless of the distribution of authority that has been made in a society, all members remain equal in the fundamental sense that each is under authority by her own decision or choice. And even if authorizations are made in part in recognition of inequality in respect to a particular subject matter or activity, equality in respect to actions concerning that subject matter can in principle be reasserted at any time. Moreover, in all other respects the presupposition of equality remains unqualified.

In light of these considerations we cannot be surprised at the recurrence of efforts to build other more specifically political modes of authority on the foundation of individual authorizations. At least from Hobbes, the classic versions of consent and contractarian theories of authority have followed this path. The chief and remarkably constant suppositions of the theory are closely similar to those I "read into" Aristotle's discussion of ruling and being ruled in turn. Citizens (or in Hobbes's case subjects) are equal one to the other in that no one of them is sufficiently superior in morally and politically relevant respects to be entitled to personal authority over any others. "By nature" or "in the nature of things" the only authority that is politically germane is the authority that each person has over her own decisions and actions. Political authority can be justified only if it takes its origins from authorizations through which equal individuals transfer some of their authority over themselves to some other agent or agency. If such authorizations are given, and if they yield a distribution of authority and correlative obligations that is fair, then political authority can be justified.

Reconciling Authority and Citizenship

The consensus on these points, of course, coexists with very sharp disagreement on vital questions about the relationship between citizenship and authority. Debate concerning these questions, which has been waged from Hobbes to the present, can be viewed as a continuing attempt to resolve tensions already evident in Aristotle's theory of citizenship. Very roughly, the debate is between Hobbes and his (in respects to be discussed) followers on the one hand and Rousseau and later Rousseaueans on the other. The former give explicit and insistent development to Aristotle's foreshadowing of the notion of formal authority and embrace the inference that any very high citizenship is incompatible with authority and everything that depends on it. The imperative generated by the fact of natural moral equality is more or less fully satisfied by consent to the creation of offices of authority. From the moment of that consent on, ruling is and ought to be done primarily by those invested with that authority. The latter, proponents of high citizenship, may allow that authority can be created, perhaps that it can only be created, in this way. Individual consent or authorization provides a solution to the problem of how offices invested with binding authority—above all the office of citizen—can be justified. These theorists, however, insist on high citizenship and they struggle to reconcile their commitment to that ideal with their own acceptance of formal authority grounded in a collection of authorizations.

Aristotle and Hobbes

I proceed by examining Hobbes's classic version of the first of these modes of argumentation. I argued above that Aristotle gets into difficulties by trying to maintain authority as a feature of political life despite rejecting Plato's contention that political authority is founded on natural inequality. I now suggest that Hobbes tries to justify a more decisive role for political authority (more decisive than the role Aristotle assigns it) by deepening and extending the egalitarianism of Aristotle's theory of citizenship. It must be recognized, however, that the problem of justifying authority presents itself in importantly different terms in the two theories. They agree that there is no natural basis for personal authority in political life. But Aristotle thinks the equality that excludes personal authority opens up the possibility of cooperative, mutually beneficial political interactions among citizens. Thus, for him the question would seem to be why political authority is necessary at all; why should the values of unrestricted, fully equal participation be qualified in any way in the political realm? Insofar as he answers this question, he does so by arguing that rule through offices of authority and the laws they promulgate maximizes the influence of that human characteristic—namely, the capacity for rational self-rule—the possession of which distinguishes citizens from slaves, from women, and from barbarians. Law is "reason without passion" and rule by its means is thus rule by reason itself rather than rule by "men" in the sense of rule by creatures with a variety of characteristics in addition to reason. Authority qualifies but does not replace citizenship. Or as we might better put it, authority contributes to a politics of high citizenship by helping to insure that those human beings with the capacities necessary to citizenship act largely or primarily out of those capacities and not out of the characteristics that they share with noncitizens.

A variety of modulations on this theme achieved prominence in the later theory of the rule of law and of constitutionalism. But no such argument is available to Hobbes. He believes that the very equalities that forbid personal authority make human interactions conflictive and deeply destructive. The most notorious feature of Hobbes's theory of equality is his insistence that every person is vulnerable to being killed by any other.[25] Equality in this raw respect excludes the possibility that any of us will be able, by our own efforts, to assure our security. Natural equality excludes dominance on the basis of violence, power, and deception or manipulation as well as dominance on the basis of authority.

But it had scarcely been left to Hobbes to discover that human beings are rudely vulnerable to one another. The more interesting question that Hobbes addresses is why, in the absence of authority or some form of effective domination, personal security must be the constant, the overweening, human concern. Granting that others are physically capable of taking my life, why should they be disposed to do so? The explanation, Hobbes says, lies in the fact that human beings are equal in three further respects. First, although human interests and desires, purposes and objectives, vary in content from person to person, all human beings are interested and purposeful.[26] Second, human beings share an environment in which the supply of resources necessary to satisfy their desires and achieve their objectives is inadequate to the demand for them.[27] Third, and for present purposes most important, every person's well-being or satisfaction, as she defines or conceives them, are as good or deserving or legitimate as any other person's.[28] There neither is nor can be any convincing reason why one person should sacrifice or subordinate her interests or objectives to those of anyone else. Equality in the first two respects guarantees that human beings will come into conflict; equality in the third respect excludes the possibility that the conflict can be contained or even moderated by the parties to it. Taken together, the three equalities exclude the possibilities that inform Aristotle's theory—namely, that equal citizens, acting in a setting of shared authority and law, can readily interact in a cooperative and mutually beneficial manner.

Ever in quest of parsimony and consistency, and finding uncommon delight in the intellectually arresting, Hobbes's solution to the problem is formed largely out of the very elements that constitute the problem itself. Individual interests and purposes remain of equal legitimacy, but with the crucial qualification that each and every one of them is subordinate to the one overriding interest—namely, avoiding the "contranatural dissolution" that prematurely terminates the pursuit of all interests and purposes. Persons who are equal in the respects indicated, and hence equal in the further, supervenient respect that they know only the authority each exercises over herself, agree one with the other to create an office of authority to which they are severally and equally subject. The occupant of that office differs from others in no respect save that she is invested with the authority of the office. In particular, the interests and desires, the beliefs and values, the judgments and decisions, of the occupant of the office (*qua* natural person) possess no distinctive epistemic, moral, or prudential virtues or qualities. Subjects do not conform to the Sovereign's laws and commands because they approve of the content or the likely consequences of doing so. If, as Aristotle seems to assume, they could agree on (even in the sense of jointly recognizing once put before them) the merits of the laws and commands, laws and commands would be largely if not entirely superfluous. Subjects conform, rather, because the matters regulated by the laws and commands have proven to be the sources of intractable disagreement and mutually destructive conflict. In short, subjects obey the Sovereign for the same reasons that they created the office of Sovereign and made themselves its subjects—namely, to escape the horrendous consequences of their natural equality.

It would be no worse than a slight exaggeration to say that Hobbes's political theory seeks to "resolve" the difficulty of reconciling citizenship and political authority by eliminating citizenship and making relations in terms of authority the exclusive *political* relationship. Human beings as such may relate to one another in a wide variety of ways, but political persons, persons *qua* subjects, must relate to one another as subscribers to an office invested with authority. If they severally achieve the self-discipline necessary to maintain this thin but essential relationship, they may therefore find greater profit in their non- or extrapolitical relations; some among them may even hope to attain the felicity that consists in assurance of the more or less continuing satisfaction of their personal interests and desires and that is the highest estate God has permitted earthly humankind.[29] If they fail in the requisite discipline, if they succumb to the temptation to pursue what Aristotle called the good life in and through politics and the political relationships of citizenship, they will succeed only in recreating—perhaps in a yet more dangerous form—their original predicament.

With these reflections—which some find dispiriting—in mind, I return to my earlier suggestion that arguments for authority have both a factual and an instrumental premise. The factual premise is that human beings are by nature equal in the several respects already discussed. This premise excludes personal authority. But it also opens the possibility of formal authority grounded in authorizations and yielding a distribution of obligations that is fair to all subjects. The premise that, despite the differences among their interests and purposes, all persons require security sufficient to allow them to pursue their interests, is an instrumental argument for accepting authority. If the condition specified by the factual premise is satisfied, the second premise implies that it is rational for each person to subscribe to authority in order to obtain the security.

This argument alters the specific form but does not resolve the generic character of the difficulties in Aristotle's theory. To restate them in the light of the intervening discussion, those difficulties consist in a tension between the factual premise of equality and the instrumental premise that some undeniable good or advantage is provided by authority. Using authority to pursue the good is problematic because doing so qualifies and encroaches on equality and the goods represented by it and served by respecting it fully. In abandoning the particular goods that Aristotle sees in equal citizenship, Hobbes renounces the attempt to reconcile authority and citizenship. But Hobbes's argument fails to resolve the closely analogous problem posed by his own recognition of equality. Is authority compatible with equality among (not citizens but) persons? Granted that all subjects have authorized the creation of the Sovereign, and granted also that they are equally subordinate to that office, there is an enormous inequality between the occupant of that office and each subject. And that inequality is at least as threatening to the values Hobbes treasures as authority is to Aristotle's values. Thus, there is serious question whether Hobbes has made any progress toward justifying authority in a society of equals.

Hobbes's response to these objections depends heavily on two related ideas. The first is that the good sought by instituting authority has been reduced to minimal and incontrovertible proportions. The second is that the authority is formal or positional, not personal or substantive. The first point invites further comparison with Aristotle. The latter looks to politics—and hence in part to the authority that is an integral element of politics—for the highest (or perhaps the next to highest) and most complex aspects of the good for humankind. By contrast, Hobbes insists that each person must define and pursue her own good in her own way and he looked to politics and its authority to do nothing more than maintain a condition necessary to (but far from sufficient for) such private activity. By thus restricting the objectives of politics and its authority, by reducing those objectives to a common denominator on which all persons could be expected to agree, he hopes to make authority acceptable to all. As to the second point, Hobbes is of course aware that the office of authority will be occupied by a person or persons with the usual complement of passions and desires. He makes no attempt to deny that the occupant(s) of the office will use its authority in self-interested ways, and he firmly opposes all proposals to prevent such abuses by limiting or restraining the exercise of the authority of the office. (Hobbes prefers monarchy on the sobering ground that it reduces to the minimum the number of officeholders, thereby allowing satisfaction of the officeholder's personal interests at the lowest possible cost to the subjects.)[30] But he insists on a sharp distinction between the *authority* of the decisions of the office and the *merits* of those decisions. Subjects are to obey laws and commands not because they approve of or agree with their contents, but simply and exclusively because they are invested with authority. They are to obey authority because it is only when authority is obeyed that security can be maintained.

Hobbes's argument concerning the second point is of undeniable cogency and significance. To put the point in conceptual terms, if our sole reason for conforming our actions with laws and commands is our agreement with their content, we are acting on agreement or advice, not on obligation to authority. "Authority" and "law" are doing no work in our thought and action. Aristotle's argument that law is reason without passion, suggesting as it seems to do that citizens should obey laws because reason is embodied in them, confuses this point. Similarly, Rousseau's argument that in a politics of high citizenship "justice and utility may in no case be divided,"[31] and indeed the assumption of the entire tradition of which he is a chief exemplar—that a politics of high citizenship will yield better law and policy than any other mode of politics—might be thought to involve the same confusion. In language that Hobbes himself might have used, to take this stance would be to recreate the very difficulty that prompted the attempt to create authority. Authority cannot be the same as, cannot be equated with or reduced to, agreement concerning the substantive merits of policies or laws. Individuals and groups who disagree about the desired content of policies and laws cannot sustain political arrangements and relationships on the basis of agreement concerning that content. In a characteristically trenchant formulation, Hobbes says that "this device therefore of them that will make civil laws first, and then a civil body afterwards (as if policy made a body politic and not a body politic made policy) is of no effect."[32]

Despite the seeming clarity of his understanding on this point, Hobbes does not in fact break the connection between the authority of laws and their content and purpose. His subjects create and obey authority in order to achieve what Michael Oakeshott calls an "imagined and wished-for" outcome or state of affairs—namely, peace and security. Agreement on the overwhelming importance of this objective is what explains and justifies the agreement to create and maintain authority. Accordingly, obedience to authority that does not in fact yield this outcome is irrational. Of course Hobbes *urges* subjects largely to forgo judgment on this question. Except in those cases in which laws or commands themselves directly and unequivocally threaten the life of a subject, the subject is urged to let the Sovereign decide what will and will not conduce to security. But the logic of Hobbes's own argument prevents this from being more than advice, more than prudential counsel. Owing to the instrumental, end-oriented character of Hobbes's argument for authority and obedience to it, it is logically impossible for the authority of any law or command to be a sufficient reason for obeying it. Agreement on the proposition that peace and security are of paramount importance, and agreement on the further proposition that *these* laws and commands will yield peace and security here and now, is precisely what "makes" the Hobbesean body politic.

These considerations might tempt us to say that, appearances to the contrary notwithstanding, neither Hobbes nor Aristotle has a theory of authority. If it is a condition of such a theory that it make authority a sufficient, an invariably decisive, reason for action, then neither of these theories qualifies. This requirement is too stringent; if we insist on it, authority among human agents becomes both a theoretical and a practical impossibility. Just below, I develop this argument by examining Michael Oakeshott's more vigorous attempt to satisfy the requirement in question. Assuming in advance that I can make good on the contention I just advanced, a better way to describe my conclusions to this juncture is to say that neither Hobbes nor Aristotle succeed in eliminating the tensions that we first encountered in discussing Aristotle's theory. In both cases persons aware of their natural equality and concerned about sustaining the good represented by it must recognize that subscription to authority deeply qualifies the equality and puts the good it represents in serious and continuing jeopardy. They may nevertheless decide that, all things considered, the qualification and the jeopardy are preferable to the available alternatives. Hence, they may make the authorization, engage in the subscription, requisite to the creation of authority. But extraordinary good fortune apart, some laws and commands will threaten the very values that induced them to subscribe to authority. Thus, whether on the perhaps depressing Hobbesean assumptions about politics and political interactions, or on the more elevated and gratifying Aristotelian assumptions, authority may be tolerated and sustained but it can hardly be celebrated. Once the assumption that there is some inequality that (in company with an agreed objective) justifies authority was abandoned, it became impossible to arrive at an unproblematic theory of authority.

As I indicated at the beginning of this chapter, my own response to this circumstance is to recognize, or rather to insist, that political authority *is* a deeply problematic feature of our arrangements. Arguments for it are inescapably less than conclusive or dispositive, are irremediably vulnerable to objections that are not only cogent but also powerful. To accept authority and authority relations as a feature of human arrangements is to make a dangerous compromise; it is to act contrary to beliefs and to risk values of the first importance. And because it is certain that there is no such thing as citizenship without authority, highly doubtful that there is any such thing as a political society without authority, it follows that accepting citizenship and political society takes on these same characteristics.

This conclusion might be thought to amount to the proposition that "human affairs are not all that one might have hoped" or perhaps "there is a tragic dimension to the human condition." Human beings cannot live together without political society and political authority, but salient and indeed highly valued character- istics of human beings should render both of these objectionable to them. This conclusion may be thought jejeune, trite, or at least morally and politically irrelevant. One can of course mount these objections against authority and citizenship, but pursuing them yields no program, no course of action, no even partial solution to the difficulties the recognition of which prompts the objections.

I suggest that reactions such as these are inappropriate. True, if the difficulties and objections I have been discussing are as general and as deeply grounded as I have suggested, they will not be entirely resolved or eliminated by awareness of them or by action informed by such awareness. But such an awareness may temper hopes, deflect quixotic initiatives, and contribute to the sobriety necessary if the difficulties are to be kept within tolerable proportions.

These perhaps unwelcome reflections presume what numerous theorists of authority and citizenship fervently deny—namely, that there are indeed insuperable theoretical and practical obstacles to overcoming the difficulties that have been my focus. So far from treating my objections as trivial or irrelevant, leading modern theorists of authority and citizenship have labored to overcome them. The conclusions I have just been anticipating would be justified only if their efforts could be shown to be unsuccessful.

The attempts that require consideration can be subsumed under the two broad categories that I have denominated Hobbesean and Rousseauist. The first seeks (in various ways) to render authority acceptable to political equals by limiting the activities, including the activities of citizens, of those who share in it. The second seeks to make authority effective in pursuing lofty ends and purposes by democratizing it radically, that is, by insisting that its possession and exercise be equally and continuously shared among all citizens who are within its jurisdiction.

Michael Oakeshott

I will focus my examination of developments in the Hobbesean tradition on Michael Oakeshott's attempt to achieve a purified version of an F-P theory of authority. I noted that Hobbes's theory maintains a vital connection between authority and an end or purpose alleged to be of overwhelming importance to all human beings. Hobbesean subjects authorize and subscribe to the authority of the Sovereign in order to achieve the peace and security that, in his judgment, can be attained in no other way. I argued, however, that this feature of Hobbes's argument puts authority in constant jeopardy. Rational subjects can be expected to maintain their subscription only insofar as doing so actually contributes to the end for which they instituted authority.

It is a major objective of Oakeshott's theorizing to secure the authority of political society against this jeopardy. He seeks to remedy this defect in Hobbes's theory by jettisoning the notion that political authority exists for the sake of achieving some end or purpose. In pursuing this objective, Oakeshott formulates a severely uncompromising version of the F-P theory of authority. As in all versions, the key notions (in addition to equality among those who subscribe to authority) are rules, offices, and procedures created by rules.

> The authority of rulings and of administrative requisitions is recognized in terms of the rules which permit them to be made and which specify their jurisdiction. The authority of an office lies in the rules which constitute it and endow it with powers and duties and is to be recognized in terms of those rules. The authority of the occupant of an office lies in the rules which constitute it and endow it with powers and duties and is to be recognized in terms of those rules. The authority of the occupant of an office, his right to exercise its powers, is the license he acquires in coming to occupy it according to the rules of a prescribed procedure of appointment or succession. The authority of legislators to make, to amend, or to repeal. . . [law] is recognized in the rules which specify the conditions to be subscribed to in order to occupy the office, and the. . .[law] they declare is recognizable as authentic law in having been enacted in subscription to a prescribed procedure and in the exercise of powers conferred in this procedure.[33]

Rules are constitutive of authority: to understand authority is to understand rules; to subscribe to authority is to subscribe to and to know how to act in relation to rules.

Thus far Oakeshott's formulation differs from other F-P theories only in the single-minded, relentless reliance it places on the notion of rules. The special quality of his version, and its distinctive interest for present purposes, resides in its insistence that the system of rules which constitutes political authority must be understood entirely without reference to desires and interests, ends and purposes, or even beliefs and values shared among those who make, enforce, and subscribe to those rules. The rules of civil authority are said by him to be purely "adverbial" in character; these rules speak exclusively to the manner in which individual citizens act on beliefs and values, pursue ends and purposes, to the choice of which authority, its rules, and the civil society they constitute are altogether indifferent.[34] Speaking of rules of this kind, Oakeshott says: "A rule (and *a fortiori* something less exacting, like a maxim) can never tell a performer what choice he shall make; it announces only conditions to be subscribed to in making choices." The criminal law "does not forbid killing or lighting a fire, it forbids killing 'murderously' or lighting a fire 'arsonically.' " The system of rules that makes up the practice of political authority in a civil society should be understood as "an instrument to be played upon, not a tune to be played."[35]

It is not difficult to understand the motivation behind Oakeshott's development of this view. If the rules that constitute a practice of authority do not serve assignable interests or objectives, then it is impossible to decide whether to subscribe to them by deciding whether one approves the objectives they are intended to serve or by deciding whether in one's judgment the rules actually contribute to their intended objectives. Instrumental, utilitarian, or any other teleological reasoning is categorially and hence categorically excluded from the practice of authority. Members or citizens in a civil political association invested with authority relate to one another exclusively as subscribers to adverbial rules. For this reason, the question of whether they share ends or purposes, interests or objectives, beliefs or values, is irrelevant to whether they will be able to maintain authority. Or to put the point more positively, the common subscription to the procedural or adverbial rules that constitute political authority makes it possible for them to pursue their individual or group ends and interests, to sustain and act on their beliefs and values, without falling into destructive conflict.

It should be noted that this understanding of authority accords an important place to, places a deep reliance on, something that might just as well be called citizenship. Citizens must maintain and act on, indeed are properly characterized by, a "disciplined imagination." There will be a standing temptation to use political authority to advance some substantive project or purpose, to achieve some anticipated and wished-for outcome. If a rule that contributes to such an objective can be invested with authority so that all citizens acquire an obligation to accept and obey it, then (as long as authority remains effective in commanding obedience) those who favor the objective will have materially advanced their cause. But to succumb to this temptation is to put authority and hence civil life in jeopardy. The turn to authority to pursue the objective indicates that there is disagreement concerning it, that those who favor the objective have failed to convince their fellow citizens of its merits. Investing a rule that serves the objective with authority adds nothing to the arguments for the objective itself. It asks, or rather purports to require, those who do not share it to accommodate themselves to it for some other reason—most likely to sustain authority. But there will be very good reasons for them to refuse to do so. In their view authority will have become a weapon in the service of the partisan objectives. To submit to it will be simply and straightforwardly to submit to a tyranny in the classical sense of rule in the perceived interests of the rulers and contrary to the perceived interests of the ruled. Thus, citizens in the true sense are persons who understand the distinctions between adverbial rules on the one hand and substantive rules on the other and who act to assure that only the former are invested with the authority of the civil society.

This understanding of citizenship and its relationship to authority is directly relevant to the difficulties in that relationship that I have been considering. It is compatible with the essential features of the understanding that all citizens will participate in the offices that adopt and promulgate adverbial rules. (Which is not to say that Oakeshott himself favors a notably inclusive or democratized conception of citizenship, and it is certainly not to say that he favors active citizenship in the sense of a role that occupies large quantities of the time and energies of citizens.) Moreover, if authority is never used to pursue controversial or divisive objectives, there will be no instances in which subscription to it will qualify or compromise the equality, freedom, autonomy, or dignity of individual citizens. On this understanding, the very fact that citizenship is inseparable from authority appears to mean that citizenship guarantees the equality that has been the supposition of theories of authority since Aristotle.

Oakeshott has given up on Hobbes's expectation that agreement could be achieved concerning the overriding importance of peace and defense, agreement sufficient to engender and sustain a stable and effective system of authority in a political society. In place of agreement on that (or, allegedly, any other) end or purpose, he proposes to substitute subscription to adverbial rules said to be indifferent to all ends and purposes. For reasons already considered, this proposal is both apposite and meritorious. Short of reverting to a fully Platonic conception of substantive-purpose authority, there can be no authority without distinctions between procedure on the one hand and substance on the other, between formal credentials and material desirabilities.

But Oakeshott's distinctions cannot do anything like all of the work he asks of them. A rule that prohibits killing "murderously" or lighting fires "arsonically" is a rule against murder or arson; it is a rule that prohibits a class of actions through the taking of which agents seek imagined and wished-for ends and purposes. Most generally, subscription to authority is itself human action and, as with all species of this genus, is done for a reason, to achieve some objective.[36] If there is no agreement whatsoever concerning the objectives of subscription, the subscription can be maintained only by sacrificing equality among subscribers. A civil society on the Oakeshottian model might well diminish the conflict between authority and citizenship, but it could not eliminate that conflict. Although I will not be able to defend it here, I assert that the same is true of the numerous more mechanical devices proposed for the same purpose by other theorists in the F-P tradition.

Rousseau and the Ideal of High Citizenship

Oakeshott seeks to render authority and citizenship compatible by severely limiting the objectives or purposes of each. The limitations he seeks are to be achieved through understanding and self-discipline on the part of participants in civil society. They must appreciate what is distinctive about such a society and they must think and act in ways consonant with that appreciation. In this respect he differs from Hobbes and from most other thinkers who, like himself, have been concerned to limit the activities of those in authority. Hobbes relies on rulers to limit their own uses of their authority, looking to subjects primarily for obedience and for restraint in respect to the reasons for it. Others who have sought limitations on authority have placed little faith in either ruler or ruled, looking rather to a variety of devices such as constitutions, bills of rights, divisions of authority of various kinds, countervailing forces in society, and so forth. In the perspective given by these comparisons, we might even characterize Oakeshott as a theorist of high citizenship.

Writers in what I have called the "Rousseauean" mode nevertheless firmly reject Oakeshott's outlook. Citizens may play a role in his conception of civil society, but that role is woefully limited, woefully negative in character. Citizens act to protect their equality as individuals; they act to prevent political society from imposing collective goals and preferences on individuals who do not share them. This of course means that political society will almost certainly be debarred from acting to eliminate the innumerable and highly destructive inequalities that coexist with the essential but unsatisfactorily thin equality that obtains among its members by virtue of the fact that they are human agents. More important, it means that citizenship is not a role in and through which individuals pursue, in company with one another, the moral excellences (however encompassing) of which they are capable. For Rousseau, the theory and practice of authority and citizenship takes "men as they are" but seeks to achieve "laws as they might be" in order not only that "justice and utility may in no case be divided" but that man's "faculties" will be "so stimulated and developed, his ideas so extended, his feelings so ennobled, and his whole soul so uplifted" that he attains to a "moral liberty."[37] For Oakeshott, the objective of the theory and practice of *citizenship and authority* is to take human beings as they are—and leave them that way.

Crucial to the position of Rousseau and his followers are a pair of assumptions that at least appear to be highly plausible. The first of these is that the possession and exercise of authority enlarges and enhances one's capacity for effective decision and action. To possess the authority to do X is to have a kind of right to take that action. It is to have a warrant for doing X that is established in one's community, a warrant that other members of the community have an obligation to respect. Thus, acquiring authority is in principle equivalent to eliminating or freeing oneself from a whole array of limitations on and obstacles to action that might be posed by the objections of other parties. The latter might disagree or object, but they are bound by their subscription to go along or stand aside. The second assumption gives a communal or collectivist cast to the first. At bottom it is the notion that authority will not be objectionable to those who possess and exercise it. If a system of authority enhances the possibility of effective action, and if we exercise authority under that system, then we should welcome the system of authority.

The objections to authority, in other words, always, and reasonably enough it would seem, come from those who do not have it. From these assumptions there is drawn what seems to be the impeccable inference that authority could be made welcome to all by the device of extending its possession and exercise to the entirety of those who make up the community in which it is established. If each and every member of the community participated fully in the possession and exercise of whatever authority is established in it, the efficacy of collective action would be enhanced and no member would have reason to complain about either the existence or the use of authority. If authority is thoroughly democratized, it becomes acceptable in a society of equals. More positively, by virtue of their status as members of the citizenry, each citizen is in the attractive position of possessing and exercising authority, and hence the attractive aspects of both citizenship and authority complement rather than conflict one with the other.

Of course no proponent of democratized authority and/or high citizenship has ever seriously envisaged distributing authority to *all* members of any political society. The assumption of political equality has without exception been withheld from children and from certain classes of criminals and those judged to be mentally deficient or deranged, and it has been extended only hesitatingly and grudgingly to those of alien religious conviction, to the unpropertied, and above all to women. These large qualifications aside, from the perspective of this essay much of the theory of high citizenship can be viewed as taking a highly favorable attitude toward authority and attempting, through citizenship, to extend the supposed benefits of its possession and exercise. Whereas the line of thought running from Hobbes to Oakeshott views authority as contributing certain essential but narrowly confined advantages, the Aristotelian and more especially the Rousseauean tradition looks upon it as, potentially, a highly desirable feature of human affairs. If authority is suitably arranged and distributed, those who possess and exercise it can be ennobled by the experience.[38]

The key assumption that political authority enhances individual and collective action seems to be challenged by much of our experience with systems of authority. Systems in which authority is firmly established, seldom if ever resisted or challenged, are nevertheless characterized by dispute and division, often by deadlock that is broken, if at all, by compromises satisfying to no one. Rather than facilitating action, the existence of established political authority motivates and organizes opposition to it.

Rousseaueans are likely to argue that this evidence, although abundant, is irrelevant to their argument because it is as it were an artifact of the very views that their argument confutes. Those who have failed to appreciate the potential advantages of political authority, those whose thinking is dominated by experience with authority improperly arranged and distributed, have deliberately incapacitated the systems of authority in or under which they live. The claims of the Rousseauean theory can be tested only in systems that have eliminated artificial limitations on and complications in the exercise of authority and have established an organic connection between authority and high citizenship.

It will be instructive to pause here to note points of agreement between Hobbes and the Rousseaueans. At least as concerned as the latter with the efficacy of authority, Hobbes argued that it would be maximized where (a) its scope and (b) its location or possession were as little in doubt, as little subject to debate, as could be. Dispute about (a) would be excluded by making the authority of the Sovereign unlimited, without qualification of any kind, the solution Hobbes comes very close to adopting. So far as Hobbes can see, dispute about (b) can be eliminated by investing all authority in one person *and* by treating that person as "representing" all those over whom the authority is to be exercised; it can be kept minimal by investing it in a small number of persons also treated as "representing" all of the others; or it can be maximized by distributing it throughout the populace (making, of course, unavailable the valuable notion of representation). Hobbes of course favors the first over the second and abhors the third.

Hobbes's handling of (*a*) is often and on the whole correctly attributed to Rousseau himself and to other recognizably Rousseauean positions. Without going into controversial exegetical details, theorists of high citizenship hope for too much from authority to allow them to be comfortable with notions of constitutional, institutional, and other limitations on it.

As to (*b*), Rousseaueans also share Hobbes's concern with plurality, diversity, and conflict among the possessors of authority. Of course they must reject monarchy (albeit there is the Legislator!), aristocracy (albeit there are the noncitizens!), and all notions of representation that permit one party or set of parties to act on behalf of—that is, in place but in the name of and in a manner binding on—another party or parties. In fact, therefore, a Rousseauean polity necessarily distributes authority in what Hobbes thinks is the worst possible way—that is, among a great many individuals each of whom, by virtue of occupying the office of citizen, can do as she wishes with her measure of political authority. How, then, are confusion and stalemate to be avoided, efficacy of action to be achieved?

Despite the obvious differences between Rousseau and Hobbes, commentators concerned with this question have discerned in Rousseau and other theorists of high citizenship notions akin to the "unity" that Hobbes claims is produced when Leviathan is created by the "authorization" of its "subjects."[39] But Rousseau's rejection of representation means that this unity can not be "artificial" in the sense of Hobbes's "*unity* of the represener, not the *unity* of the represented."[40] For this reason, and perhaps owing to the prominence of obscure notions such as general will in theories of high citizenship, it has frequently been suggested that the desired "efficacy" would be achieved at the expense of plurality and individuality—that is, by fostering an all too "real unity" consisting of stultifying conformism maintained by democratic tyranny.

We should note at once that a requirement of *some* degree of consensus, of broad if not unqualified agreement on at least some matters, is a feature of any theory of authority and any theory of citizenship. Even Hobbes and Oakeshott, who are as anxious to minimize this requirement as any thinkers known to me, recognize that the requirement must be satisfied in some measure. As a bare minimum, there must be agreement that *this* and not *that* is an office invested with authority, that *these* and not *those* are the rules and procedures by and through which authority is exercised. But even this much agreement cannot be achieved or sustained unless there is also something close to consensus on some number of further values and beliefs. For Hobbes, peace and security must be accorded overweening importance and there must be a shared belief that they can be achieved and maintained only if there is political authority. For Oakeshott the comparable value seems to be the desirability of "abating" somewhat the "contingency" that conditions all human conduct,[41] this objective or value being conjoined with the belief that contingency is best abated by fidelity to an adverbially defined civility constituting a practice of authority. I elaborate somewhat on this point below, but it is manifest that to criticize the ideal of high citizenship for supposing consensus on *something* is frivolous if not captious.

Second, it would clearly be a mistake to interpret the major theorists of high citizenship as *pre*suming deep and extensive consensus. They do presuppose the degree of commonality represented by acceptance of the natural moral equality that forbids a politics of personal authority. They argue, however, that further and more substantive commonalities will develop in the course and as a consequence of a life of shared citizenship. Citizenship is a remedy for the fragmentation, division, and conflict that exists in its absence. Rousseau's work is especially striking in this regard, containing both biting denunciations of the selfishness, competitiveness, and antagonism rife in his society and paeans to the mutuality that could be expected if Frenchmen became genuine citizens. The same contrast between reality and potentiality is sharply drawn by contemporary theorists of high citizenship such as Arendt, Barber, and Pateman. Whether inspired by classical city-states, eighteenth-century Geneva, Swiss cantons, or Yugoslavian factories, these theorists describe high citizenship as a kind of bootstrap operation; active, continuing involvement in the life of a suitably organized political association will itself create such commonalities as are necessary to politics in this mode. To the objection that their ideal is irrelevant because the conditions of its realization are nowhere satisfied, they rejoin that serious pursuit of the ideal will itself create those conditions.

Third, there is no reason to think that there is any very large inventory of items on which consensus is specifically required. The scope of the consensus that is expected varies depending on the theorist's conception of the aspects of life that are fit subjects for political deliberation and interaction. There is, for example, no need for Aristotelian or Arendtian *citizens* to agree on the principles of a household economy. Critics who represent the ideal as requiring or aspiring to an encompassing uniformity simply misrepresent it.

These interpretations can be restated to give a better focus to the question of whether high citizenship contributes distinctively to easing the authority-citizenship relationship. The theory of high citizenship presents an ideal that is primarily procedural. It does not celebrate political outcomes or states of affairs—for example, those in which everyone agrees with the substance of all decisions, or those in which everyone ought to agree because the decisions are correct, just, or otherwise meritorious. True, some proponents of the ideal have believed that decisions made by an active citizenry will, as a generalization, be better decisions better supported. If true, these generalizations provide ancillary support for the kind of politics the theory promotes. But it would be imprudent to argue for high citizenship primarily on these grounds, even less prudent to argue that citizens should obey laws for these reasons. The first argument tends either to make authority irrelevant or to disqualify citizen involvement wherever the generalization fails to hold. On the second argument authority becomes equivalent to that about which consensus obtains and hence is again either superfluous when available or unavailable when needed.

In its most persuasive formulations, then, the theory of high citizenship favors a particular kind of political process because it generates and sustains distinctive characteristics and attitudes among the citizenry. Perhaps the most appropriate general term for the characteristics and attitudes the theory hopes to engender is identification: self-identification as citizen and shared identifications as members of a citizenry pursuing the good of the collectivity of citizens. In place of fragmenting, conflict-generating attitudes such as self-interestedness and competitiveness, it encourages cooperation and trustful acceptance of interdependencies. As sharers in the authority of the polity, citizens engage in deliberations addressed not to the question of which interests will prevail (albeit most decisions will in fact benefit some interests and disserve others) but what they as conjoint authorities should best do. They are to think of authority not as a weapon to be fought over but as a communal asset to be wisely used.

As citizens develop these characteristics their disagreements become "friendly" in the sense of a "friendly amendment" to a motion, one offered in the spirit of a contribution to a common enterprise. Thus, those who oppose proposals, who argue and vote unavailingly against them, can not only accept but also identify with their adoption. They can do so not only because they have participated in the process that yielded that outcome but also because they identify with the spirit that animates it and with the enterprise of which that spirit is the vital center.

Understood in this manner, high citizenship is more than an attractive ideal. It captures qualities that are, in some measure, almost certainly indispensable to any encompassing, politically organized association. Most pertinent here, it specifies features without which no such association could develop or sustain authority. Authority is a kind of reason for action: to acknowledge the authority of a rule is to acknowledge that there is a reason for conforming to it. But it is a reason of a very special kind. Although it cannot be entirely divorced from the content of the rules in which it is invested, neither can it be equated with or reduced to the merits of those rules. It is therefore a conceptual as well as a practical impossibility to sustain subscription to authority in the absence of considerations—including considerations in addition to assessments of the substantive merits of the rules—which support the judgment that the authority of a rule is a reason for obeying it. In the entire absence of identifications of the kinds promoted by the theory of high citizenship such considerations would be unavailable.

Should we not enlist ourselves in the cause of high citizenship?

Conclusion: Citizens and Individuals

My own answer to this question is a qualified negative. It is negative primarily because the ideal of high citizenship accommodates itself too readily to political authority. Stated somewhat ironically, my answer is negative primarily because the theory of high citizenship is too successful in the task that I, in company with some of its most distinguished proponents, set for it, the task of reconciling citizenship and authority.

Early in this essay I argued that citizenship is inseparable from authority. I then asked whether this is reason to be suspicious of citizenship as well as of authority. The theory of high citizenship returns a negative answer to my question. It encourages citizens to identify with authority.

This response has its share of attractions. If authority became what the ideal of high citizenship portrays it to be, why shouldn't we as citizens identify with it? It is of course appropriate to be wary of authority in conflict-ridden societies in which authority is paternalistic at its best and tyrannical at its more usual worst. Because these have been and continue to be the circumstances of most human beings, resistance to the alternative understanding proposed by the theory of high citizenship is more than under-standable. Unfortunately, that resistance perpetuates the very circumstance that prompts and sustains it. Authority will cease to be suspect only when we create for ourselves a politics of high citizenship in which we no longer have reason to suspect it.

In my judgment, however, authority is *on principle* suspect, on principle objectionable. It is more objectionable under some circumstances than others, but it is *always* objectionable. The reasons it is always objectionable can be stated in a number of ways and could take us into a moderately technical literature.[42] At bottom, its objectionable qualities reside in a fact we have encountered several times, namely, that (certain special cases aside) it has a role to play only when we disagree concerning the merits of the actions we should and should not take, the policies we should and should not adopt. Where there is consensus concerning what should and should not be done we simply act or refrain from acting on reasons specific to the actions in question. But if we disagree or are uncertain (but nevertheless judge that a decision must be made) authority may be invoked as a reason for accepting a particular decision. Thus, as a logical matter (the psychology of the situation may of course be less clear-cut) either authority has no work to do or it works to give us a reason for an action that we would not otherwise (that is, in the absence of authority) take. To subscribe to authority is to commit oneself to take actions that one would not take if considered exclusively on the merits of the actions themselves.[43] Under suitable circumstances, there may on balance be convincing reasons for such a commitment; I at least do not see how a reflective person could make that commitment without regret.

Neither the theory of high citizenship nor any other theory alters this characteristic of authority. Insofar as action is taken in the absence of consensus, or is continued after that consensus has disappeared, some citizens will be required to accommodate to policies with the content of which they disagree. If or insofar as the idea of high citizenship is realized, however, this fact will not so much as give them pause; they will not find it objectionable or even mildly regrettable. Having come to identify themselves as citizens and hence as sharers in authority, when a decision has been made they will focus not on its content but on the fact that authority of which they are a part has made it. Identifying themselves as they do with authority, they cannot regard that which is invested with authority as infringing on or derogating from them.

The politics of high citizenship may begin in plurality and disagreement, but (insofar as it acts in a determinate manner on any specific question) it *must* end in unchallengeable agreement (concerning that question). But of course agreement cannot alter (what as likely as not will be) the fact that there are excellent reasons against the decision or policy. In short, the politics of high citizenship would not change the fundamental character of authority; it would change the attitudes of citizens toward authority.[44]

I said that my answer to the question "Should high citizenship be our ideal?" is a qualified negative. It remains to say something about why, from the perspectives of this essay, the negative is qualified, about why our attitude toward citizenship and politics should be chastened not withdrawalist.

I argued that Plato's theory is incoherent because it relies on *an* authority while denying a condition thereof, that is, denying the availability of persons who are not themselves authorities but who have sufficient knowledge or understanding to accord that standing to others, to recognize and acknowledge the authority of the pronouncements or performances of others. This argument can be restated as follows: Plato makes unintelligible the relationships among authority, its pronouncements and performances, and those to whom those pronouncements are addressed (for whom they are to bear authority or be authoritative).

Although typically (not invariably and seldom clearly) employing the concept of *in* authority, withdrawalist and "low" citizenship theories are in constant danger of an analogous incoherence (and its practical consequences). The characteristic pronouncements or performances of *in* authorities are laws and commands promulgated to those who have authorized or otherwise subscribed to the system of authority in question (who are in the jurisdiction of that system of authority). With the qualification that they depersonalize authority by making it a property of offices and rules, these theories claim (as in Hobbes and Oakeshott) or tacitly allow (as in much of the "low" theory of citizenship) that there is an intelligible relationship among the three elements analogous to those that compose *an* authority relationships *à la* Plato, that is, offices invested with authority, laws and commands issuing from those offices, and the citizens or subjects to whom the laws and commands are promulgated. If those laws and commands are *intra vires*, that fact about them is said (by these and numerous other theories) to create—or rather to constitute—an obligation, the obligation of obedience to the laws and commands, for everyone in the jurisdiction. For present purposes let us concede (what deserves challenge) that abstractly (conceptually) these relationships are intelligible.

Insofar as they are successful in discouraging the interactions between officeholders and citizens or subjects, withdrawalist and low citizenship theories reduce the relationships in question to the terms just stated, that is, they reduce "politics" to authority, law, and to the obligation of obedience. While all forms of "legal absolutism" and numerous explications of *in* authority construe the obligation to obey as independent of the merits of laws, these theories go further and argue that citizens or subjects should disavow (as in Hobbes) or suppress to the greatest possible extent (as in most of the theories cited in note 1, above) concern with the reasons for or merits of laws and commands. It may be (as in Hobbes but rarely in other theories of political withdrawalism and low citizenship) deemed valuable for them to understand why authority and law are necessary, but it is not valuable, may be harmful, for them to consider or even to be made aware of the reasons for and against the adoption (as distinct from the enforcement once adopted and until repealed) of this, that, or the next law.

The strongest formulation of the argument I am advancing against these theories (strongest, that is, if we continue to assume the intelligibility of the conceptual relationships discussed just above) is that this position is incoherent because citizens and subjects who do not understand the reasons for a law *cannot* discharge their obligation to obey it; they cannot do so because knowing what counts as obeying a rule, knowing *what* the rule demands or forbids, requires understanding the reasons for it. Although I think there is a convincing version of this argument, because presenting it here would take us far afield, I instead make the (for present purposes sufficient) arguments that (*a*) such an understanding is *often* necessary to knowing how to obey (or disobey) a rule and (*b*) that in any case in the absence of such understanding the occurrence of obedience or disobedience becomes random, ceases to be explainable and to that extent expectable in terms of thought and action within politics.

This charge, frequently stated in terms of volatility or a tendency to lurch from sullen but otherwise lifeless submission to destructive disorder, is often brought against, as it were, the other side of the equation, that is, against authoritarianism and the unwillingness of authoritarian rulers and their apologists to justify or even explain the reasons for their laws and commands. By eschewing or discrediting concern with and involvement in the political processes that produce laws and commands, withdrawalism and theories of low citizenship make it difficult if not impossible for those subject to authority to augment or enrich the (at best) thin intelligibility of their relation to political authority as such by an understanding of the reasons for and against the laws and commands they are expected to obey.

Stripped of what is often their arrogant and aggrandizing moralism and perfectionism, the promise of theories of high citizenship is that they will eliminate this randomness, will give intelligibility and the possibility of stability to the relationship between political authority, law, and obedience and disobedience.

For the reasons I have given, this promise is worse than false. There is no unproblematic theory of authority, no sure way to maintain intelligibility—let alone yet more attractive or satisfying connections—among the components of authority relationships. But as programs for public life, withdrawalism and low citizenship give up on the attempt to sustain these relationships in so much as a tolerable condition.[45]

There is no formula for making political life tolerable, but there are two languages that may assist us as we make the continuing and inherently problematic effort to do so. The more prosaic of these features the distinction between persons—or better, individuals— and their statuses and roles. "Citizen" is one status (office) that most of us occupy, citizenship one of the roles that we play. As individuals we are also parents, plumbers, and professors, consumers, coworkers, and colleagues. As individuals, one of our concerns is to try to understand and maintain in a satisfactory condition the relationships among our several statuses and roles. Doing so requires something by no means easy to achieve or maintain, that disciplined imagination of which Michael Oakeshott has written. Theories of high citizenship privilege the status and role of citizenship at the expense of all others (and of individuality); theories of low citizenship privilege all others at the expense of citizenship (and the protections and other advantages that it, properly understood, can afford to individuality).

Our self-awareness as individuals may afford critical perspective on the several partial and more specialized roles that we play, including the role of citizen. As Aristotle's sometimes poetic discussions of the relationship between a good man and a good citizen may also be interpreted as suggesting, such perspective may allow us to understand that citizenship implicates us in the perhaps necessary but nevertheless objectionable mode of relationship that is subscription to political authority. Such an understanding yields no argument for withdrawing from citizenship and politics, a course that could put our individuality and hence all of our roles in jeopardy. It does give us reason to conduct ourselves as citizens in a manner befitting our individuality; it gives us reason to adopt a chastened view of citizenship.

Notes

1. See Joseph Schumpeter, *Capitalism, Socialism, and Democracy*, 4th ed. (New York: Harper & Row, 1954); Anthony Downs, *An Economic Theory of Democracy* (New York: Harper & Row, 1957); Seymour Martin Lipset, *Political Man* (Garden City, N.Y.: Doubleday, 1960); Bernard Berelson et al., *Voting* (Chicago: University of Chicago Press, 1954); Robert Dahl, *A Preface to Democratic Theory* (Chicago: University of Chicago Press, 1967), *After the Revolution* (New Haven: Yale University Press, 1970), and *Polyarchy* (New Haven: Yale University Press, 1971); Giovanni Sartori, *Democratic Theory* (New York: Praeger, 1965).

2. See Hannah Arendt, *The Human Condition* (Garden City, N.Y.: Doubleday, 1959), *Between Past and Future*, enl. ed (New York: Viking, 1968), and *On Revolution* (New York: Viking, 1963); Benjamin R. Barber, *The Death of Communal Liberty* (Princeton: Princeton University Press, 1974), *Superman and Common Men* (New York: Penguin, 1971), and *Strong Democracy* (Berkeley: University of California Press, 1984); Carole Pateman, *Participation and Democratic Theory* (Cambridge: Cambridge University Press, 1970), and *The Problem of Political Obligation* (Berkeley: University of California Press, 1979); Dennis F. Thompson, *The Democratic Citizen* (Cambridge: Cambridge University Press, 1970), and *Political Participation* (Washington, D.C.: American Political Science Association, 1977); Michael Walzer, *Obligations* (Cambridge: Harvard University Press, 1970) and *Radical Principles* (New York: Basic Books, 1980).

3. See esp. Thompson, *Democratic Citizen*; Pateman, *Participation and Democratic Theory*; Barber, *Strong Democracy*.

4. See Gabriel Almond and Sidney Verba, *The Civic Culture* (Princeton: Princeton University Press, 1963); J. David Greenstone and Paul E. Peterson, *Race and Authority in Urban Politics* (Chicago: University of Chicago Press, 1973).

5. Of course withdrawalism was not anarchistic in its most notable premodern expressions. Political withdrawalists such as the Stoics, Augustine, Pascal, Montaigne, and Hobbes found it possible to be in but no more than marginally of (as opposed to against) their political societies, a position revived by recent libertarian thinkers and, to my mind more interestingly, by Michael Oakeshott.

6. Aristotle, *Politics*, 1275b, 1279a.

7. Jean-Jacques Rousseau, *The Social Contract* (New York: E. P. Dutton, 1950), I, vi.

8. I have elaborated the understanding of authority that informs this criticism of Plato (and much of the discussion in this essay) in *The Practice of Political Authority* (Chicago: University of Chicago Press, 1980).

9. I am thinking of Hannah Arendt's argument that there is no genuine, differentiated concept of political authority in either Plato or Aristotle, that the concept was an invention of the Romans. See her "What Is Authority?" in *Between Past and Future*, pp. 91–141, esp. p. 104. See also Elizabeth Anscombe, "Modern Moral Philosophy," in *Ethics*, ed. Judith J. Thomson and Gerald Dworkin (New York: Harper & Row, 1968).

10. An exception is Dahl's *After the Revolution*.

11. I elaborate the following distinctions in *The Practice of Political Authority*. See also Richard B. Friedman, "On the Concept of Authority in Political Philosophy," in *Concepts in Social and Political Philosophy*, ed. Richard E. Flathman (New York: Macmillan, 1973).

12. See the selections from Weber in ibid.

13. See esp. Oakeshott's *On Human Conduct* (Oxford: Clarendon Press, 1975).

14. It is primarily because Plato describes subjects as incapable of understanding and acting on such further argumentation that authority—as distinct from power or domination—is an impossibility in his theory.

15. Cf. the discussions cited in n. 9, above.

16. See Aristotle, *Politics*, 1279a *et seq.*

17. Ibid., 1277b.

18. To put this difficulty somewhat differently and in a manner that anticipates discussion below of a further problem, if a citizen hasn't already learned to be ruled, how can that citizen safely be permitted to participate in ruling?

19. Rousseau, *Social Contract*, II, i.

20. Aristotle, *Politics*, 1278b, 1282b.

21. Aristotle, *Nicomachean Ethics*, 1140a–43a.

22. Ibid., 1104b–43a.

23. Or rather, the two coincide only under an ideal constitution: Aristotle, *Politics*, III, iv.

24. Ibid., VII, iii; I, ii; *Nichomachean Ethics*, IX, ix; I, vii.

25. Thomas Hobbes, *Leviathan* (Oxford: Basil Blackwell, 1955), chap. 13.

26. Ibid., chap. 6.

27. Ibid., chap. 13.

28. Ibid., chap. 6.

29. Ibid.

30. Ibid., chap. 19.

31. Rousseau, *Social Contract*, I, 1.

32. Thomas Hobbes, *Elements of Law* (Cambridge: Cambridge University Press, 1928), p. 152.

33. Oakeshott, *On Human Conduct*, pp. 150–51.

34. Ibid., pp. 116–17. In this discussion, I leave aside Oakeshott's importantly different account of authority in what he calls an "enterprise association" or *universitas* as opposed to civil association or *societas*. He develops the distinction between the two modes of association and their authority in the second and third essays of *On Human Conduct*, pp. 108–84, 185–326.

35. Ibid., p. 58.

36. Oakeshott himself gives us an excellent analysis of these features of human conduct. See ibid., esp. the first essay.

37. Rousseau, *Social Contract*, I, viii.

38. For suggestive reflections that bear on this theme from a somewhat different angle of approach, see Nannerl Keohane, *Philosophy and the State in France* (Princeton: Princeton University Press, 1980), esp. her interpretation of Rousseau as continuing and in a sense completing the tradition of absolutist thought in France.

39. Hobbes, *Leviathan*, chap. 17.

40. Ibid., chap. 16.

41. Oakeshott, *On Human Conduct*, p. 180.

42. See, for example, Richard B. Friedman, "On the Concept of Authority in Political Philosophy," in Flathman, *Concepts in Social and Political Philosophy*; Joseph P. Raz, *Practical Reason and Norms* (London: Hutchinson, 1975) and "On Legitimate Authority," in *Philosophical Law*, ed. Richard Bronaugh (Westport, Conn.: Greenwood Press, 1978).

43. More precisely, it is to commit oneself to the proposition that one may (if authority is in fact invoked) acquire obligations to take actions that one would not take on their merits. The obligation, of course, need not be regarded—in my judgment, ought not to be regarded—as an invariably decisive reason for action.

44. Much of this argument can be abbreviated by reference to the complications mentioned in n. 43, above. If we regard the obligation to obey authority as less than an invariably decisive reason for action, we in effect open up space for civil disobedience. If I have correctly construed the ideal of high citizenship, in a politics that fully realized that ideal civil disobedience could never be justified. Or rather, civil disobedience would be both a logical and a psychological impossibility. I have argued elsewhere that a defensible theory of political authority must provide a place for justifiable civil disobedience. See my *Practice of Political Authority*, pt. II.

45. I say programs because theories of *politics*, that is, attempts to theorize the present form of human association which is both encompassing and coercive, must maintain accommodations for individual and group exceptionalism and idiosyncrasy. But individuals and groups who want to universalize or even generalize their withdrawalism are obliged, it seems to me, to adopt philosophical anarchism. Nothing in this essay is intended to discredit or diminish the immense attractiveness of the latter view.

— 5 —

The Civil Society Argument

Michael Walzer

I

My aim here is to defend a complex, imprecise and, at crucial points, uncertain account of society and politics. I have no hope of theoretical simplicity, not at this historical moment when so many stable oppositions of political and intellectual life have collapsed; but I also have no desire for simplicity, since a world that theory could fully grasp and neatly explain would not, I suspect, be a pleasant place. In the nature of things, then, my argument will not be elegant, and though I believe that arguments should march, the sentences following one another like soldiers on parade, the route of my march today will be twisting and roundabout. I shall begin with the idea of civil society, recently revived by Central and East European intellectuals, and go on to discuss the state, the economy, and the nation, and then civil society and the state again. These are the crucial social formations that we inhabit, but we do not at this moment live comfortably in any of them. Nor is it possible to imagine, in accordance with one or another of the great simplifying theories, a way to choose among them—as if we were destined to find, one day, the best social formation. I mean to argue against choosing, but I shall also claim that it is from within civil society that this argument is best understood.

The words "civil society" name the space of uncoerced human association and also the set of relational networks—formed for the sake of family, faith, interest, and ideology—that fill this space. Central and East European dissidence flourished within a highly restricted version of civil society, and the first task of the new democracies created by the dissidents, so we are told, is to rebuild the networks: unions, churches, political parties and movements, cooperatives, neighborhoods, schools of thought, societies for promoting or preventing this and that. In the West, by contrast, we have lived in civil society for many years without knowing it. Or, better, since the Scottish Enlightenment, or since Hegel, the words have been known to the knowers of such things, but they have rarely served to focus anyone else's attention. Now writers in Hungary, Czechoslovakia, and Poland invite us to think about how this social formation is secured and invigorated.

We have reasons of our own for accepting the invitation. Increasingly, associational life in the 'advanced' capitalist and social democratic countries seems at risk. Publicists and preachers warn us of a steady attenuation of everyday cooperation and civic friendship. And this time it is possible that they are not, as they usually are, foolishly alarmist. Our cities really are noisier and nastier than they once were. Familial solidarity, mutual assistance, political likemindedness—all these are less certain and less substantial than they once were. Other people, strangers on the street, seem less trustworthy than they once did. The Hobbesian account of society is more persuasive than it once was.

Perhaps this worrisome picture follows—in part, no more, but what else can a political theorist say?—from the fact that we have not thought enough about solidarity and trust or planned for their future. We have been thinking too much about social formations different from, in competition with, civil society. And so we have neglected the networks through which civility is produced and reproduced. Imagine that the following questions were posed, one or two centuries ago, to political theorists and moral philosophers: What is the preferred setting, the most supportive environment, for the good life? What sorts of institution should we work for? Nineteenth- and twentieth-century social thought provides four different, by now familiar, answers to these questions. Think of them as four rival ideologies, each with its own claim to completeness and correctness. Each of them is importantly wrong. Each of them neglects the necessary pluralism of any *civil* society. Each of them is predicated on an assumption I mean to attack: that such questions must receive a singular answer.

II

I shall begin, since this is for me the best-known ground, with two leftist answers. The first of the two holds that the preferred setting for the good life is the political community, the democratic state, within which we can be citizens: freely engaged, fully committed, decision-making members. And a citizen, on this view, is much the best thing to be. To live well is to be politically active, working with our fellow citizens, collectively determining our common destiny—not for the sake of this or that determination but for the work itself, in which our highest capacities as rational and moral agents find expression. We know ourselves best as persons who propose, debate, and decide.

This argument goes back to the Greeks, but we are most likely to recognize its neoclassical versions. It is Rousseau's argument, or the standard leftist interpretation of Rousseau's argument. His understanding of citizenship as moral agency is one of the key sources of democratic idealism. We can see it at work in liberals like John Stuart Mill, in whose writings it produced an unexpected defense of syndicalism (what is today called "workers' control") and, more generally, of social democracy. It appeared among nineteenth- and twentieth-century democratic radicals, often with a hard populist edge. It played a part in the reiterated demand for social inclusion by women, workers, blacks, and new immigrants, all of whom based their claims on their capacity as agents. And this same neoclassical idea of citizenship resurfaced in the 1960s in New Left theories of participation, where it was, however, like many latter-day revivals, highly theoretical and without local resonance.

Today, perhaps in response to the political disasters of the late 1960s, "communitarians" in the United States struggle to give Rousseauian idealism a historical reference, looking back to the early American Republic and calling for a renewal of civic virtue. They prescribe citizenship as an antidote to the fragmentation of contemporary society—for these theorists, like Rousseau, are disinclined to value the fragments. In their hands, republicanism is still a simplifying creed. If politics is our highest calling, then we are called away from every other activity (or, every other activity is redefined in political terms); our energies are directed towards policy formation and decision-making in the democratic state.

I don't doubt that the active and engaged citizen is an attractive figure—even if some of the activists that we actually meet carrying placards and shouting slogans aren't all that attractive. The most penetrating criticism of this first answer to the question about the good life is not that the life isn't good but that it isn't the "real life" of very many people in the modern world. This is so in two senses. First, though the power of the democratic state has grown enormously, partly (and rightly) in response to the demands of engaged citizens, it cannot be said that the state is fully in the hands of its citizens. And the larger it gets, the more it takes over those smaller associations still subject to hands-on control. The rule of the *demos* is in significant ways illusory; the participation of ordinary men and women in the activities of the state (unless they are state employees) is largely vicarious; even party militants are more likely to argue and complain than actually to decide.

Second, despite the single-mindedness of republican ideology, politics rarely engages the full attention of the citizens who are supposed to be its chief protagonists. They have too many other things to worry about. Above all, they have to earn a living. They are more deeply engaged in the economy than in the political community. Republican theorists (like Hannah Arendt) recognize this engagement only as a threat to civic virtue. Economic activity belongs to the realm of necessity, they argue; politics to the realm of freedom. Ideally, citizens should not have to work; they should be served by machines, if not by slaves, so that they can flock to the assemblies and argue with their fellows about affairs of state. In practice, however, work, though it begins in necessity, takes on value of its own—expressed in commitment to a career, pride in a job well done, a sense of camaraderie in the workplace. All of these are competitive with the values of citizenship.

III

The second leftist position on the preferred setting for the good life involves a turning away from republican politics and a focus instead on economic activity. We can think of this as the socialist answer to the questions I began with; it can be found in Marx and also, though the arguments are somewhat different, among the utopians he hoped to supersede. For Marx, the preferred setting is the cooperative economy, where we can all be producers—artists (Marx was a romantic), inventors and craftsmen. (Assembly line workers don't quite seem to fit.) This again is much the best thing to be. The picture Marx paints is of creative men and women making useful and beautiful objects, not for the sake of this or that object but for the sake of creativity itself, the highest expression of our "species-being" as *homo faber*, man-the-maker.

The state, in this view, ought to be managed in such a way as to set productivity free. It doesn't matter who the managers are so long as they are committed to this goal and rational in its pursuit. Their work is technically important but not substantively interesting. Once productivity is free, politics simply ceases to engage anyone's attention. Before that time, in the Marxist here and now, political conflict is taken to be the superstructural enactment of economic conflict, and democracy is valued mainly because it enables socialist movements and parties to organize for victory. The value is instrumental and historically specific. A democratic state is the preferred setting not for the good life but for the class struggle; the purpose of the struggle is to win, and victory brings an end to democratic instrumentality. There is no intrinsic value in democracy, no reason to think that politics has, for creatures like us, a permanent attractiveness. When we are all engaged in productive activity, social division and the conflicts it engenders will disappear, and the state, in the once-famous phrase, will wither away.

In fact, if this vision were ever realized, it is politics that would wither away. Some kind of administrative agency would still be necessary for economic coordination, and it is only a Marxist conceit to refuse to call this agency a state. "Society regulates the general production," Marx wrote in *The German Ideology*, "and thus makes it possible for me to do one thing today and another tomorrow. . . just as I have a mind." Since this regulation is nonpolitical, the individual producer is freed from the burdens of citizenship. He attends instead to the things he makes and to the cooperative relationships he establishes. Exactly how he can work with other people and still do whatever he pleases is unclear to me and probably to most other readers of Marx. The texts suggest an extraordinary faith in the virtuosity of the regulators. No one, I think, quite shares this faith today, but something like it helps to explain the tendency of some leftists to see even the liberal and democratic state as an obstacle that has to be, in the worst of recent jargons, "smashed."

The seriousness of Marxist antipolitics is nicely illustrated by Marx's own dislike of syndicalism. What the syndicalists proposed was a neat amalgam of the first and second answers to the question about the good life: for them, the preferred setting was the worker-controlled factory, where men and women were simultaneously citizens and producers, making decisions and making things. Marx seems to have regarded the combination as impossible; factories could not be both democratic and productive. This is the point of Engels's little essay on authority, which I take to express Marx's view also. More generally, self-government on the job called into question the legitimacy of "social regulation" or state planning, which alone, Marx thought, could enable individual workers to devote themselves, without distraction, to their work.

But this vision of the cooperative economy is set against an unbelievable background—a nonpolitical state, regulation without conflict, "the administration of things." In every actual experience of socialist politics, the state has moved rapidly into the foreground, and most socialists, in the West at least, have been driven to make their own amalgam of the first and second answers. They call themselves "democratic socialists," focusing on the state as well as (in fact, much more than) on the economy and doubling the preferred settings for the good life. Since I believe that two are better than one, I take this to be progress. But before I try to suggest what further progress might look like, I need to describe two more ideological answers to the question about the good life, one of them capitalist, the other nationalist. For there is no reason to think that only leftists love singularity.

IV

The third answer holds that the preferred setting for the good life is the marketplace, where individual men and women, consumers rather than producers, choose among a maximum number of options. The autonomous individual confronting his, and now her, possibilities—this is much the best thing to be. To live well is not to make political decisions or beautiful objects; it is to make personal choices. Not any particular choices, for no choice is substantively the best: it is the activity of choosing that makes for autonomy. And the market within which choices are made, like the socialist economy, largely dispenses with politics; it requires at most a minimal state—not "social regulation," only the police.

Production, too, is free even if it isn't, as in the Marxist vision, freely creative. More important than the producers, however, are the entrepreneurs, heroes of autonomy, consumers of opportunity, who compete to supply whatever all the other consumers want or might be persuaded to want. Entrepreneurial activity tracks consumer preference. Though not without its own excitements, it is mostly instrumental: the aim of all entrepreneurs (and all producers) is to increase their market power, maximize their options. Competing with one another, they maximize everyone else's option too, filling the marketplace with desirable objects. The market is preferred (over the political community and the cooperative economy) because of its fullness. Freedom, in the capitalist view, is a function of plenitude. We can only choose when we have many choices.

It is also true, unhappily, that we can only make effective (rather than merely speculative or wistful) choices when we have resources to dispose of. But people come to the marketplace with radically unequal resources—some with virtually nothing at all. Not everyone can compete successfully in commodity production, and therefore not everyone has access to commodities. Autonomy turns out to be a high-risk value, which many men and women can only realize with help from their friends. The market, however, is not a good setting for mutual assistance, for I cannot help someone else without reducing (for the short term, at least) my own options. And I have no reason, as an autonomous individual, to accept any reductions of any sort for someone else's sake. My argument here is not that autonomy collapses into egotism, only that autonomy in the marketplace provides no support for social solidarity. Despite the successes of capitalist production, the good life of consumer choice is not universally available. Large numbers of people drop out of the market economy or live precariously on its margins.

Partly for this reason, capitalism, like socialism, is highly dependent on state action—not only to prevent theft and enforce contracts but also to regulate the economy and guarantee the minimal welfare of its participants. But these participants, in so far as they are market activists, are not active in the state: capitalism in its ideal form, like socialism again, does not make for citizenship. Or, its protagonists conceive of citizenship in economic terms, so that citizens are transformed into autonomous consumers, looking for the party or program that most persuasively promises to strengthen their market position. They need the state, but have no moral relation to it, and they control its officials only as consumers control the producers of commodities, by buying or not buying what they make.

Since the market has no political boundaries, capitalist entrepreneurs also evade official control. They need the state but have no loyality to it; the profit motive brings them into conflict with democratic regulation. So arms merchants sell the latest military technology to foreign powers and manufacturers move their factories overseas to escape safety codes or minimum wage laws. Multinational corporations stand outside (and to some extent against) every political community. They are known only by their brand names, which, unlike family names and country names, evoke preferences but not affections or solidarities.

V

The fourth answer to the question about the good life can be read as a response to market amorality and disloyalty, though it has, historically, other sources as well. According to the fourth answer, the preferred setting is the nation, within which we are loyal members, bound to one another by ties of blood and history. And a member, secure in his membership, literally part of an organic whole—this is much the best thing to be. To live well is to participate with other men and women in remembering, cultivating, and passing on a national heritage. This is so, on the nationalist view, without reference to the specific content of the heritage, so long as it is one's own, a matter of birth, not choice. Every nationalist will, of course, find value in his own heritage, but the highest value is not in the finding but in the willing: the firm identification of the individual with a people and a history.

Nationalism has often been a leftist ideology, historically linked to democracy and even to socialism. But it is most characteristically an ideology of the right, for its understanding of membership is ascriptive; it requires no political choices and no activity beyond ritual affirmation. When nations find themselves ruled by foreigners, however, ritual affirmation is not enough. Then nationalism requires a more heroic loyalty: self-sacrifice in the struggle for national liberation. The capacity of the nation to elicit such sacrifices from its members is proof of the importance of this fourth answer. Individual members seek the good life by seeking autonomy not for themselves but for their people. Ideally, this attitude ought to survive the liberation struggle and provide a foundation for social solidarity and mutual assistance. Perhaps, to some extent, it does: certainly the welfare state has had its greatest successes in ethnically homogeneous countries. It is also true, however, that once liberation has been secured, nationalist men and women are commonly content with a vicarious rather than a practical participation in the community. There is nothing wrong with vicarious participation, on the nationalist view, since the good life is more a matter of identity than activity—faith, not works, so to speak, though both of these are understood in secular terms.

In the modern world, nations commonly seek statehood, for their autonomy will always be at risk if they lack sovereign power. But they don't seek states of any particular kind. No more do they seek economic arrangements of any particular kind. Unlike religious believers who are their close kin and (often) bitter rivals, nationalists are not bound by a body of authoritative law or a set of sacred texts. Beyond liberation, they have no program, only a vague commitment to continue a history, to sustain "a way of life." Their own lives, I suppose, are emotionally intense, but in relation to society and economy this is a dangerously free-floating intensity. In time of trouble, it can readily be turned against other nations, particularly against the internal others: minorities, aliens, strangers. Democratic citizenship, worker solidarity, free enterprise and consumer autonomy—all these are less exclusive than nationalism but not always resistant to its power. The ease with which citizens, workers and consumers become fervent nationalists is a sign of the inadequacy of the first three answers to the question about the good life. The nature of nationalist fervor signals the inadequacy of the fourth.

VI

All these answers are wrong-headed because of their singularity. They miss the complexity of human society, the inevitable conflicts of commitment and loyalty. Hence I am uneasy with the idea that there might be a fifth and finally correct answer to the question about the good life. Still, there is a fifth answer, the newest one (it draws upon less central themes of nineteenth- and twentieth-century social thought), which holds that the good life can only be lived in civil society, the realm of fragmentation and struggle but also of concrete and authentic solidarities, where we fulfill E. M. Forster's injunction "only connect," and become sociable or communal men and women. And this is, of course, much the best thing to be. The picture here is of people freely associating and communicating with one another, forming and reforming groups of all sorts, not for the sake of any particular formation—family, tribe, nation, religion, commune, brotherhood or sisterhood, interest group or ideological movement— but for the sake of sociability itself. For we are by nature social, before we are political or economic, beings.

I would rather say that the civil society argument is a corrective to the four ideological accounts of the good life—part-denial, part-incorporation—rather than a fifth to stand alongside them. It challenges their singularity, but it has no singularity of its own. The phrase "social being" describes men and women who are citizens, producers, consumers, members of the nation, and much else besides—and none of these by nature or because it is the best thing to be. The associational life of civil society is the actual ground where all versions of the good are worked out and tested...and proven to be partial, incomplete, ultimately unsatisfying. It cannot be the case that living on this ground is good-in-itself; there isn't any other place to live. What is true is that the quality of our political and economic activity and of our national culture is intimately connected to the stength and vitality of our associations.

Ideally, civil society is a *setting of settings*: all are included, none is preferred. The argument is a liberal version of the four answers, accepting them all, insisting that each leave room for the others, therefore not finally accepting any of them. Liberalism appears here as an anti-ideology, and this is an attactive position in the contemporary world. I shall stress this attractiveness as I try to explain how civil society might actually incorporate and deny the four answers. Later on, however, I shall have to argue that this position too, so genial and benign, has its problems.

Let's begin with the political community and the cooperative economy, taken together. These two leftist versions of the good life systematically undervalued all associations except the *demos* and the working class. Their protagonists could imagine conflicts between political communities and between classes, but not within either; they aimed at the abolition or transcendence of particularism and all its divisions. Theorists of civil society, by contrast, have a more realistic view of communities and economies. They are more accommodating to conflict, that is, to political opposition and economic competition. Associational freedom serves for them to legitimate a set of market relations, though not necessarily the capitalist set. The market, when it is entangled in the network of associations, when the forms of ownership are pluralized, is without doubt the economic formation most consistent with the civil society argument. This same argument also serves to legitimate a kind of state, liberal and pluralist more than republican (not so radically dependent upon the virtue of its citizens). Indeed, a state of this sort, as we will see, is necessary if associations are to flourish.

Once incorporated into civil society, neither citizenship nor production can ever again be all-absorbing. They will have their votaries, but these people will not be models for the rest of us—or they will be partial models only, for some people at some time of their lives, not for other people, not at other times. This pluralist perspective follows in part, perhaps, from the lost romance of work, from our experience with the new productive technologies and the growth of the service economy. Service is more easily reconciled with a vision of man as a social animal than with *homo faber*. What can a hospital attendant or a school teacher or a marriage counselor or a social worker or a television repairman or a government official be said to *make*? The contemporary economy does not offer many people a chance for creativity in the Marxist sense. Nor does Marx (or any socialist thinker of the central tradition) have much to say about those men and women whose economic activity consists entirely in helping other people. The helpmate, like the housewife, was never assimilated to the class of workers.

In similar fashion, politics in the contemporary democratic state does not offer many people a chance for Rousseauian self-determination. Citizenship, taken by itself, is today mostly a passive role: citizens are spectators who vote. Between elections, they are served, well or badly, by the civil service. They are not at all like those heroes of republican mythology, the citizens of ancient Athens meeting in assembly and (foolishly, as it turned out) deciding to invade Sicily. But in the associational networks of civil society, in unions, parties, movements, interest groups, and so on, these same people make many smaller decisions and shape to some degree the more distant determinations of state and economy. And in a more densely organized, more egalitarian civil society, they might do both these things to greater effect.

These socially engaged men and women—part-time union officers, movement activists, party regulars, consumer advocates, welfare volunteers, church members, family heads—stand outside the republic of citizens as it is commonly conceived. They are only intermittently virtuous; they are too caught up in particularity. They look, most of them, for many partial fulfillments, no longer for the one clinching fulfillment. On the ground of actuality (unless the state usurps the ground), citizenship shades off into a great diversity of (sometimes divisive) decision-making roles; and, similarly, pro-duction shades off into a multitude of (sometimes competitive) socially useful activities. It is, then, a mistake to set politics and work in opposition to one another. There is no ideal fulfillment and no essential human capacity. We require many settings so that we can live different kinds of good lives.

All this is not to say, however, that we need to accept the capitalist version of competition and division. Theorists who regard the market as the preferred setting for the good life aim to make it the actual setting for as many aspects of life as possible. Their single-mindedness takes the form of market imperialism; confronting the democratic state, they are advocates of privatization and laissez-faire. Their ideal is a society in which all goods and services are provided by entrepreneurs to consumers. That some entrepreneurs would fail and many consumers find themselves helpless in the marketplace—this is the price of individual autonomy. It is, obviously, a price we already pay: in all capitalist societies, the market makes for inequality. The more successful its imperialism, the greater the inequality. But were the market to be set firmly within civil society, politically constrained, open to communal as well as private initiatives, limits might be fixed on its unequal outcomes. The exact nature of the limits would depend on the strength and density of the associational networks (including, now, the political community).

The problem with inequality is not merely that some individuals are more capable, others less capable, of making their consumer preferences effective. It's not that some individuals live in fancier apartments than others, or drive better-made cars, or take vacations in more exotic places. These are conceivably the just rewards of market success. The problem is that inequality commonly translates into domination and radical deprivation. But the verb "translates" here describes a socially mediated process, which is fostered or inhibited by the structure of its mediations. Dominated and deprived individuals are likely to be disorganized as well as impoverished, whereas poor people with strong families, churches, unions, political parties, and ethnic alliances are not likely to be dominated or deprived for long. Nor need these people stand alone even in the marketplace. The capitalist answer assumes that the good life of entrepreneurial initiative and consumer choice is a life led most importantly by individuals. But civil society encompasses or can encompass a variety of market agents: family businesses, publicly owned or municipal companies, worker communes, consumer cooperatives, nonprofit organizations of many different sorts. All these function in the market though they have their origins outside. And just as the experience of democracy is expanded and enhanced by groups that are in but not of the state, so consumer choice is expanded and enhanced by groups that are in but not of the market.

It is only necessary to add that among the groups in but not of the state are market organizations, and among the groups in but not of the market are state organizations. All social forms are relativized by the civil society argument—and on the actual ground too. This also means that all social forms are contestable; moreover, contests can't be won by invoking one or another account of the preferred setting—as if it were enough to say that market organizations, in so far as they are efficient, do not have to be democratic or that state firms, in so far as they are democratically controlled, do not have to operate within the constraints of the market. The exact character of our associational life is something that has to be argued about, and it is in the course of these arguments that we also decide about the forms of democracy, the nature of work, the extent and effects of market inequalities, and much else.

The quality of nationalism is also determined within civil society, where national groups coexist and overlap with families and religious communities (two social formations largely neglected in modernist answers to the question about the good life) and where nationalism is expressed in schools and movements, organizations for mutual aid, cultural and historical societies. It is because groups like these are entangled with other groups, similar in kind but different in aim, that civil society holds out the hope of a domesticated nationalism. In states dominated by a single nation, the multiplicity of the groups pluralizes nationalist politics and culture; in states with more than one nation, the density of the networks prevents radical polarization.

Civil society as we know it has its origin in the struggle for religious freedom. Though often violent, the struggle held open the possibility of peace. "The establishment of this one thing," John Locke wrote about toleration, "would take away all ground of complaints and tumults upon account of conscience." One can easily imagine groundless complaints and tumults, but Locke believed (and he was largely right) that tolerance would dull the edge of religious conflict. People would be less ready to take risks once the stakes were lowered. Civil society simply is that place where the stakes are lower, where, in principle, at least, coercion is used only to keep the peace and all associations are equal under the law. In the market, this formal equality often has no substance, but in the world of faith and identity, it is real enough. Though nations do not compete for members in the same way as religions (sometimes) do, the argument for granting them the associational freedom of civil society is similar. When they are free to celebrate their histories, remember their dead, and shape (in part) the education of their children, they are more likely to be harmless than when they are unfree. Locke may have put the claim too strongly when he wrote that "There is only one thing which gathers people into seditious commotions, and that is oppression," but he was close enough to the truth to warrant the experiment of radical tolerance.

But if oppression is the cause of seditious commotion, what is the cause of oppression? I don't doubt that there is a materialist story to tell here, but I want to stress the central role played by ideological single-mindedness: the intolerant universalism of (most) religions, the exclusivity of (most) nations. The actual experience of civil society, when it can be had, seems to work against these two. Indeed, it works so well, some observers think, that neither religious faith nor national identity is likely to survive for long in the network of free associations. But we really don't know to what extent faith and identity depend upon coercion or whether they can reproduce themselves under conditions of freedom. I suspect that they both respond to such deep human needs that they will outlast their current organizational forms. It seems, in any case, worthwhile to wait and see.

VII

But there is no escape from power and coercion, no possibility of choosing, like the old anarchists, civil society alone. A few years ago, in a book called *Anti-Politics*, the Hungarian dissident George Konrad described a way of living alongside the totalitarian state but, so to speak, with one's back turned towards it. He urged his fellow dissidents to reject the very idea of seizing or sharing power and to devote their energies to religious, cultural, economic, and professional associations. Civil society appears in his book as an alternative to the state, which he assumes to be unchangeable and irredeemably hostile. His argument seemed right to me when I first read his book. Looking back, after the collapse of the communist regimes in Hungary and elsewhere, it is easy to see how much it was a product of its time—and how short that time was! No state can survive for long if it is wholly alienated from civil society. It cannot outlast its own coercive machinery; it is lost, literally, without its firepower. The production and reproduction of loyalty, civility, political competence, and trust in authority are never the work of the state alone, and the effort to go it alone—one meaning of totalitarianism—is doomed to failure.

The failure, however, has carried with it terrible costs, and so one can understand the appeal of contemporary antipolitics. Even as Central and East European dissidents take power, they remain, and should remain, cautious and apprehensive about its uses. The totalitarian project has left behind an abiding sense of bureaucratic brutality. Here was the ultimate form of political single-mindedness, and though the "democratic" (and, for that matter, the "communist") ideology on which it rested was false, the intrusions even of a more genuine democracy are rendered suspect by the memory. Post-totalitarian politicians and writers have, in addition, learned the older antipolitics of free enterprise—so that the laissez-faire market is defended in the East today as one of the necessary institutions of civil society, or, more strongly, as the dominant social formation. This second view takes on plausibility from the extraordinary havoc wrought by totalitarian economic planning. But it rests, exactly like political single-mindedness, on a failure to recognize the pluralism of associational life. The first view leads, often, to a more interesting and more genuinely liberal mistake: it suggests that pluralism is self-sufficient and self-sustaining.

This is, indeed, the experience of the dissidents; the state could not destroy their unions, churches, free universities, illegal markets, *samizdat* publications. None the less, I want to warn against the antipolitical tendencies that commonly accompany the celebration of civil society. The network of associations incorporates, but it cannot dispense with, the agencies of state power; neither can socialist cooperation or capitalist competition dispense with the state. That's why so many dissidents are ministers now. It is indeed true that the new social movements in the East and the West—concerned with ecology, feminism, the rights of immigrants and national minorities, workplace and product safety, and so on—do not aim, as the democratic and labor movements once aimed, at taking power. This represents an important change, in sensibility as much as in ideology, reflecting a new valuation of parts over wholes and a new willingness to settle for something less than total victory. But there can be no victory at all that does not involve some control over, or use of, the state appararus. The collapse of totalitarianism is empowering for the members of civil society precisely because it renders the state accessible.

Here is the paradox of the civil society argument. Citizenship is one of many roles that members play, but the state itself is unlike all the other associations. It both frames civil society and occupies space within it. It fixes the boundary conditions and the basic rules of all associational activity (including political activity). It compels association members to think about a common good, beyond their own conceptions of the good life. Even the failed totalitarianism of, say, the Polish communist state had this much impact upon the Solidarity union: it determined that Solidarity was a Polish union, focused on economic arrangements and labor policy within the borders of Poland. A democratic state, which is continuous with the other associations, has at the same time a greater say about their quality and vitality. It serves, or it doesn't serve, the needs of the associational networks as these are worked out by men and women who are simultaneously members and citizens. I will give only a few obvious examples, drawn from American experience.

Families with working parents need state help in the form of publicly funded day-care and effective public schools. National minorities need help in organizing and sustaining their own educational programs. Worker-owned companies and consumer cooperatives need state loans or loan guarantees; so (even more often) do capitalist entrepreneurs and firms. Philanthropy and mutual aid, churches and private universities, depend upon tax exemptions. Labor unions need legal recognition and guarantees against "unfair labor practices." Professional associations need state support for their licensing procedures. And across the entire range of association, individual men and women need to be protected against the power of officials, employers, experts, party bosses, factory supervisers, directors, priests, parents, patrons; and small and weak groups need to be protected against large and powerful ones. For civil society, left to itself, generates radically unequal power relationships, which only state power can challenge.

Civil society also challenges state power, most importantly when associations have resources or supporters abroad: world religions, pan-national movements, the new environmental groups, multi-national corporations. We are likely to feel differently about these challenges, especially after we recognize the real but relative importance of the state. Multinational corporations, for example, need to be constrained, much like states with imperial ambitions; and the best constraint probably lies in collective security, that is, in alliances with other states that give economic regulation some international effect. The same mechanism may turn out to be useful to the new environmental groups. In the first case, the state pressures the corporation; in the second it responds to environmentalist pressure. The two cases suggest, again, that civil society requires political agency. And the state is an indispensable agent—even if the associational networks also, always, resist the organizing impulses of state bureaucrats.

Only a democratic state can create a democratic civil society; only a democratic civil society can sustain a democratic state. The civility that makes democratic politics possible can only be learned in the associational networks; the roughly equal and widely dispersed capabilities that sustain the networks have to be fostered by the democratic state. Confronted with an overbearing state, citizens, who are also members, will struggle to make room for autonomous associations and market relationships (and also for local governments and decentralized bureaucracies). But the state can never be what it appears to be in liberal theory, a mere framework for civil society. It is also the instrument of the struggle, used to give a paricular shape to the common life. Hence, citizenship has a certain practical preeminence among all our actual and possible memberships. That's not to say that we must be citizens all the time, finding in politics, as Rousseau urged, the greater part of our happiness. Most of us will be happier elsewhere, involved only sometimes in affairs of state. But we must have a state open to our sometime involvement.

Nor need we be involved all the time in our associations. A democratic civil society is one controlled by its members, not through a single process of self-determination but through a large number of different and uncoordinated processes. These need not all be democratic, for we are likely to be members of many associations, and we will want some of them to be managed in our interests, but also in our absence. Civil society is sufficiently democratic when in some, at least, of its parts we are able to recognize ourselves as authoritative and responsible participants. States are tested by their capacity to sustain this kind of participation—which is very different from the heroic intensity of Rousseauian citizenship. And civil society is tested by its capacity to produce citizens whose interests, at least sometimes, reach further than themselves and their comrades, who look after the political community that fosters and protects the associational networks.

VIII

I mean to defend a perspective that might be called, awkwardly, "critical associationalism." I want to join, but I am somewhat uneasy with, the civil society argument. It cannot be said that nothing is lost when we give up the single-mindedness of democratic citizenship or socialist cooperation or individual autonomy or national identity. There was a kind of heroism in those projects—a concentration of energy, a clear sense of direction, an unblinking recognition of friends and enemies. To make one of them one's own was a serious commitment. The defense of civil society does not quite seem comparable. Associational engagement is conceivably as important a project as any of the others, but its greatest virtue lies in its inclusiveness, and inclusiveness does not make for heroism. "Join the associations of your choice" is not a slogan to rally political militants, and yet that is what civil society requires: men and women actively engaged—in state, economy, and nation, and also in churches, neighborhoods, and families, and in many other settings too. To reach this goal is not as easy as it sounds; many people, perhaps most people, live very loosely within the networks, a growing number of people seem to be radically disengaged—passive clients of the state, market drop-outs, resentful and posturing nationalists. And the civil society project doesn't confront an energizing hostility, as all others do; its protagonists are more likely to meet sullen indifference, fear, despair, apathy, and withdrawal.

In Central and Eastern Europe, civil society is still a battle cry, for it requires a dismantling of the totalitarian state and it brings with it the exhilarating experience of associational independence. Among ourselves what is required is nothing so grand; nor does it lend itself to a singular description (but this is what lies ahead in the East too). The civil society project can only be described in terms of all the other projects, against their singularity. Hence, my account here, which suggests the need (1) to decentralize the state, so that there are more opportunities for citizens to take responsibility for (some of) its activities; (2) to socialize the economy so that there is a greater diversity of market agents, communal as well as private; and (3) to pluralize and domesticate nationalism, on the religious model, so that there are different ways to realize and sustain historical identities.

None of this can be accomplished without using political power to redistribute resources and to underwrite and subsidize the most desirable associational activities. But political power alone cannot accomplish any of it. The kinds of "action" discussed by theorists of the state need to be supplemented (not, however, replaced) by something radically different: more like union organizing than political mobilization, more like teaching in a school than arguing in the assembly, more like volunteering in a hospital than joining a political party, more like working in an ethnic alliance or a feminist support group than canvassing in an election, more like shaping a co-op budget than deciding on national fiscal policy. But can any of these local and small-scale activities ever carry with them the honor of citizenship? Sometimes, certainly, they are narrowly conceived, partial and particularist; they need political correction. The greater problem, however, is that they seem so ordinary. Living in civil society, one might think, is like speaking in prose.

But just as speaking in prose implies an understanding of syntax, so these forms of action (when they are pluralized) imply an understanding of civility. And that is not an understanding about which we can be entirely confident these days. There is something to be said for the neoconservative argument that in the modern world we need to recapture the density of associational life and relearn the activities and understandings that go with it. And if this is the case, then a more strenuous argument is called for from the Left: we have to reconstruct that same density under new conditions of freedom and equality. It would appear to be an elementary requirement of social democracy that there exist a *society* of lively, engaged, and effective men and women—where the honor of "action" belongs to the many and not to the few.

Against a background of growing disorganization—violence, homelessness, divorce, abandonment, alienation, and addiction—a society of this sort looks more like a necessary achievement than a comfortable reality. In truth, however, it was never a comfortable reality, except for the few. Most men and women have been trapped in one or another subordinate relationship, where the "civility" they learned was deferential rather than independent and active. That is why democratic citizenship, socialist production, free enterprise, and nationalism were all of them liberating projects. But none of them has yet produced a general, coherent or sustainable liberation. And their more single-minded adherents, who have exaggerated the effectiveness of the state or the market or the nation and neglected the networks, have probably contributed to the disorder of contemporary life. The projects have to be relativized and brought together, and the place to do that is in civil society, the setting of settings, where each can find the partial fulfillment that is all it deserves.

Civil society itself is sustained by groups much smaller than the *demos* or the working class or the mass of consumers or the nation. All these are necessarily pluralized as they are incorporated. They become part of the world of family, friends, comrades, and colleagues, where people are connected to one another and made responsible for one another. Connected and responsible: without that, "free and equal" is less attractive than we once thought it would be. I have no magic formula for making connections or strengthening the sense of responsibility. These are not aims that can be underwritten with historical guarantees or achieved through a single unified struggle. Civil society is a project of projects; it requires many organizing strategies and new forms of state action. It requires a new sensitivity for what is local, specific, contingent—and, above all, a new recognition (to paraphrase a famous sentence) that the good life is in the details.

— 6 —

Polity and Group Difference: A Critique of the Ideal of Universal Citizenship

Iris Marion Young

An ideal of universal citizenship has driven the emancipatory momentum of modern political life. Ever since the bourgeoisie challenged aristocratic privileges by claiming equal political rights for citizens as such, women, workers, Jews, blacks, and others have pressed for inclusion in that citizenship status. Modern political theory asserted the equal moral worth of all persons, and social movements of the oppressed took this seriously as implying the inclusion of all persons in full citizenship status under the equal protection of the law.

Citizenship for everyone, and everyone the same qua citizen. Modern political thought generally assumed that the universality of citizenship in the sense of citizenship for all implies a universality of citizenship in the sense that citizenship status transcends particularity and difference. Whatever the social or group differences among citizens, whatever their inequalities of wealth, status, and power in the everyday activities of civil society, citizenship gives everyone the same status as peers in the political public. With equality conceived as sameness, the ideal of universal citizenship carries at least two meanings in addition to the extension of citizenship to everyone: (*a*) universality defined as general in opposition to particular; what citizens have in common as opposed to how they differ, and (*b*) universality in the sense of laws and rules that say the same for all and apply to all in the same way; laws and rules that are blind to individual and group differences.

During this angry, sometimes bloody, political struggle in the nineteenth and twentieth centuries, many among the excluded and disadvantaged thought that winning full citizenship status, that is, equal political and civil rights, would lead to their freedom and equality. Now in the late twentieth century, however, when citizenship rights have been formally extended to all groups in liberal capitalist societies, some groups still find themselves treated as second-class citizens. Social movements of oppressed and excluded groups have recently asked why extension of equal citizenship rights has not led to social justice and equality. Part of the answer is straightforwardly Marxist: those social activities that most determine the status of individuals and groups are anarchic and oligarchic; economic life is not sufficiently under the control of citizens to affect the unequal status and treatment of groups. I think this is an important and correct diagnosis of why equal citizenship has not eliminated oppression, but in this article I reflect on another reason more intrinsic to the meaning of politics and citizenship as expressed in much modern thought.

The assumed link between citizenship for everyone, on the one hand, and the two other senses of citizenship—having a common life with and being treated in the same way as the other citizens— on the other, is itself a problem. Contemporary social movements of the oppressed have weakened the link. They assert a positivity and pride in group specificity against ideals of assimilation. They have also questioned whether justice always means that law and policy should enforce equal treatment for all groups. Embryonic in these challenges lies a concept of *differentiated* citizenship as the best way to realize the inclusion and participation of everyone in full citizenship.

In this article I argue that far from implying one another, the universality of citizenship, in the sense of the inclusion and participation of everyone, stands in tension with the other two meanings of universality embedded in modern political ideas: universality as generality, and universality as equal treatment. First, the ideal that the activities of citizenship express or create a general will that transcends the particular differences of group affiliation, situation, and interest has in practice excluded groups judged not capable of adopting that general point of view; the idea of citizenship as expressing a general will has tended to enforce a homogeneity of citizens. To the degree that contemporary proponents of revitalized citizenship retain that idea of a general will and common life, they implicitly support the same exclusions and homogeneity. Thus, I argue that the inclusion and participation of everyone in public discussion and decision making requires mechanisms for group representation. Second, where differences in capacities, culture, values, and behavioral styles exist among groups, but some of these groups are privileged, strict adherence to a principle of equal treatment tends to perpetuate oppression or disadvantage. The inclusion and participation of everyone in social and political institutions therefore sometimes requires the articulation of special rights that attend to group differences in order to undermine oppression and disadvantage.

I.

Citizenship as Generality

Many contemporary political theorists regard capitalist welfare society as depoliticized. Its interest group pluralism privatizes policymaking, consigning it to back room deals and autonomous regulatory agencies and groups. Interest group pluralism fragments both policy and the interests of the individual, making it difficult to assess issues in relation to one another and set priorities. The fragmented and privatized nature of the political process, moreover, facilitates the dominance of the more powerful interests.[1]

In response to this privatization of the political process, many writers call for a renewed public life and a renewed commitment to the virtues of citizenship. Democracy requires that citizens of welfare corporate society awake from their privatized consumerist slumbers, challenge the experts who claim the sole right to rule, and collectively take control of their lives and institutions through processes of active discussion that aim at reaching collective decisions.[2] In participatory democratic institutions citizens develop and exercise capacities of reasoning, discussion, and socializing that otherwise lie dormant, and they move out of their private existence to address others and face them with respect and concern for justice.

Many who invoke the virtues of citizenship in opposition to the privatization of politics in welfare capitalist society assume as models for contemporary public life the civic humanism of thinkers such as Machiavelli or, more often, Rousseau.[3]

With these social critics I agree that interest group pluralism, because it is privatized and fragmented, facilitates the domination of corporate, military, and other powerful interests. With them I think democratic processes require the institutionalization of genuinely public discussion. There are serious problems, however, with uncritically assuming as a model the ideals of the civic public that come to us from the tradition of modern political thought.[4] The ideal of the public realm of citizenship as expressing a general will, a point of view and interest that citizens have in common and that transcends their differences, has operated in fact as a demand for homogeneity among citizens. The exclusion of groups defined as different was explicitly acknowledged before this century. In our time, the excluding consequences of the universalist ideal of a public that embodies a common will are more subtle, but they still obtain.

The tradition of civic republicanism stands in critical tension with the individualist contract theory of Hobbes or Locke. Where liberal individualism regards the state as a necessary instrument to mediate conflict and regulate action so that individuals can have the freedom to pursue their private ends, the republican tradition locates freedom and autonomy in the actual public activities of citizenship. By participating in public discussion and collective decision making, citizens transcend their particular self-interested lives and the pursuit of private interests to adopt a general point of view from which they agree on the common good. Citizenship is an expression of the universality of human life; it is a realm of rationality and freedom as opposed to the heteronomous realm of particular need, interest, and desire.

Nothing in this understanding of citizenship as universal as opposed to particular, common as opposed to differentiated, implies extending full citizenship status to all groups. Indeed, at least some modern republicans thought just the contrary. While they extolled the virtues of citizenship as expressing the universality of humanity, they consciously excluded some people from citizenship on the grounds that they could not adopt the general point of view, or that their inclusion would disperse and divide the public. The ideal of a common good, a general will, a shared public life leads to pressures for a homogeneous citizenry.

Feminists in particular have analyzed how the discourse that links the civic public with fraternity is not merely metaphorical. Founded by men, the modern state and its public realm of citizenship paraded as universal values and norms which were derived from specifically masculine experience: militarist norms of honor and homoerotic camaraderie; respectful competition and bargaining among independent agents; discourse framed in unemotional tones of dispassionate reason.

Several commentators have argued that in extolling the virtues of citizenship as participation in a universal public realm, modern men expressed a flight from sexual difference, from having to recognize another kind of existence that they could not entirely understand, and from the embodiment, dependency on nature, and morality that women represent.[5] Thus, the opposition between the universality of the public realm of citizenship and the particularity of private interest became conflated with oppositions between reason and passion, masculine and feminine.

The bourgeois world instituted a moral division of labor between reason and sentiment, identifying masculinity with reason and femininity with sentiment, desire, and the needs of the body. Extolling a public realm of manly virtue and citizenship as independence, generality, and dispassionate reason entailed creating the private sphere of the family as the place to which emotion, sentiment, and bodily needs must be confined.[6] The generality of the public thus depends on excluding women, who are responsible for tending to that private realm, and who lack the dispassionate rationality and independence required of good citizens.

In his social scheme, for example, Rousseau excluded women from the public realm of citizenship because they are the caretakers of affectivity, desire, and the body. If we allowed appeals to desires and bodily needs to move public debates, we would undermine public deliberation by fragmenting its unity. Even within the domestic realm, moreover, women must be dominated. Their dangerous, heterogeneous sexuality must be kept chaste and confined to marriage. Enforcing chastity on women will keep each family a separated unity, preventing the chaos and blood mingling that would be produced by illegitimate children. Chaste, enclosed women in turn oversee men's desire by tempering its potentially disruptive impulses through moral education. Men's desire for women itself threatens to shatter and disperse the universal, rational realm of the public, as well as to disrupt the neat distinction between the public and private. As guardians of the private realm of need, desire, and affectivity, women must ensure that men's impulses do not subvert the universality of reason. The moral neatness of the female-tended hearth, moreover, will temper the possessively individualistic impulses of the particularistic realm of business and commerce, since competition, like sexuality, constantly threatens to explode the unity of the polity.[7]

It is important to recall that universality of citizenship conceived as generality operated to exclude not only women but other groups as well. European and American republicans found little contradiction in promoting a universality of citizenship that excluded some groups, because the idea that citizenship is the same for all translated in practice to the requirement that all citizens be the same. The white male bourgeoisie conceived republican virtue as rational, restrained, and chaste, not yielding to passion or desire for luxury, and thus able to rise above desire and need to a concern for the common good. This implied excluding poor people and wage workers from citizenship on the grounds that they were too motivated by need to adopt a general perspective. The designers of the American constitution were no more egalitarian than their European brethren in this respect; they specifically intended to restrict the access of the laboring class to the public, because they feared disruption of commitment to the general interests.

These early American republicans were also quite explicit about the need for the homogeneity of citizens, fearing that group differences would tend to undermine commitment to the general interest. This meant that the presence of blacks and Indians, and later Mexicans and Chinese, in the territories of the republic posed a threat that only assimilation, extermination, or dehumanization could thwart. Various combinations of these three were used, of course, but recognition of these groups as peers in the public was never an option. Even such republican fathers as Jefferson identified the red and black people in their territories with wild nature and passion, just as they feared that women outside the domestic realm were wanton and avaricious. They defined moral, civilized republican life in opposition to this backward-looking, uncultivated desire that they identified with women and nonwhites.[8] A similar logic of exclusion operated in Europe, where Jews were particular targets.[9]

These republican exclusions were not accidental, nor were they inconsistent with the ideal of universal citizenship as understood by these theorists. They were a direct consequence of a dichotomy between public and private that defined the public as a realm of generality in which all particularities are left behind, and defined the private as the particular, the realm of affectivity, affiliation, need, and the body. As long as that dichotomy is in place, the inclusion of the formerly excluded in the definition of citizenship—women, workers, Jews, blacks, Asians, Indians, Mexicans—imposes a homogeneity that suppresses group differences in the public and in practice forces the formerly excluded groups to be measured according to norms derived from and defined by privileged groups.

Contemporary critics of interest group liberalism who call for a renewed public life certainly do not intend to exclude any adult persons or groups from citizenship. They are democrats, convinced that only the inclusion and participation of all citizens in political life will make for wise and fair decisions and a polity that enhances rather than inhibits the capacities of its citizens and their relations with one another. The emphasis by such participatory democrats on generality and commonness, however, still threatens to suppress differences among citizens.

I shall focus on the text of Benjamin Barber, who, in his book *Strong Democracy*, produces a compelling and concrete vision of participatory democratic processes. Barber recognizes the need to safeguard a democratic public from intended or inadvertent group exclusions, though he offers no proposals for safeguarding the inclusion and participation of everyone. He also argues fiercely against contemporary political theorists who construct a model of political discourse purified of affective dimensions. Thus, Barber does not fear the disruption of the generality and rationality of the public by desire and the body in the way that nineteenth-century republican theorists did. He retains, however, a conception of the civic public as defined by generality, as opposed to group affinity and particular need and interest. He makes a clear distinction between the public realm of citizenship and civic activity, on the one hand, and a private realm of particular identities, roles, affiliations, and interests on the other. Citizenship by no means exhausts people's social identities, but it takes moral priority over all social activities in a strong democracy. The pursuit of particular interests, the pressing of the claims of particular groups, all must take place within a framework of community and common vision established by the public realm. Thus Barber's vision of participatory democracy continues to rely on an opposition between the public sphere of a general interest and a private sphere of particular interest and affiliation.[10]

While recognizing the need for majority rule procedures and means of safeguarding minority rights, Barber asserts that "the strong democrat regrets every division and regards the existence of majorities as a sign that mutualism has failed" (p. 207). A community of citizens, he says, "owes the character of its existence to what its constituent members have in common" (p. 232), and this entails transcending the order of individual needs and wants to recognize that "we are a moral body whose existence depends on the common ordering of individual needs and wants into a single vision of the future in which all can share" (p. 224). This common vision is not imposed on individuals from above, however, but is forged by them in talking and working together. Barber's models of such common projects, however, reveal his latent biases: "Like players on a team or soldiers at war, those who practice a common politics may come to feel ties that they never felt before they commenced their common activity. This sort of bonding, which emphasizes common procedures, common work, and a shared sense of what a community needs to succeed, rather than monolithic purposes and ends, serves strong democracy most successfully" (p. 244).

The attempt to realize an ideal of universal citizenship that finds the public embodying generality as opposed to particularity, commonness versus difference, will tend to exclude or to put at a disadvantage some groups, even when they have formally equal citizenship status. The idea of the public as universal and the concomitant identification of particularity with privacy makes homogeneity a requirement of public participation. In exercising their citizenship, all citizens should assume the same impartial, general point of view transcending all particular interests, perspectives, and experiences.

But such an impartial general perspective is a myth.[11] People necessarily and properly consider public issues in terms influenced by their situated experience and perception of social relations. Different social groups have different needs, cultures, histories, experiences, and perceptions of social relations which influence their interpretation of the meaning and consequences of policy proposals and influence the form of their political reasoning. These differences in political interpretation are not merely or even primarily a result of differing or conflicting interests, for groups have differing interpretations even when they seek to promote justice and not merely their own self-regarding ends. In a society where some groups are privileged while others are oppressed, insisting that as citizens persons should leave behind their particular affiliations and experiences to adopt a general point of view serves only to reinforce that privilege; for the perspectives and interests of the privileged will tend to dominate this unified public, marginalizing or silencing those of other groups.

Barber asserts that responsible citizenship requires transcending particular affiliations, commitments, and needs, because a public cannot function if its members are concerned only with their private interests. Here he makes an important confusion between plurality and privatization. The interest group pluralism that he and others criticize indeed institutionalizes and encourages an egoistic, self-regarding view of the political process, one that sees parties entering the political competition for scarce goods and privileges only in order to maximize their own gain, and therefore they need not listen to or respond to the claims of others who have their own point of view. The processes and often the outcomes of interest group bargaining, moreover, take place largely in private; they are neither revealed nor discussed in a forum that genuinely involves all those potentially affected by decisions.

Privacy in this sense of private bargaining for the sake of private gain is quite different from plurality, in the sense of the differing group experiences, affiliations, and commitments that operate in any large society. It is possible for persons to maintain their group identity and to be influenced by their perceptions of social events derived from their group-specific experience, and at the same time to be public spirited, in the sense of being open to listening to the claims of others and not being concerned for their own gain alone. It is possible and necessary for people to take a critical distance from their own immediate desires and gut reactions in order to discuss public proposals. Doing so, however, cannot require that citizens abandon their particular affiliations, experiences, and social location. As I will discuss in the next section, having the voices of particular group perspectives other than one's own explicitly represented in public discussion best fosters the maintenance of such critical distance without the pretense of impartiality.

A repoliticization of public life should not require the creation of a unified public realm in which citizens leave behind their particular group affiliations, histories, and needs to discuss a general interest or common good. Such a desire for unity suppresses but does not eliminate differences and tends to exclude some perspectives from the public.[12] Instead of a universal citizenship in the sense of this generality, we need a group differentiated citizenship and a heterogeneous public. In a heterogeneous public, differences are publicly recognized and acknowledged as irreducible, by which I mean that persons from one perspective or history can never completely understand and adopt the point of view of those with other group-based perspectives and histories. Yet commitment to the need and desire to decide together the society's policies fosters communication across those differences.

II.

Differentiated Citizenship As Group Representation

In her study of the functioning of a New England Town Meeting government, Jane Mansbridge discusses how women, blacks, working-class people, and poor people tend to participate less and have their interests represented less than whites, middle-class professionals, and men. Even though all citizens have the right to participate in the decision-making process, the experience and perspectives of some groups tend to be silenced for many reasons. White middle-class men assume authority more than others and they are more practiced at speaking persuasively; mothers and old people often find it more difficult than others to get to meetings.[13] Amy Gutmann also discusses how participatory democratic structures tend to silence disadvantaged groups. She offers the example of community control of schools, where increased democracy led to increased segregation in many cities because the more privileged and articulate whites were able to promote their perceived interests against blacks' just demand for equal treatment in an integrated system.[14] Such cases indicate that when participatory democratic structures define citizenship in universalistic and unified terms, they tend to reproduce existing group oppression.

Gutmann argues that such oppressive consequences of democratization imply that social and economic equality must be achieved before political equality can be instituted. I cannot quarrel with the value of social and economic equality, but I think its achievement depends on increasing political equality as much as the achievement of political equality depends on increasing social and economic equality. If we are not to be forced to trace a utopian circle, we need to solve now the "paradox of democracy" by which social power makes some citizens more equal than others, and equality of citizenship makes some people more powerful citizens. That solution lies at least in part in providing institutionalized means for the explicit recognition and representation of oppressed groups. Before discussing principles and practices involved in such a solution, however, it is necessary to say something about what a group is and when a group is oppressed.

The concept of a social group has become politically important because recent emancipatory and leftist social movements have mobilized around group identity rather than exclusively class or economic interests. In many cases such mobilization has consisted in embracing and positively defining a despised or devalued ethnic or racial identity. In the women's movement, gay rights movement, or elders' movements, differential social status based on age, sexuality, physical capacity, or the division of labor has been taken up as a positive group identity for political mobilization.

I shall not attempt to define a social group here, but I shall point
to several marks which distinguish a social group from other
collectivities of people. A social group involves first of all an affinity
with other persons by which they identify with one another, and
by which other people identify them. A person's particular sense
of history, understanding of social relations and personal possibilities, her or his mode of reasoning, values, and expressive styles
are constituted at least partly by her or his group identity. Many
group definitions come from the outside, from other groups that
label and stereotype certain people. In such circumstances the
despised group members often find their affinity in their oppression.
The concept of social group must be distinguished from two concepts with which it might be confused: aggregate and association.

An aggregate is any classification of persons according to some
attribute. Persons can be aggregated according to any number of
attributes, all of them equally arbitrary—eye color, the make of car
we drive, the street we live on. At times the groups that have
emotional and social salience in our society are interpreted as
aggregates, as arbitrary classifications of persons according to
attributes of skin color, genitals, or years lived. A social group,
however, is not defined primarily by a set of shared attributes, but
by the sense of identity that people have. What defines black
Americans as a social group is not primarily their skin color; this
is exemplified by the fact that some persons whose skin color is
fairly light, for example, identify as black. Though sometimes
objective attributes are a necessary condition for classifying oneself
or others as a member of a certain social group, it is the identification
of certain persons with a social status, a common history that social
status produces, and a self-identification that defines the group as
a group.

Political and social theorists tend more often to elide social
groups with associations rather than aggregates. By an association
I mean a collectivity of persons who come together voluntarily—
such as a club, corporation, political party, church, college, union,
lobbying organization, or interest group. An individualist contract
model of society applies to associations but not to groups. Individuals constitute associations; they come together as already

formed persons and set them up, establishing rules, positions, and offices.

Since one joins an association, even if membership in it fundamentally affects one's life, one does not take that association membership to define one's very identity in the way, for example, being Navajo might. Group affinity, on the other hand, has the character of what Heidegger calls "thrownness": one finds oneself as a member of a group, whose existence and relations one experiences as always already having been. For a person's identity is defined in relation to how others identify him or her, and others do so in terms of groups which always already have specific attributes, stereotypes, and norms associated with them, in reference to which a person's identity will be formed. From the thrownness of group affinity it does not follow that one cannot leave groups and enter new ones. Many women become lesbian after identifying as heterosexual, and anyone who lives long enough becomes old. These cases illustrate thrownness precisely in that such changes in group affinity are experienced as a transformation in one's identity.

A social group should not be understood as an essence or nature with a specific set of common attributes. Instead, group identity should be understood in relational terms. Social processes generate groups by creating relational differentiations, situations of clustering and affective bonding in which people feel affinity for other people. Sometimes groups define themselves by despising or excluding others whom they define as other, and whom they dominate and oppress. Although social processes of affinity and separation define groups, they do not give groups a substantive identity. There is no common nature that members of a group have.

As products of social relations, groups are fluid; they come into being and may fade away. Homosexual practices have existed in many societies and historical periods, for example, but gay male group identification exists only in the West in the twentieth century. Group identity may become salient only under specific circumstances, when in interaction with other groups. Most people in modern societies have multiple group identifications, moreover, and therefore groups themselves are not discrete unities. Every group has group differences cutting across it.

I think that group differentiation is an inevitable and desirable process in modern societies. We need not settle that question, however. I merely assume that ours is now a group differentiated society, and that it will continue to be so for some time to come. Our political problem is that some of our groups are privileged and others are oppressed.

But what is oppression? In another place I give a fuller account of the concept of oppression.[15] Briefly, a group is oppressed when one or more of the following conditions occurs to all or a large portion of its members: (1) the benefits of their work or energy go to others without those others reciprocally benefiting them (exploitation); (2) they are excluded from participation in major social activities, which in our society means primarily a workplace (marginalization); (3) they live and work under the authority of others, and have little work autonomy and authority over others themselves (powerlessness); (4) as a group they are stereotyped at the same time that their experience and situation is invisible in the society in general, and they have little opportunity and little audience for the expression of their experience and perspective on social events (cultural imperialism); (5) group members suffer random violence and harassment motivated by group hatred or fear. In the United States today at least the following groups are oppressed in one or more of these ways: women, blacks, Native Americans, Chicanos, Puerto Ricans and other Spanish-speaking Americans, Asian Americans, gay men, lesbians, working-class people, poor people, old people, and mentally and physically disabled people.

Perhaps in some utopian future there will be a society without group oppression and disadvantage. We cannot develop political principles by starting with the assumption of a completely just society, however, but must begin from within the general historical and social conditions in which we exist. This means that we must develop participatory democratic theory not on the assumption of an undifferentiated humanity, but rather on the assumption that there are group differences and that some groups are actually or potentially oppressed or disadvantaged.

I assert, then, the following principle: a democratic public, however that is constituted, should provide mechanisms for the effective representation and recognition of the distinct voices and perspectives of those of its constituent groups that are oppressed or disadvantaged within it. Such group representation implies institutional mechanisms and public resources supporting three activities: (1) self-organization of group members so that they gain a sense of collective empowerment and a reflective understanding of their collective experience and interests in the context of the society; (2) voicing a group's analysis of how social policy proposals affect them, and generating policy proposals themselves, in institutionalized contexts where decision makers are obliged to show that they have taken these perspectives into consideration; (3) having veto power regarding specific policies that affect a group directly, for example, reproductive rights for women, or use of reservation lands for Native Americans.

The principles call for specific representation only for oppressed or disadvantaged groups, because privileged groups already are represented. Thus, the principle would not apply in a society entirely without oppression. I do not regard the principle as merely provisional, or instrumental, however, because I believe that group difference in modern complex societies is both inevitable and desirable, and that wherever there is group difference, disadvantage or oppression always looms as a possibility. Thus, a society should always be committed to representation for oppressed or disadvantaged groups and ready to implement such representation when it appears. These considerations are rather academic in our own context, however, since we live in a society with deep group oppressions the complete elimination of which is only a remote possibility.

Social and economic privilege means, among other things, that the groups which have it behave as though they have a right to speak and be heard, that others treat them as though they have that right, and that they have the material, personal, and organizational resources that enable them to speak and be heard in public. The privileged are usually not inclined to protect and further the interests of the oppressed partly because their social position prevents them from understanding those interests, and partly because to some degree their privilege depends on the continued oppression of others. So a major reason for explicit representation of oppressed groups in discussion and decision making is to undermine oppression. Such group representation also exposes in public the specificity of the assumptions and experience of the privileged. For unless confronted with different perspectives on social relations and events, different values and language, most people tend to assert their own perspective as universal.

Theorists and politicians extol the virtues of citizenship because through public participation persons are called on to transcend merely self-centered motivation and acknowledge their dependence on and responsibility to others. The responsible citizen is concerned not merely with interests but with justice, with acknowledging that each other person's interest and point of view is as good as his or her own, and that the needs and interests of everyone must be voiced and be heard by the others, who must acknowledge, respect, and address those needs and interests. The problem of universality has occurred when this responsibility has been interpreted as transcendence into a general perspective.

I have argued that defining citizenship as generality avoids and obscures this requirement that all experiences, needs, and perspectives on social events have a voice and are respected. A general perspective does not exist which all persons can adopt and from which all experiences and perspectives can be understood and taken into account. The existence of social groups implies different, though not necessarily exclusive, histories, experiences, and perspectives on social life that people have, and it implies that they do not entirely understand the experience of other groups. No one can claim to speak in the general interest, because no one of the groups can speak for another, and certainly no one can speak for them all. Thus, the only way to have all group experience and social perspectives voiced, heard, and taken account of is to have them specifically represented in the public.

Group representation is the best means to promote just outcomes to democratic decision-making processes. The argument for this claim relies on Habermas's conception of communicative ethics. In the absence of a Philosopher King who reads transcendent normative verities, the only ground for a claim that a policy or decision is just is that it has been arrived at by a public which has truly promoted free expression of all needs and points of view. In his formulation of a communicative ethic, Habermas retains inappropriately an appeal to a universal or impartial point of view from which claims in a public should be addressed. A communicative ethic that does not merely articulate a hypothetical public that would justify decisions, but proposes actual conditions tending to promote just outcomes of decision-making processes, should promote conditions for the expression of the concrete needs of all individuals in their particularity.[16] The concreteness of individual lives, their needs and interests, and their perception of the needs and interests of others, I have argued, are structured partly through group-based experience and identity. Thus, full and free expression of concrete needs and interests under social circumstances where some groups are silenced or marginalized requires that they have a specific voice in deliberation and decision making.

The introduction of such differentiation and particularity into democratic procedures does not encourage the expression of narrow self-interest; indeed, group representation is the best antidote to self-deceiving self-interest masked as an impartial or general interest. In a democratically structured public where social inequality is mitigated through group representation, individuals or groups cannot simply assert that they want something; they must say that justice requires or allows that they have it. Group representation provides the opportunity for some to express their needs or interests who would not likely be heard without that representation. At the same time, the test of whether a claim on the public is just, or a mere expression of self-interest, is best made when persons making it must confront the opinion of others who have explicitly different, though not necessarily conflicting, experiences, priorities, and needs. As a person of social privilege, I am not likely to go outside of myself and have a regard for social justice unless I am forced to listen to the voice of those my privilege tends to silence.

Group representation best institutionalizes fairness under circumstances of social oppression and domination. But group representation also maximizes knowledge expressed in discussion, and thus promotes practical wisdom. Group differences not only involve different needs, interests, and goals, but probably more important different social locations and experiences from which social facts and policies are understood. Members of different social groups are likely to know different things about the structure of social relations and the potential and actual effects of social policies. Because of their history, their group-specific values or modes of expression, their relationship to other groups, the kind of work they do, and so on, different groups have different ways of understanding the meaning of social events, which can contribute to the others' understanding if expressed and heard.

Emancipatory social movements in recent years have developed some political practices committed to the idea of a heterogeneous public, and they have at least partly or temporarily instituted such publics. Some political organizations, unions, and feminist groups have formal caucuses for groups (such as blacks, Latinos, women, gay men and lesbians, and disabled or old people) whose perspectives might be silenced without them. Frequently these organizations have procedures for caucus voice in organization discussion and caucus representation in decision making, and some organizations also require representation of members of specific groups in leadership bodies. Under the influence of these social movements asserting group difference, during some years even the Democratic party, at both national and state levels, has instituted delegate rules that include provisions for group representation.

Though its realization is far from assured, the ideal of a "rainbow coalition" expresses such a heterogeneous public with forms of group representation. The traditional form of coalition corresponds to the idea of a unified public that transcends particular differences of experience and concern. In traditional coalitions, diverse groups work together for ends which they agree interest or affect them all in a similar way, and they generally agree that the differences of perspective, interests, or opinion among them will not surface in the public statements and actions of the coalition. In a rainbow coalition, by contrast, each of the constituent groups affirms the presence of the others and affirms the specificity of its experience and perspective on social issues.[17] In the rainbow public, blacks do not simply tolerate the participation of gays, labor activists do not grudgingly work alongside peace movement veterans, and none of these paternalistically allow feminist participation. Ideally, a rainbow coalition affirms the presence and supports the claims of each of the oppressed groups or political movements constituting it, and it arrives at a political program not by voicing some "principles of unity" that hide differences but rather by allowing each constituency to analyze economic and social issues from the perspective of its experience. This implies that each group maintains autonomy in relating to its constituency and that decision-making bodies and procedures provide for group representation.

To the degree that there are heterogeneous publics operating according to the principles of group representation in contemporary politics, they exist only in organizations and movements resisting the majority politics. Nevertheless, in principle participatory democracy entails commitment to institutions of a heterogeneous public in all spheres of democratic decision making. Until and unless group oppression or disadvantages are eliminated, political publics, including democratized workplaces and government decision-making bodies, should include the specific representation of those oppressed groups, through which those groups express their specific understanding of the issues before the public and register a group-based vote. Such structures of group representation should not replace structures of regional or party representation but should exist alongside them.

Implementing principles of group representation in national politics in the United States, or in restructured democratic publics within particular institutions such as factories, offices, universities, churches, and social service agencies, would require creative thinking and flexibility. There are no models to follow. European models of consociational democratic institutions, for example, cannot be taken outside of the contexts in which they have evolved, and even within them they do not operate in a very democratic fashion. Reports of experiments with publicly institutionalized self-organization among women, indigenous peoples, workers, peasants, and students in contemporary Nicaragua offer an example closer to the conception I am advocating.[18]

The principle of group representation calls for such structures of representation for oppressed or disadvantaged groups. But what groups deserve representation? Clear candidates for group representation in policy making in the United States are women, blacks, Native Americans, old people, poor people, disabled people, gay men and lesbians, Spanish-speaking Americans, young people, and nonprofessional workers. But it may not be necessary to ensure specific representation of all these groups in all public contexts and in all policy discussions. Representation should be designated whenever the group's history and social situation provide a particular perspective on the issues, when the interests of its members are specifically affected, and when its perceptions and interests are not likely to receive expression without that representation.

An origin problem emerges in proposing a principle such as this, which no philosophical argument can solve. To implement this principle a public must be constituted to decide which groups deserve specific representation in decision-making procedures. What are the principles guiding the composition of such a "constitutional convention?" Who should decide what groups should receive representation, and by what procedures should this decision take place? No program or set of principles can found a politics, because politics is always a process in which we are already engaged; principles can be appealed to in the course of political discussion, they can be accepted by a public as guiding their action. I propose a principle of group representation as a part of such potential discussion, but it cannot replace that discussion or determine its outcome.

What should be the mechanisms of group representation? Earlier I stated that the self-organization of the group is one of the aspects of a principle of group representation. Members of the group must meet together in democratic forums to discuss issues and formulate group positions and proposals. This principle of group representation should be understood as part of a larger program for democratized decision-making processes. Public life and decision-making processes should be transformed so that all citizens have significantly greater opportunities for participation in discussion and decision making. All citizens should have access to neighborhood or district assemblies where they participate in discussion and decision making. In such a more participatory democratic scheme, members of oppressed groups would also have group assemblies, which would delegate group representatives.

One might well ask how the idea of a heterogeneous public which encourages self-organization of groups and structures of group representation in decision making is different from the interest group pluralism, criticism of which I endorsed earlier in this article. First, in the heterogeneous public not any collectivity of persons that chooses to form an association counts as a candidate for group representation. Only those groups that describe the major identities and major status relationships constituting the society or particular institution, and which are oppressed or disadvantaged, deserve specific representation in a heterogeneous public. In the structures of interest group pluralism, Friends of the Whales, the National Association for the Advancement of Colored People, the National Rifle Association, and the National Freeze Campaign all have the same status, and each influences decision making to the degree that their resources and ingenuity can win out in the competition for policymakers' ears. While democratic politics must maximize freedom of the expression of opinion and interest, that is a different issue from ensuring that the perspective of all groups has a voice.

Second, in the heterogeneous public the groups represented are not defined by some particular interest or goal, or some particular political position. Social groups are comprehensive identities and ways of life. Because of their experiences their members may have some common interests that they seek to press in the public. Their social location, however, tends to give them distinctive under-standings of all aspects of the society and unique perspectives on social issues. For example, many Native Americans argue that their traditional religion and relation to land gives them a unique and important understanding of environmental problems.

Finally, interest group pluralism operates precisely to forestall the emergence of public discussion and decision making. Each interest group promotes only its specific interest as thoroughly and forcefully as it can, and it need not consider the other interests competing in the political marketplace except strategically, as potential allies or adversaries in the pursuit of its own. The rules of interest group pluralism do not require justifying one's interest as right or as compatible with social justice. A heterogeneous public, however, is a *public*, where participants discuss together the issues before them and are supposed to come to a decision that they determine as best or most just.

III.

Universal Rights and Special Rights

A second aspect of the universality of citizenship is today in tension with the goal of full inclusion and participation of all groups in political and social institutions: universality in the formulation of law and policies. Modern and contemporary liberalism hold as basic the principle that the rules and policies of the state, and in contemporary liberalism also the rules of private institutions, ought to be blind to race, gender, and other group differences. The public realm of the state and law properly should express its rules in general terms that abstract from the particularities of individual and group histories, needs, and situations to recognize all persons equally and treat all citizens in the same way.

As long as political ideology and practice persisted in defining some groups as unworthy of equal citizenship status because of supposedly natural differences from white male citizens, it was important for emancipatory movements to insist that all people are the same in respect of their moral worth and deserve equal citizenship. In this context, demands for equal rights that are blind to group differences were the only sensible way to combat exclusion and degradation.

Today, however, the social consensus is that all persons are of equal moral worth and deserve equal citizenship. With the near achievement of equal rights for all groups, with the important exception of gay men and lesbians, group inequalities nevertheless remain. Under these circumstances many feminists, black liberation acivists, and others struggling for the full inclusion and participation of all groups in this society's institutions and positions of power, reward, and satisfaction, argue that rights and rules that are universally formulated and thus blind to differences of race, culture, gender, age, or disability, perpetuate rather than undermine oppression.

Contemporary social movements seeking full inclusion and participation of oppressed and disadvantaged groups now find themselves faced with a dilemma of difference.[19] On the one hand, they must continue to deny that there are any essential differences between men and women, whites and blacks, able-bodied and disabled people, which justify denying women, blacks, or disabled people the opportunity to do anything that others are free to do or to be included in any institution or position. On the other hand, they have found it necessary to affirm that there are often group-based differences between men and women, whites and blacks, able-bodied and disabled people that made application of a strict principle of equal treatment, especially in competition for positions, unfair because these differences put those groups at a disadvantage. For example, white middle-class men as a group are socialized into the behavioral styles of a particular kind of articulateness, coolness, and competent authoritativeness that are most rewarded in professional and managerial life. To the degree that there are group differences that disadvantage, fairness seems to call for acknowledging rather than being blind to them.

Though in many respects the law is now blind to group differences, the society is not, and some groups continue to be marked as deviant and as the other. In everyday interactions, images, and decision making, assumptions continue to be made about women, blacks, Latinos, gay men, lesbians, old people, and other marked groups, which continue to justify exclusions, avoidances, paternalism, and authoritarian treatment. Continued racist, sexist, homophobic, ageist, and ableist behaviors and institutions create particular circumstances for these groups, usually disadvantaging them in their opportunity to develop their capacities and giving them particular experiences and knowledge. Finally, in part because they have been segregated and excluded from one another, and in part because they have particular histories and traditions, there are cultural differences among social groups—differences in language, style of living, body comportment and gesture, values, and perspectives on society.

Acknowledging group difference in capacities, needs, culture, and cognitive styles poses a problem for those seeking to eliminate oppression only if difference is understood as deviance or deficiency. Such understanding presumes that some capacities, needs, culture, or cognitive styles are normal. I suggested earlier that their privilege allows dominant groups to assert their experience of and perspective on social events as impartial and objective. In a similar fashion, their privilege allows some groups to project their group-based capacities, values, and cognitive and behavioral styles as the norm to which all persons should be expected to conform. Feminists in particular have argued that most contemporary workplaces, especially the most desirable, presume a life rhythm and behavioral style typical of men, and that women are expected to accommodate to the workplace expectations that assume those norms.

Where group differences in capacities, values, and behavioral or cognitive styles exist, equal treatment in the allocation of reward according to rules of merit composition will reinforce and perpetuate disadvantage. Equal treatment requires everyone to be measured according to the same norms, but in fact there are no "neutral" norms of behavior and performance. Where some groups are privileged and others oppressed, the formulation of law, policy, and the rules of private institutions tend to be biased in favor of the privileged groups, because their particular experience implicitly sets the norm. Thus, where there are group differences in capacities, socialization, values, and cognitive and cultural styles, only attending to such differences can enable the inclusion and participation of all groups in political and economic institutions. This implies that instead of always formulating rights and rules in universal terms that are blind to difference, some groups sometimes deserve special rights.[20] In what follows, I shall review several contexts of contemporary policy debate where I argue such special rights for oppressed or disadvantaged groups are appropriate.

The issue of a right to pregnancy and maternity leave, and the right to special treatment for nursing mothers, is highly controversial among feminists today. I do not intend here to wind through the intricacies of what has become a conceptually challenging and interesting debate in legal theory. As Linda Krieger argues, the issue of rights for pregnant and birthing mothers in relation to the workplace has created a paradigm crisis for our understanding of sexual equality, because the application of a principle of equal treatment on this issue has yielded results whose effects on women are at best ambiguous and at worst detrimental.[21]

In my view, an equal treatment approach on this issue is inadequate because it either implies that women do not receive any right to leave and job security when having babies, or it assimilates such guarantees under a supposedly gender neutral category of "disability." Such assimilation is unacceptable because pregnancy and childbirth are normal conditions of normal women, they themselves count as socially necessary work, and they have unique and variable characteristics and needs.[22] Assimilating pregnancy into disability gives a negative meaning to these processes as "unhealthy." It suggests, moreover, that the primary or only reason that a woman has a right to leave and job security is that she is physically unable to work at her job, or that doing so would be more difficult than when she is not pregnant and recovering from childbirth. While these are important reasons, depending on the individual woman, another reason is that she ought to have the time to establish breast feeding and develop a relationship and routine with her child, if she chooses.

The pregnancy leave debate has been heated and extensive because both feminists and nonfeminists tend to think of biological sex difference as the most fundamental and irradicable difference. When difference slides into deviance, stigma, and disadvantage, this impression can engender the fear that sexual equality is not attainable. I think it is important to emphasize that reproduction is by no means the only context in which issues of same versus different treatment arise. It is not even the only context where it arises for issues involving bodily difference. The last twenty years have seen significant success in winning special rights for persons with physical and mental disabilities. Here is a clear case where promoting equality in participation and inclusion requires attending to the particular needs of different groups.

Another bodily difference which has not been as widely discussed in law and policy literature, but should be, is age. With increasing numbers of willing and able old people marginalized in our society, the issue of mandatory retirement has been increasingly discussed. This discussion has been muted because serious consideration of working rights for all people able and willing to work implies major restructuring of the allocation of labor in an economy with already socially volatile levels of unemployment. Forcing people out of their workplaces solely on account of their age is arbitrary and unjust. Yet I think it is also unjust to require old people to work on the same terms as younger people. Old people should have different working rights. When they reach a certain age they should be allowed to retire and receive income benefits. If they wish to continue working, they should be allowed more flexible and part-time schedules than most workers currently have.

Each of these cases of special rights in the workplace—pregnancy and birthing, physical disability, and being old—has its own purposes and structures. They all challenge, however, the same paradigm of the "normal, healthy" worker and "typical work situation." In each case, the circumstance that calls for different treatment should not be understood as lodged in the differently treated workers, per se, but in their interaction with the structure and norms of the workplace. Even in cases such as these, that is, difference does not have its source in natural, unalterable, biological attributes, but in the relationship of bodies to conventional rules and practices. In each case the political claim for special rights emerges not from a need to compensate for an inferiority, as some would interpret it, but from a positive assertion of specificity in different forms of life.[23]

Issues of difference arise for law and policy not only regarding bodily being, but just as importantly for cultural integrity and invisibility. By culture I mean group-specific phenomena of behavior, temperament, or meaning. Cultural differences include phenomena of language, speaking style or dialect, body comportment, gesture, social practices, values, group-specific socialization, and so on. To the degree that groups are culturally different, however, equal treatment in many issues of social policy is unjust because it denies these cultural differences or makes them a liability. There are a vast number of issues where fairness involves attention to cultural differences and their effects, but I shall briefly discuss three: affirmative action, comparable worth, and bilingual, bicultural education and service.

Whether they involve quotas or not, affirmative action programs violate a principle of equal treatment because they are race or gender conscious in setting criteria for school admissions, jobs, or promotions. These policies are usually defended in one of two ways. Giving preference to race or gender is understood either as just compensation for groups that have suffered discrimination in the past, or as compensation for the present disadvantage these groups suffer because of that history of discrimination and exclusion.[24] I do not wish to quarrel with either of these justifications for the differential treatment based on race or gender implied by affirmative action policies. I want to suggest that in addition we can understand affirmative action policies as compensating for the cultural biases of standards and evaluators used by the schools or employers. These standards and evaluators reflect at least to some degree the specific life and cultural experience of dominant groups—whites, Anglos, or men. In a group-differentiated society, moreover, the development of truly neutral standards and evaluations is difficult or impossible, because female, black, or Latino cultural experience and the dominant cultures are in many respects not reducible to a common measure. Thus, affirmative action policies compensate for the dominance of one set of cultural attributes. Such an interpretation of affirmative action locates the "problem" that affirmative action solves partly in the understandable biases of evaluators and their standards, rather than only in specific differences of the disadvantaged group.

Although they are not a matter of different treatment as such, comparable worth policies similarly claim to challenge cultural biases in traditional evaluation in the worth of female-dominated occupations, and in doing so require attending to differences. Schemes of equal pay for work of comparable worth require that predominantly male and predominantly female jobs have similar wage structures if they involve similar degrees of skill, difficulty, stress, and so on. The problem in implementing these policies, of course, lies in designing methods of comparing the jobs, which often are very different. Most schemes of comparison choose to minimize sex differences by using supposedly gender-neutral criteria, such as educational attainment, speed of work, whether it involves manipulation of symbols, decision making, and so on. Some writers have suggested, however, that standard classifications of job traits may be systematically biased to keep specific kinds of tasks involved in many female-dominated occupations hidden.[25] Many female-dominated occupations involve gender-specific kinds of labor—such as nurturing, smoothing over social relations, or the exhibition of sexuality—which most task observation ignores.[26] A fair assessment of the skills and complexity of many female-dominated jobs may therefore involve paying explicit attention to gender differences in kinds of jobs rather than applying gender-blind categories of comparison.

Finally, linguistic and cultural minorities ought to have the right to maintain their language and culture and at the same time be entitled to all the benefits of citizenship, as well as valuable education and career opportunities. This right implies a positive obligation on the part of governments and other public bodies to print documents and to provide services in the native language of recognized linguistic minorities, and to provide bilingual instruction in schools. Cultural assimilation should not be a condition of full social participation, because it requires a person to transform his or her sense of identity, and when it is realized on a group level it means altering or annihilating the group's identity. This principle does not apply to any persons who do not identify with majority language or culture within a society but only to sizeable linguistic or cultural minorities living in distinct though not necessarily segregated communities. In the United States, then, special rights for cultural minorities applies at least to Spanish-speaking Americans and Native Americans.

The universalist finds a contradiction in asserting both that formerly segregated groups have a right to inclusion and that these groups have a right to different treatment. There is no contradiction here, however, if attending to difference is necessary in order to make participation and inclusion possible. Groups with different circumstances or forms of life should be able to participate together in public institutions without shedding their distinct identities or suffering disadvantage because of them. The goal is not to give special compensation to the deviant until they achieve normality, but rather to denormalize the way institutions formulate their rules by revealing the plural circumstances and needs that exist, or ought to exist, within them.

Many opponents of oppression and privilege are wary of claims for special rights because they fear a restoration of special classifications that can justify exclusion and stigmatization of the specially marked groups. Such fear has been particularly pro-nounced among feminists who oppose affirming sexual and gender difference in law and policy. It would be foolish for me to deny that this fear has some significant basis.

Such fear is founded, however, on accession to traditional identification of group difference with deviance, stigma, and inequality. Contemporary movements of oppressed groups, however, assert a positive meaning to group difference, by which a group claims its identity as a group and rejects the stereotypes and labeling by which others mark it as inferior or inhuman. These social movements engage the meaning of difference itself as a terrain of political struggle, rather than leave difference to be used to justify exclusion and subordination. Supporting policies and rules that attend to group difference in order to undermine oppression and disadvantage is, in my opinion, a part of that struggle.

Fear of claims to special rights points to a connection of the principle of group representation with the principle of attending to difference in policy. The primary means of defense from the use of special rights to oppress or exclude groups is the self-organization and representation of those groups. If oppressed and disadvantaged groups are able to discuss among themselves what procedures and policies they judge will best further their social and political equality and have access to mechanisms, to make their judgments known to the larger public, then policies that attend to difference are less likely to be used against them than for them. If they have the institutionalized right to veto policy proposals that directly affect them, and them primarily, moreover, such danger is further reduced.

In this article I have distinguished three meanings of universality that have usually been collapsed in discussions of the universality of citizenship and the public realm. Modern politics properly promotes the universality of citizenship in the sense of the inclusion and participation of everyone in public life and democratic processes. The realization of genuinely universal citizenship in this sense today is impeded rather than furthered by the commonly held conviction that when they exercise their citizenship, persons should adopt a universal point of view and leave behind the perceptions they derive from their particular experience and social position. The full inclusion and participation of all in law and public life is also sometimes impeded by formulating laws and rules in universal terms that apply to all citizens in the same way.

In response to these arguments, some people have suggested to me that such challenges to the ideal of universal citizenship threaten to leave no basis for rational normative appeals. Normative reason, it is suggested, entails universality in a Kantian sense: when a person claims that something is good or right he or she is claiming that everyone in principle could consistently make that claim, and that everyone should accept it. This refers to a fourth meaning of universality, more epistemological than political. There may indeed be grounds for questioning a Kantian-based theory of the universality of normative reason, but this is a different issue from the substantive political issues I have addressed here, and the arguments in this paper neither imply nor exclude such a possibility. In any case, I do not believe that challenging the ideal of a unified public or the claim that rules should always be formally universal subverts the possibility of making rational normative claims.

Notes

1. Theodore Lowi's classic analysis of the privatized operations of interest group liberalism remains descriptive of American politics: see *The End of Liberalism* (New York: Norton, 1969). For more recent analyses, see Jürgen Habermas, *Legitimation Crisis* (Boston: Beacon, 1973); Claus Offe, *Contradictions of the Welfare State* (Cambridge, Mass.: MIT Press, 1984); John Keane, *Public Life in Late Capitalism* (Cambridge, Mass.: MIT Press, 1984); Benjamin Barber, *Strong Democracy* (Berkeley: University of California Press, 1984).

2. For an outstanding recent account of the virtues of and conditions for such democracy, see Philip Green, *Retrieving Democracy* (Totowa, N.J.: Rowman & Allanheld, 1985).

3. Barber and Keane both appeal to Rousseau's understanding of civic activity as a model for contemporary participatory democracy, as does Carole Pateman in her classic work, *Participation and Democratic Theory* (Cambridge: Cambridge University Press, 1970). (Pateman's position has, of course, changed.) See also James Miller, *Rousseau: Dreamer of Democracy* (New Haven, Conn.: Yale University Press, 1984).

4. Many who extol the virtues of the civic public, of course, appeal also to a model of the ancient *polis*. For a recent example, see Murray

Bookchin, *The Rise of Urbanization and the Decline of Citizenship* (San Francisco: Sierra Club Books, 1987). In this article, however, I choose to restrict my claims to modern political thought. The idea of the ancient Greek *polis* often functions in both modern and contemporary discussion as a myth of lost origins, the paradise from which we have fallen and to which we desire to return: in this way, appeals to the ancient Greek *polis* are often contained within appeals to modern ideas of civic humanism.

5. Hannah Pitkin performs a most detailed and sophisticated analysis of the virtues of the civic public as a flight from sexual difference through a reading of the texts of Machiavelli; see *Fortune Is a Woman* (Berkeley: University of California Press, 1984). Carole Pateman's recent writing also focuses on such analysis. See, e.g., Carole Pateman, *The Social Contract* (Stanford, Calif.: Stanford University Press, 1988). See also Nancy Hartsock, *Money, Sex and Power* (New York: Longman, 1983), chaps. 7 and 8.

6. See Susan Okin, "Women and the Making of the Sentimental Family," *Philosophy and Public Affairs* 11 (1982): 65–88; see also Linda Nicholson, *Gender and History: The Limits of Social Theory in the Age of the Family* (New York: Columbia University Press, 1986).

7. For analyses of Rousseau's treatment of women, see Susan Okin, *Women in Western Political Thought* (Princeton, N.J.: Princeton University Press, 1978); Lynda Lange, "Rousseau: Women and the General Will," in *The Sexism of Social and Political Theory*, ed. Lorenne M. G. Clark and Lynda Lange (Toronto: University of Toronto Press, 1979); Jean Bethke Elshtain, *Public Man, Private Woman* (Princeton, N.J.: Princeton University Press, 1981), chap. 4. Mary Dietz develops an astute critique of Elshtain's "maternalist" perspective on political theory; in so doing, however, she also seems to appeal to a universalist ideal of the civic public in which women will transcend their particular concerns and become general; see "Citizenship with a Feminist Face: The Problem with Maternal Thinking," *Political Theory* 13 (1985): 19–37. On Rousseau on women, see also Joel Schwartz, *The Sexual Politics of Jean-Jacques Rousseau* (Chicago: University of Chicago Press, 1984).

8. See Ronald Takaki, *Iron Cages: Race and Culture in 19th Century America* (New York: Knopf, 1979). Don Herzog discusses the exclusionary prejudices of some other early American republicans; see "Some Questions for Republicans," *Political Theory* 14 (1986): 473–93.

9. George Mosse, *Nationalism and Sexuality* (New York: Fertig, 1985).

10. Barber, *Strong Democracy*, chaps. 8 and 9. Future page references in parentheses are to this book.

11. I have developed this account more thoroughly in my paper, Iris Marion Young, "Impartiality and the Civic Public: Some Implications of Feminist Critiques of Moral and Political Theory," in *Feminism as Critique*, ed. S. Benhabib and D. Cornell (Oxford: Polity Press, 1987), pp. 56–76.

12. On feminism and participatory democracy, see Pateman.

13. Jane Mansbridge, *Beyond Adversarial Democracy* (New York: Basic Books, 1980).

14. Amy Gutmann, *Liberal Equality* (Cambridge: Cambridge University Press, 1980), pp. 191–202.

15. See Iris Marion Young, "Five Faces of Oppression," *Philosophical Forum* 19 (1988): 270–90.

16. Jürgen Habermas, *Reason and the Rationalization of Society* (Boston: Beacon, 1983), pt. 3. For criticism of Habermas as retaining too universalist a conception of communicative action, see Seyla Benhabib, *Critique, Norm and Utopia* (New York: Columbia University Press, 1986); and Young, "Impartiality and the Civic Public."

17. The Mel King for mayor campaign organization exhibited the promise of such group representation in practice, which was only partially and haltingly realized; see special double issue of *Radical America* 17, no. 6, and 18, no. 1 (1984). Sheila Collins discusses how the idea of a rainbow coalition challenges traditional American political assumptions of a "melting pot," and she shows how lack of coordination between the national level rainbow departments and the grassroots campaign committees prevented the 1984 Jackson campaign from realizing the promise of group representation; see *The Rainbow Challenge: The Jackson Campaign and the Future of U.S. Politics* (New York: Monthly Review Press, 1986).

18. See Gary Ruchwarger, *People in Power: Forging a Grassroots Democracy in Nicaragua* (Hadley, Mass.: Bergin & Garvey, 1985).

19. Martha Minow, "Learning to Live with the Dilemma of Difference: Bilingual and Special Education," *Law and Contemporary Problems*, no. 48 (1985), pp. 157–211.

20. I use the term "special rights" in much the same way as Elizabeth Wolgast, in *Equality and the Rights of Women* (Ithaca, N.Y.: Cornell University Press, 1980). Like Wolgast, I wish to distinguish a class of rights that all

persons should have, general rights, and a class of rights that categories of persons should have by virtue of particular circumstances. That is, the distinction should refer only to different levels of generality, where "special" means only "specific." Unfortunately, "special rights" tends to carry a connotation of *exceptional*, that is, specially marked and deviating from the norm. As I assert below, however, the goal is not to compensate for deficiencies in order to help people be "normal," but to denormalize, so that in certain contexts and at certain levels of abstraction everyone has "special" rights.

21. Linda J. Krieger, "Through a Glass Darkly: Paradigms of Equality and the Search for a Women's Jurisprudence," *Hypatia: A Journal of Feminist Philosophy* 2 (1987): 45–62. Deborah Rhode provides an excellent synopsis of the dilemmas involved in this pregnancy debate in feminist legal theory in "Justice and Gender" (typescript), chap. 9.

22. See Ann Scales, "Towards a Feminist Jurisprudence," *Indiana Law Journal* 56 (1980): 375–444. Christine Littleton provides a very good analysis of the feminist debate about equal vs. different treatment regarding pregnancy and childbirth, among other legal issues for women, in "Reconstructing Sexual Equality," *California Law Review* 25 (1987): 1279–1337. Littleton suggests, as I have stated above, that only the dominant male conception of work keeps pregnancy and birthing from being conceived of as work.

23. Littleton suggests that difference should be understood not as a characteristic of particular sorts of people, but of the interaction of particular sorts of people with specific institutional structures. Minow expresses a similar point by saying that difference should be understood as a function of the relationship among groups, rather than located in attributes of a particular group.

24. For one among many discussions of such "backward looking" and "forward looking" arguments, see Bernard Boxill, *Blacks and Social Justice* (Totowa, N.J.: Rowman & Allanheld, 1984), chap. 7.

25. See R. W. Beatty and J. R. Beatty, "Some Problems with Contemporary Job Evaluation Systems," and Ronnie Steinberg, "A Want of Harmony: Perspectives on Wage Discrimination and Comparable Worth," both in *Comparable Worth and Wage Discrimination: Technical Possibilities and Political Realities*, ed. Helen Remick (Philadelphia: Temple University Press, 1981); D. J. Treiman and H. I. Hartmann, eds., *Women, Work and Wages* (Washington, D.C.: National Academy Press, 1981), p. 81.

26. David Alexander, "Gendered Job Traits and Women's Occupations" (Ph.D. diss., University of Massachusetts, Department of Economics, 1987).

– 7 –

Is Patriotism A Virtue?

Alasdair MacIntyre

I

One of the central tasks of the moral philosopher is to articulate the convictions of the society in which he or she lives so that these convictions may become available for rational scrutiny. This task is all the more urgent when a variety of conflicting and incompatible beliefs are held within one and the same community, either by rival groups who differ on key moral questions or by one and the same set of individuals who find within themselves competing moral allegiances. In either of these types of case the first task of the moral philosopher is to render explicit what is at issue in the various disagreements and it is a task of this kind that I have set myself in this lecture.

For it is quite clear that there are large disagreements about patriotism in our society. And although it would be a mistake to suppose that there are only two clear, simple and mutually opposed sets of beliefs about patriotism, it is at least plausible to suggest that the range of conflicting views can be placed on a spectrum with two poles. At one end is the view, taken for granted by almost everyone in the nineteenth century, a commonplace in the literary culture of the McGuffey readers, that "patriotism" names a virtue. At the other end is the contrasting view, expressed with sometimes shocking clarity in the 1960s, that "patriotism" names a vice. It would be misleading for me to suggest that I am going to be able to offer good reasons for taking one of these views rather than the other. What I do hope to achieve is a clarification of the issues that divide them.

A necessary first step in the direction of any such clarification is to distinguish patriotism properly so called from two other sets of attitudes that are all too easily assimilated to it. The first is that exhibited by those who are protagonists of their own nation's causes because and only because, so they assert, it is their nation which is *the* champion of some great moral ideal. In the Great War of 1914–1918 Max Weber claimed that Imperial Germany should be supported because its was the cause of *Kultur*, while Emile Durkheim claimed with equal vehemence that France should be supported because its was the cause of *civilisation*. And here and now there are those American politicians who claim that the United States deserves our allegiance because it champions the goods of freedom against the evils of communism. What distinguishes their attitude from patriotism is twofold: first it is the ideal and not the nation which is the primary object of their regard; and secondly insofar as their regard for the ideal provides good reasons for allegiance to their country, it provides good reasons for anyone at all to uphold their country's cause, irrespective of their nationality or citizenship.

Patriotism by contrast is defined in terms of a kind of loyalty to a particular nation which only those possessing that particular nationality can exhibit. Only Frenchmen can be patriotic about France, while anyone can make the cause of *civilisation* their own. But it would be all too easy in noticing this to fail to make a second equally important distinction. Patriotism is not to be confused with a mindless loyalty to one's own particular nation which has no regard at all for the characteristics of that particular nation. Patriotism does generally and characteristically involve a peculiar regard not just for one's own nation, but for the particular characteristics and merits and achievements of one's own nation. These latter are indeed valued *as* merits and achievements and their character as merits and achievements provides reasons supportive of the patriot's attitudes. But the patriot does not value in the same way precisely similar merits and achievements when they are the merits and achievements of some nation other than his or hers. For he or she—at least in the role of patriot—values them not just as merits and achievements, but as the merits and achievements of this particular nation.

To say this is to draw attention to the fact that patriotism is one of a class of loyalty-exhibiting virtues (that is, if it *is* a virtue at all), other members of which are marital fidelity, the love of one's own family and kin, friendship, and loyalty to such institutions as schools and cricket or baseball clubs. All these attitudes exhibit a peculiar action-generating regard for particular persons, institutions or groups, a regard founded upon a particular historical relationship of association between the person exhibiting the regard and the relevant person, institution or group. It is often, although not always, the case that associated with this regard will be a felt gratitude for the benefits which the individual takes him or herself to have received from the person, institution or group. But it would be one more mistake to suppose patriotism or other such attitudes of loyalty to be at their core or primarily responses of gratitude. For there are many persons, institutions, and groups to which each of us have good reason to feel grateful without this kind of loyalty being involved. What patriotism and other such attitudes involve is not just gratitude, but a particular kind of gratitude; and what those who treat patriotism and other such loyalties as virtues are committed to believing is not that what they owe their nation or whomever or whatever it is is simply a requital for benefits received, based on some relationship of reciprocity of benefits.

So although one may as a patriot love one's country, or as a husband or wife exhibit marital fidelity, and cite as partially supporting reasons one's country's or one's spouse's merits and one's own gratitude to them for benefits received these can be no more than *partially* supporting reasons, just because what is valued is valued precisely as the merits of *my* country or spouse or as the benefits received by *me* from *my* country or spouse. The particularity of the relationship is essential and ineliminable, and in identifying it as such we have already specified one central problem. What *is* the relationship between patriotism as such, the regard for this particular nation, and the regard which the patriot has for the merits and achievements of his or her nation and for the benefits which he or she has received? The answer to this question must be delayed for it will turn out to depend upon the answer to an apparently even more fundamental question, one that can best be framed in terms of the thesis that, if patriotism is understood as I have understood it, then "patriotism" is not merely not the name of a

virtue, but must be the name of a vice, since patriotism thus understood and morality are incompatible.

II.

The presupposition of this thesis is an account of morality which
has enjoyed high prestige in our culture. According to that account
to judge from a moral standpoint is to judge impersonally. It is to
judge as any rational person would judge, independently of his or
her interests, affections and social position. And to act morally is
to act in accordance with such impersonal judgments. Thus, to think
and to act morally involve the moral agent in abstracting him or
herself from all social particularity and partiality. The potential
conflict between morality so understood and patriotism is at once
clear. For patriotism requires me to exhibit peculiar devotion to my
nation and you to yours. It requires me to regard such contingent
social facts as where I was born and what government ruled over
that place at that time, who my parents were, who my great-great-
grandparents were and so on, as deciding for me the question of
what virtuous action is—at least insofar as it is the virtue of
patriotism which is in question. Hence, the moral standpoint and
the patriotic standpoint are systematically incompatible.

Yet although this is so, it might be argued that the two
standpoints need not be in conflict. For patriotism and all other such
particular loyalties can be restricted in their scope so that their
exercise is always within the confines imposed by morality.
Patriotism need be regarded as nothing more than a perfectly proper
devotion to one's own nation which must never be allowed to violate
the constraints set by the impersonal moral standpoint. This is
indeed the kind of patriotism professed by certain liberal moralists
who are often indignant when it is suggested by their critics that
they are not patriotic. To those critics however patriotism thus limited
in its scope appears to be emasculated, and it does so because in
some of the most important situations of actual social life either the
patriotic standpoint comes into serious conflict with the standpoint
of a genuinely impersonal morality or it amounts to no more than

a set of practically empty slogans. What kinds of circumstances are these? They are at least twofold.

The first kind arises from scarcity of essential resources, often historically from the scarcity of land suitable for cultivation and pasture, and perhaps in our own time from that of fossil fuels. What your community requires as the material prerequisites for your survival as a distinctive community and your growth into a distinctive nation may be exclusive use of the same or some of the same natural resources as my community requires for its survival and growth into a distinctive nation. When such a conflict arises, the standpoint of impersonal morality requires an allocation of goods such that each individual person counts for one and no more than one, while the patriotic standpoint requires that I strive to further the interests of my community and you strive to further those of yours, and certainly where the survival of one community is at stake, and sometimes perhaps even when only large interests of one community are at stake, patriotism entails a willingness to go to war on one's community's behalf.

The second type of conflict-engendering circumstance arises from differences between communities about the right way for each to live. Not only competition for scarce natural resources, but incompatibilities arising from such conflict-engendering beliefs may lead to situations in which once again the liberal moral standpoint and the patriotic standpoint are radically at odds. The administration of the *pax Romana* from time to time required the Roman *imperium* to set its frontiers at the point at which they could be most easily secured, so that the burden of supporting the legions would be reconcilable with the administration of Roman law. And the British Empire was no different in its time. But this required infringing upon the territory and the independence of barbarian border peoples. A variety of such peoples—Scottish Gaels, Iroquois Indians, Bedouin—have regarded raiding the territory of their traditional enemies living within the confines of such large empires as an essential constituent of the good life; whereas the settled urban or agricultural communities, which provided the target for their depredations, have regarded the subjugation of such peoples and their reeducation into peaceful pursuits as one of their central responsibilities. And on such issues once again the impersonal moral standpoint and that of patriotism cannot be reconciled.

For the impersonal moral standpoint, understood as the philosophical protagonists of modern liberalism have understood it, requires neutrality not only between rival and competing interests but also between rival and competing sets of beliefs about the best way for human beings to live. Each individual is to be left free to pursue in his or her own way that way of life which he or she judges to be best; while morality by contrast consists of rules which, just because they are such that any rational person, independently of his or her interests or point of view on the best way for human beings to live, would assent to them, are equally binding on all persons. Hence, in conflicts between nations or other communities over ways of life, the standpoint of morality will once again be that of an impersonal arbiter, adjudicating in ways that give equal weight to each individual person's needs, desires, beliefs about the good and the like, while the patriot is once again required to be partisan.

Notice that in speaking of the standpoint of liberal impersonal morality in the way in which I have done I have been describing a standpoint whose truth is both presupposed by the political actions and utterances of a great many people in our society and explicitly articulated and defended by most modern moral philosophers; and that it has at the level of moral philosophy a number of distinct versions—some with a Kantian flavor, some utilitarian, some contractarian. I do not mean to suggest that the disagreements between these positions are unimportant. Nonetheless the five central positions that I have ascribed to that standpoint appear in all these various philosophical guises: first, that morality is constituted by rules to which any rational person would under certain ideal conditions give assent; second, that those rules impose constraints upon and are neutral between rival and competing interests— morality itself is not the expression of any particular interest; third, that those rules are also neutral between rival and competing sets of beliefs about what the best way for human beings to live is; fourth, that the units which provide the subject matter of morality as well as its agents are individual human beings and that in moral evaluations each individual is to count for one and nobody for more than one; and fifth, that the standpoint of the moral agent constituted by allegiance to these rules is one and the same for all moral agents and as such is independent of all social particularity. What morality provides are standards by which all actual social structures may be brought to judgment from a standpoint independent of all of them. It is morality so understood allegiance to which is not only incompatible with treating patriotism as a virtue, but which requires that patriotism—at least in any substantial version—be treated as a vice.

But is this the only possible way to understand morality? As a matter of history, the answer is clearly "No." This understanding of morality invaded post-Renaissance Western culture at a particular point in time as the moral counterpart to political liberalism and social individualism and its polemical stances reflect its history of emergence from the conflicts which those movements engendered and themselves presuppose alternatives against which those polemical stances were and are directed. Let me therefore turn to considering one of those alternative accounts of morality, whose peculiar interest lies in the place that it has to assign to patriotism.

III.

According to the liberal account of morality *where* and *from whom* I learn the principles and precepts of morality are and must be irrelevant both to the question of what the content of morality is and to that of the nature of my commitment to it, as irrelevant as *where* and *from whom* I learn the principles and precepts of mathematics are to the content of mathematics and the nature of my commitment to mathematical truths. By contrast on the alternative account of morality which I am going to sketch, the questions of *where* and *from whom* I learn my morality turn out to be crucial for both the content and the nature of moral commitment.

On this view, it is an essential characteristic of the morality which each of us acquires that it is learned from, in and through the way of life of some particular community. Of course the moral rules elaborated in one particular historical community will often resemble and sometimes be identical with the rules to which allegiance is given in other particular communities, especially in communities with a shared history or which appeal to the same canonical texts. But there will characteristically be *some* distinctive features of the set of rules considered as a whole, and those distinctive features will often arise from the way in which members of that particular community responded to some earlier situation or series of situations in which particular features of difficult cases led to one or more rules being put in question and reformulated or understood in some new way. Moreover the form of the rules of morality as taught and apprehended will be intimately connected with specific institutional arrangements. The moralities of different societies may agree in having a precept enjoining that a child should honor his or her parents, but what it is so to honor and indeed what a father is and what a mother is will vary greatly between different social orders. So that what I learn as a guide to my actions and as a standard for evaluating them is never morality as such, but always the highly specific morality of some highly specific social order.

To this the reply by the protagonists of modern liberal morality might well be: doubtless this is how a comprehension of the rules of morality is first acquired. But what allows such specific rules, framed in terms of particular social institutions, to be accounted moral rules at all is the fact they are nothing other than applications of universal and general moral rules and individuals acquire genuine morality only because and insofar as they progress from particularized socially specific applications of universal and general moral rules to comprehending them as universal and general. To learn to understand oneself as a moral agent just is to learn to free oneself from social particularity and to adopt a standpoint independent of any particular set of social institutions and the fact that everyone or almost everyone has to learn to do this by starting out from a standpoint deeply infected by social particularity and partiality goes no way towards providing an alternative account of morality. But to this reply a threefold rejoinder can be made.

First, it is not just that I first apprehend the rules of morality in some socially specific and particularized form. It is also and correlatively that the goods by reference to which and for the sake of which any set of rules must be justified are also going to be goods that are socially specific and particular. For central to those goods is the enjoyment of one particular kind of social life, lived out through a particular set of social relationships and thus what I enjoy is the good of *this* particular social life inhabited by me and I enjoy *it* as what *it* is. It may well be that it follows that I would enjoy and benefit equally from similar forms of social life in other communities; but this hypothetical truth in no way diminishes the importance of the contention that my goods are as a matter of fact found *here*, among *these* particular people, in *these* particular relationships. Goods are never encountered except as thus particularized. Hence, the abstract general claim, that rules of a certain kind are justified by being productive of and constitutive of goods of a certain kind, is true only if these and these and these particular sets of rules incarnated in the practices of these and these and these particular communities are productive of or constitutive of these and these and these particular goods enjoyed at certain particular times and places by certain specifiable individuals.

It follows that *I* find *my* justification for allegiance to these rules of morality in *my* particular community; deprived of the life of that community, *I* would have no reason to be moral. But this is not all. To obey the rules of morality is characteristically and generally a hard task for human beings. Indeed were it not so, our need for morality would not be what it is. It is because we are continually liable to be blinded by immediate desire, to be distracted from our responsibilities, to lapse into backsliding and because even the best of us may at times encounter quite unusual temptations that it is important to morality that *I* can only be a moral agent because *we* are moral agents, that I need those around me to reinforce my moral strengths and assist in remedying my moral weaknesses. It is in general only within a community that individuals become capable of morality, are sustained in their morality, and are constituted as moral agents by the way in which other people regard them and what is owed to and by them as well as by the way in which they regard themselves. In requiring much from me morally the other members of my community express a kind of respect for me that has nothing to do with expectations of benefit; and those of whom nothing or little is required in respect of morality are treated with a lack of respect which is, if repeated often enough, damaging to the moral capacities of those individuals. Of course, lonely moral heroism is sometimes required and sometimes achieved. But we must not treat this exceptional type of case as though it were typical. And once we recognize that typically moral agency and continuing moral capacity are engendered and sustained in essential ways by particular institutionalized social ties in particular social groups, it will be difficult to counterpose allegiance to a particular society and allegiance to morality in the way in which the protagonists of liberal morality do.

Indeed the case for treating patriotism as a virtue is now clear. *If* first of all it is the case that I can only apprehend the rules of morality in the version in which they are incarnated in some specific community; and *if* second it is the case that the justification of morality must be in terms of particular goods enjoyed within the life of particular communities; and *if* third it is the case that I am characteristically brought into being and maintained as a moral agent only through the particular kinds of moral sustenance afforded by my community, *then* it is clear that deprived of this community, I am unlikely to flourish as a moral agent. Hence, my allegiance to the community and what it requires of me—even to the point of requiring me to die to sustain its life—could not meaningfully be contrasted with or counterposed to what morality required of me. Detached from my community, I will be apt to lose my hold upon all genuine standards of judgment. Loyalty to that community, to the hierarchy of particular kinship, particular local community and particular natural community, is on this view a prerequisite for morality. So patriotism and those loyalties cognate to it are not just virtues but central virtues. Everything however turns on the truth or falsity of the claims advanced in the three preceding if-clauses. And the argument so far affords us no resources for delivering a verdict upon that truth or falsity. Nonetheless some progress has been achieved, and not only because the terms of the debate have become clearer. For it has also become clear that this dispute is not adequately characterized if it is understood simply as a disagreement between two rival accounts of morality, as if there were some independently identifiable phenomenon situated somehow or other in the social world waiting to be described more or less accurately by the contending parties. What we have here are two rival and incompatible moralities, each of which is viewed from within by its adherents as morality-as-such, each of which makes its exclusive claim to our allegiance. How are we to evaluate such claims?

One way to begin is to be learned from Aristotle. Since we possess no stock of clear and distinct first principles or any other such epistemological resource that would provide us with a neutral and independent standard for judging between them, we shall do well to proceed dialectically. And one useful dialectical strategy is to focus attention on those accusations which the adherents of each bring against the rival position which the adherents of that rival position treat as of central importance to rebut. For this will afford at least one indication of the issues about the importance of which both sides agree and about the characterization of which their very recognition of disagreement suggests that there must also be some shared beliefs. In what areas do such issues arise?

IV.

One such area is defined by a charge which it seems reasonable at least *prima facie* for the protagonists of patriotism to bring against morality. The morality for which patriotism is a virtue offers a form of rational justification for moral rules and precepts whose structure is clear and rationally defensible. The rules of morality are justifiable if and only if they are productive of and partially constitutive of a form of shared social life whose goods are directly enjoyed by those inhabiting the particular communities whose social life is of that kind. Hence, *qua* member of this or that particular community I can appreciate the justification for what morality requires of me from within the social roles that I live out in my community. By contrast, it may be argued, liberal morality requires of me to assume an abstract and artificial—perhaps even an impossible—stance, that of a rational being as such, responding to the requirements of morality not *qua* parent or farmer or quarterback, but *qua* rational agent who has abstracted him or herself from all social particularity, who has become not merely Adam Smith's impartial spectator, but a correspondingly impartial actor, and one who in his impartiality is doomed to rootlessness, to be a citizen of nowhere. How can I justify to myself performing this act of abstraction and detachment?

The liberal answer is clear: such abstraction and detachment is defensible, because it is a necessary condition of moral freedom, of emancipation from the bondage of the social, political, and economic *status quo*. For unless I can stand back from every and any feature of that *status quo*, including the roles within it which I myself presently inhabit, I will be unable to view it critically and to decide for myself what stance it is rational and right for me to adopt towards it. This does not preclude that the outcome of such a critical evaluation may not be an endorsement of all or some of the existing social order; but even such an endorsement will only be free and rational if I have made it for myself in this way. (Making just such an endorsement of much of the economic *status quo* is the distinguishing mark of the contemporary conservative liberal, such as Milton Friedman, who is as much a liberal as the liberal liberal who finds much of the *status quo* wanting—such as J. K. Galbraith or Edward Kennedy—or the radical liberal.) Thus, liberal morality does after all appeal to an overriding good, the good of this particular kind of emancipating freedom. And in the name of this good it is able not only to respond to the question about how the rules of morality are to be justified but also to frame a plausible and potentially damaging objection to the morality of patriotism.

It is of the essence of the morality of liberalism that no limitations are or can be set upon the criticism of the social *status quo*. No institution, no practice, no loyalty can be immune from being put in question and perhaps rejected. Conversely the morality of patriotism is one which precisely because it is framed in terms of the membership of some particular social community with some particular social, political, and economic structure, must exempt at least some fundamental structures of that community's life from criticism. Because patriotism has to be a loyalty that is in some respects unconditional, so in just those respects rational criticism is ruled out. But if so the adherents of the morality of patriotism have condemned themselves to a fundamentally irrational attitude—since to refuse to examine some of one's fundamental beliefs and attitudes is to insist on accepting them, whether they are rationally justifiable or not, which is irrational—and have imprisoned themselves within that irrationality. What answer can the adherents of the morality of patriotism make to this kind of accusation? The reply must be threefold.

When the liberal moralist claims that the patriot is bound to treat his or her nation's projects and practices in some measure uncritically, the claim is not only that at any one time certain of these projects and practices will be being treated uncritically; it is that some at least must be permanently exempted from criticism. The patriot is in no position to deny this; but what is crucial to the patriot's case is to identify clearly precisely what it is that is thus exempted. And at this point it becomes extremely important that in outlining the case for the morality of patriotism—as indeed in outlining the case for liberal morality—we should not be dealing with strawmen. Liberalism and patriotism are not positions invented by me or by other external commentators; they have their own distinctive spokesmen and their own distinctive voices. And although I hope that it has been clear throughout that I have only been trying to articulate what those voices would say, it is peculiarly important to the case for patriotic morality at this point that its actual historical protagonists be identified. So what I say next is an attempt to identify the common attitudes on this point of Charles Péguy and Charles de Gaulle, of Bismarck and of Adam von Trott. You will notice that in these pairs one member is someone who was at least for a time a member of his nation's political establishment, the other someone who was always in a radical way outside that establishment and hostile to it, but that even those who were for a time identified with the *status quo* of power, were also at times alienated from it. And this makes it clear that whatever is exempted from the patriot's criticism, the *status quo* of power and government and the policies pursued by those exercising power and government never need be so exempted. What then is exempted? The answer is: the nation conceived *as a project*, a project somehow or other brought to birth in the past and carried on so that a morally distinctive community was brought into being which embodied a claim to political autonomy in its various organized and institutionalized expressions. Thus, one can be patriotic towards a nation whose political independence is yet to come—as Garibaldi was; or towards a nation which once was and perhaps might be again—like the Polish patriots of the 1860s. What the patriot is

committed to is a particular way of linking a past which has conferred a distinctive moral and political identity upon him or her with
a future for the project which is his or her nation which it is his
or her responsibility to bring into being. Only this allegiance is
unconditional and allegiance to particular governments or forms
of government or particular leaders will be entirely conditional upon
their being devoted to furthering that project rather than frustrating
or destroying it. Hence there is nothing inconsistent in a patriot's
being deeply opposed to his country's contemporary rulers, as
Péguy was, or plotting their overthrow, as Adam von Trott did.

Yet although this may go part of the way towards answering
the charge of the liberal moralist that the patriot must in certain
areas be completely uncritical and therefore irrationalist, it certainly
does not go all the way. For everything that I have said on behalf
of the morality of patriotism is compatible with it being the case
that on occasion patriotism might require me to support and work
for the success of some enterprise of my nation as crucial to its overall
project, crucial perhaps to its survival, when the success of that
enterprise would not be in the best interests of humankind, eval-
uated from an impartial and an impersonal standpoint. The case
of Adam von Trott is very much to the point.

Adam von Trott was a German patriot who was executed after
the unsuccessful assassination attempt against Hitler's life in 1944.
Trott deliberately chose to work inside Germany with the minuscule,
but highly placed, conservative opposition to the Nazis with the
aim of replacing Hitler from within, rather than to work for an
overthrow of Nazi Germany, which would result in the destruction
of the Germany brought to birth in 1871. But to do this he had to
appear to be identified with the cause of Nazi Germany and so
strengthened not only his country's cause, as was his intention, but
also as an unavoidable consequence the cause of the Nazis. This
kind of example is a particularly telling one, because the claim that
such and such a course of action is "to the best interests of mankind"
is usually at best disputable, at worst cloudy rhetoric. But there are
a very few causes in which so much was at stake—and that this
is generally much clearer in retrospect than it was at the time does
not alter that fact—that the phrase has clear application: the
overthrow of Nazi Germany was one of them.

How ought the patriot then to respond? Perhaps in two ways. The first begins by reemphasizing that from the fact that the particularist morality of the patriot is rooted in a particular community and inextricably bound up with the social life of that community, it does not follow that it cannot provide rational grounds for repudiating many features of that country's present organized social life. The conception of justice engendered by the notion of citizenship within a particular community may provide standards by which particular political institutions are found wanting: when Nazi anti-Semitism encountered the phenomena of German Jewish ex-soldiers who had won the Iron Cross, it had to repudiate German particularist standards of excellence (for the award of the Iron Cross symbolized a recognition of devotion to Germany). Moreover the conception of one's own nation having a special mission does not necessitate that this mission may not involve the extension of a justice originally at home only in the particular institutions of the homeland. And clearly particular governments or agencies of government may defect and may be understood to have defected from this mission so radically that the patriot may find that a point comes when he or she has to choose between the claims of the project which constitutes his or her nation and the claims of the morality that he or she has learnt as a member of the community whose life is informed by that project. Yes, the liberal critic of patriotism will respond, this indeed *may* happen; but it may not and it often will not. Patriotism turns out to be a permanent source of moral danger. And this claim, I take it, cannot in fact be successfully rebutted.

A second possible, but very different type of answer on behalf of the patriot would run as follows. I argued earlier that the kind of regard for one's own country which would be compatible with a liberal morality of impersonality and impartiality would be too insubstantial, would be under too many constraints, to be regarded as a version of patriotism in the traditional sense. But it does not follow that some version of traditional patriotism may not be compatible with some other morality of universal moral law, which sets limits to and provides both sanction for and correction of the particularist morality of the patriot. Whether this is so or not is too large and too distinct a question to pursue in this present paper.

But we ought to note that even if it is so—and all those who have been both patriots and Christians *or* patriots and believers in Thomistic natural law *or* patriots and believers in the Rights of Man have been committed to claiming that it is so—this would not diminish in any way the force of the liberal claim that patriotism is a morally dangerous phenomenon.

That the rational protagonist of the morality of patriotism is compelled, if my argument is correct, to concede this does not mean that there is not more to be said in the debate. And what needs to be said is that the liberal morality of impartiality and impersonality turns out also to be a morally dangerous phenomenon in an interestingly corresponding way. For suppose the bonds of patriotism to be dissolved: would liberal morality be able to provide anything adequately substantial in its place? What the morality of patriotism at its best provides is a clear account of and justification for the particular bonds and loyalties which form so much of the substance of the moral life. It does so by underlining the moral importance of the different members of a group acknowledging a shared history. Each one of us to some degree or other understands his or her life as an enacted narrative; and because of our relationships with others we have to understand ourselves as characters in the enacted narratives of other people's lives. Moreover the story of each of our lives is characteristically embedded in the story of one or more larger units. I understand the story of my life in such a way that it is part of the history of my family or of this farm or of this university or of this countryside; and I understand the story of the lives of other individuals around me as embedded in the same larger stories, so that I and they share a common stake in the outcome of that story and in what sort of story it both is and is to be: tragic, heroic, comic.

A central contention of the morality of patriotism is that I will obliterate and lose a central dimension of the moral life if I do not understand the enacted narrative of my own individual life as embedded in the history of my country. For if I do not so understand it I will not understand what I owe to others or what others owe to me, for what crimes of my nation I am bound to make reparation, for what benefits to my nation I am bound to feel gratitude. Understanding what is owed to and by me and understanding the history of the communities of which I am a part is on this view one and the same thing.

It is worth stressing that one consequence of this is that patriotism, in the sense in which I am understanding it in this paper, is only possible in certain types of national community under certain conditions. A national community, for example, which systematically disowned its own true history or substituted a largely fictitious history for it or a national community in which the bonds deriving from history were in no way the real bonds of the community (having been replaced for example by the bonds of reciprocal self-interest) would be one towards which patriotism would be—from any point of view—an irrational attitude. For precisely the same reasons that a family whose members all came to regard membership in that family as governed only by reciprocal self-interest would no longer be a family in the traditional sense, so a nation whose members took up a similar attitude would no longer be a nation and this would provide adequate grounds for holding that the project which constituted that nation had simply collapsed. Since all modern bureaucratic states tend towards reducing national communities to this condition, all such states tend towards a condition in which any genuine morality of patriotism would have no place and what paraded itself as patriotism would be an unjustifiable simulacrum.

Why would this matter? In modern communities in which membership is understood only or primarily in terms of reciprocal self-interest, only two resources are generally available when destructive conflicts of interest threaten such reciprocity. One is the arbitrary imposition of some solution by force; the other is appeal to the neutral, impartial and impersonal standards of liberal morality. The importance of this resource is scarcely to be underrated; but how much of a resource is it? The problem is that some motivation has to be provided for allegiance to the standards of impartiality and impersonality which both has rational justification and can outweigh the considerations provided by interest. Since any large need for such allegiance arises precisely and only when and insofar as the possibility of appeals to reciprocity in interests has broken down, such reciprocity can no longer provide the relevant kind of motivation. And it is difficult to identify anything that can take its place. The appeal to moral agents *qua* rational beings to place their allegiance to impersonal rationality above that to their interests has, just because it is an appeal to rationality, to furnish an adequate reason for so doing. And this is a point at which liberal accounts of morality are notoriously vulnerable. This vulnerability becomes a manifest practical liability at one key point in the social order.

Every political community except in the most exceptional conditions requires standing armed forces for its minimal security. Of the members of these armed forces it must require both that they be prepared to sacrifice their own lives for the sake of the community's security and that their willingness to do so be not contingent upon their own individual evaluation of the rightness or wrongness of their country's cause on some specific issue, measured by some standard that is neutral and impartial relative to the interests of their own community and the interests of other communities. And, that is to say, good soldiers may not be liberals and must indeed embody in their actions a good deal at least of the morality of patriotism. So the political survival of any polity in which liberal morality had secured large-scale allegiance would depend upon there still being enough young men and women who rejected that liberal morality. And in this sense liberal morality tends towards the dissolution of social bonds.

Hence, the charge that the morality of patriotism can successfully bring against liberal morality is the mirror-image of that which liberal morality can successfully urge against the morality of patriotism. For while the liberal moralist was able to conclude that patriotism is a permanent source of moral danger because of the way it places our ties to our nation beyond rational criticism, the moralist who defends patriotism is able to conclude that liberal morality is a permanent source of moral danger because of the way it renders our social and moral ties too open to dissolution by rational criticism. And each party is in fact in the right against the other.

V.

The fundamental task which confronts any moral philosopher who finds this conclusion compelling is clear. It is to enquire whether, although the central claims made on behalf of these two rival modern moralities cannot both be true, we ought perhaps not to move towards the conclusion that both sets of claims are in fact false. And this is an enquiry in which substantial progress has already been made. But history in its impatience does not wait for moral philosophers to complete their tasks, let alone to convince their fellow-citizens. The *polis* ceased to be the key institution in Greek politics even while Aristotle was still restating its rationale and any contemporary philosopher who discusses the key conceptions that have informed modern political life since the eighteenth century is in danger of reliving Aristotle's fate, even if in a rather less impressive way. The owl of Minerva really does seem to fly at dusk.

Does this mean that my argument is therefore devoid of any immediate practical significance? That would be true only if the conclusion that a morality of liberal impersonality and a morality of patriotism must be deeply incompatible itself had no practical significance for our understanding of our everyday politics. But perhaps a systematic recognition of this incompatibility will enable us to diagnose one central flaw in the political life characteristic of modern Western states, or at least of all those modern Western states which look back for their legitimation to the American and the French revolutions. For politics so established have tended to contrast themselves with the older regimes that they displaced by asserting that, while all previous politics had expressed in their lives the partiality and one-sidedness of local customs, institutions, and traditions, they have for the first time given expression in their constitutional and institutional forms to the impersonal and impartial rules of morality as such, common to all rational beings. So Robespierre proclaimed that it was an effect of the French Revolution that the cause of France and the cause of the Rights of Man were one and the same cause. And in the nineteenth century the United States produced its own version of this claim, one which at the level of rhetoric provided the content for many Fourth of July orations and at the level of education set the standards for the Americanization of the late nineteenth century and early twentieth century immigrants, especially those from Europe.

Hegel employs a useful distinction which he marks by his use of the words *Sittlichkeit* and *Moralität*. *Sittlichkeit* is the customary morality of each particular society, pretending to be no more than this. *Moralität* reigns in the realm of rational universal, impersonal morality, of liberal morality, as I have defined it. What those immigrants were taught in effect was that they had left behind countries and cultures where *Sittlichkeit* and *Moralität* were certainly distinct and often opposed and arrived in a country and a culture whose *Sittlichkeit* just is *Moralität*. And thus for many Americans the cause of America, understood as the object of patriotic regard, and the cause of morality, understood as the liberal moralist understands it, came to be identified. The history of this identification could not be other than a history of confusion and incoherence, if the argument which I have constructed in this lecture is correct. For a morality of particularist ties and solidarities has been conflated with a morality of universal, impersonal, and impartial principles in a way that can never be carried through without incoherence.

One test therefore of whether the argument that I have constructed has or has not empirical application and practical significance would be to discover whether it is or is not genuinely illuminating to write the political and social history of modern America as in key part the living out of a central conceptual confusion, a confusion perhaps required for the survival of a large-scale modern polity which has to exhibit itself as liberal in many institutional settings, but which also has to be able to engage the patriotic regard of enough of its citizens, if it is to continue functioning effectively. To determine whether that is or is not true would be to risk discovering that we inhabit a kind of polity whose moral order requires systematic incoherence in the form of public allegiance to mutually inconsistent sets of principles. But that is a task which—happily—lies beyond the scope of this lecture.

— 8 —

Aliens and Citizens:
The Case for Open Borders

Joseph H. Carens

Borders have guards and the guards have guns. This is an obvious fact of political life but one that is easily hidden from view—at least from the view of those of us who are citizens of affluent Western democracies. To Haitians in small, leaky boats confronted by armed Coast Guard cutters, to Salvadorans dying from heat and lack of air after being smuggled into the Arizona desert, to Guatemalans crawling through rat-infested sewer pipes from Mexico to California—to these people the borders, guards, and guns are all too apparent. What justifies the use of force against such people? Perhaps borders and guards can be justified as a way of keeping out criminals, subversives, or armed invaders. But most of those trying to get in are not like that. They are ordinary, peaceful people, seeking only the opportunity to build decent, secure lives for themselves and their families. On what moral grounds can these sorts of people be kept out? What gives anyone the right to point guns at *them*?

To most people the answer to this question will seem obvious. The power to admit or exclude aliens is inherent in sovereignty and essential for any political community. Every state has the legal and moral right to exercise that power in pursuit of its own national interest, even if that means denying entry to peaceful, needy foreigners. States may choose to be generous in admitting immigrants, but they are under no obligation to do so.[1]

I want to challenge that view. In this essay, I will argue that borders should generally be open and that people should normally be free to leave their country of origin and settle in another, subject only to the sorts of constraints that bind current citizens in their

229

new country. The argument is strongest, I believe, when applied
to the migration of people from third world countries to those of
the first world. Citizenship in Western liberal democracies is the
modern equivalent of feudal privilege—an inherited status that
greatly enhances one's life chances. Like feudal birthright privileges,
restrictive citizenship is hard to justify when one thinks about it
closely.

In developing this argument, I will draw upon three contemporary approaches to political theory: first that of Robert Nozick;
second that of John Rawls; third that of the utilitarians. Of the three,
I find Rawls the most illuminating, and I will spend the most time
on the arguments that flow from his theory. But I do not want to
tie my case too closely to his particular formulations (which I will
modify in any event). My strategy is to take advantage of three well-
articulated theoretical approaches that many people find persuasive
to construct a variety of arguments for (relatively) open borders.
I will argue that all three approaches lead to the same basic conclusion: there is little justification for restricting immigration. Each
of these theories begins with some kind of assumption about the
equal moral worth of individuals. In one way or another, each treats
the individual as prior to the community. These foundations provide
little basis for drawing fundamental distinctions between citizens
and aliens who seek to become citizens. The fact that all three
theories converge upon the same basic result with regard to
immigration despite their significant differences in other areas
strengthens the case for open borders. In the final part of the essay,
I will consider communitarian objections to my argument, especially
those of Michael Walzer, the best contemporary defender of the view
I am challenging.

Aliens and Property Rights

One popular position on immigration goes something like this:
"It's our country. We can let in or keep out whomever we want."
This could be interpreted as a claim that the right to exclude aliens
is based on property rights, perhaps collective or national property
rights. Would this sort of claim receive support from theories in

which property rights play a central role? I think not, because those theories emphasize *individual* property rights and the concept of collective or national property rights would undermine the individual rights that these theories wish to protect.

Consider Robert Nozick as a contemporary representative of the property rights tradition. Following Locke, Nozick assumes that individuals in the state of nature have rights, including the right to acquire and use property. All individuals have the same natural rights—that is, the assumption about moral equality that underlies this tradition—although the exercise of those rights leads to material inequalities. The "inconveniences" of the state of nature justify the creation of a minimal state whose sole task is to protect people within a given territory against violations of their rights.[2]

Would this minimal state be justified in restricting immigration? Nozick never answers this question directly, but his argument at a number of points suggests not. According to Nozick the state has no right to do anything other than enforce the rights which individuals already enjoy in the state of nature. Citizenship gives rise to no distinctive claim. The state is obliged to protect the rights of citizens and noncitizens equally because it enjoys a *de facto* monopoly over the enforcement of rights within its territory. Individuals have the right to enter into voluntary exchanges with other individuals. They possess this right as individuals, not as citizens. The state may not interfere with such exchanges so long as they do not violate someone else's rights.[3]

Note what this implies for immigration. Suppose a farmer from the United States wanted to hire workers from Mexico. The government would have no right to prohibit him from doing this. To prevent the Mexicans from coming would violate the rights of both the American farmer and the Mexican workers to engage in voluntary transactions. Of course, American workers might be disadvantaged by this competition with foreign workers. But Nozick explicitly denies that anyone has a right to be protected against competitive disadvantage. (To count that sort of thing as a harm would undermine the foundations of *individual* property rights.) Even if the Mexicans did not have job offers from an American, a Nozickean government would have no grounds for preventing them from entering the country. So long as they were peaceful and did not steal, trespass on private property, or otherwise violate the rights of other individuals, their entry and their actions would be none of the state's business.

Does this mean that Nozick's theory provides no basis for the exclusion of aliens? Not exactly. It means rather that it provides no basis for the *state* to exclude aliens and no basis for individuals to exclude aliens that could not be used to exclude citizens as well. Poor aliens could not afford to live in affluent suburbs (except in the servants' quarters), but that would be true of poor citizens too. Individual property owners could refuse to hire aliens, to rent them houses, to sell them food, and so on, but in a Nozickean world they could do the same things to their fellow citizens. In other words, individuals may do what they like with their own personal property. They may normally exclude whomever they want from land they own. But they have this right to exclude as individuals, not as members of a collective. They cannot prevent other individuals from acting differently (hiring aliens, renting them houses, etc.).[4]

Is there any room for collective action to restrict entry in Nozick's theory? In the final section of his book, Nozick draws a distinction between nations (or states) and small face-to-face communities. People may voluntarily construct small communities on principles quite different from the ones that govern the state so long as individuals are free to leave these communities. For example, people may choose to pool their property and to make collective decisions on the basis of majority rule. Nozick argues that this sort of community has a right to restrict membership to those whom it wishes to admit and to control entry to its land. But such a community may also redistribute its jointly held property as it chooses. This is not an option that Nozick (or any other property rights theorist) intends to grant to the state.[5]

This shows why the claim "It's our country. We can admit or exclude whomever we want" is ultimately incompatible with a property rights theory like Nozick's. Property cannot serve as a protection for individuals *against* the collective if property is collectively owned. If the notion of collective ownership is used to justify keeping aliens out, it opens the possibility of using the same notion to justify redistributing income or whatever else the majority decides. Nozick explicitly says that the land of a nation is not the collective property of its citizens. It follows that the control that the state can legitimately exercise over that land is limited to the enforcement of the rights of individual owners. Prohibiting people from entering a territory because they did not happen to be born there or otherwise gain the credentials of citizenship is no part of any state's legitimate mandate. The state has no right to restrict immigration.

Migration and the Original Position

In contrast to Nozick, John Rawls provides a justification for an activist state with positive responsibilities for social welfare. Even so, the approach to immigration suggested by *A Theory of Justice* leaves little room for restrictions in principle. I say "suggested" because Rawls himself explicitly assumes a closed system in which questions about immigration could not arise. I will argue, however, that Rawls's approach is applicable to a broader context than the one he considers. In what follows, I assume a general familiarity with Rawls's theory, briefly recalling the main points and then focusing on those issues that are relevant to my inquiry.

Rawls asks what principles people would choose to govern society if they had to choose from behind a "veil of ignorance," knowing nothing about their own personal situations (class, race, sex, natural talents, religious beliefs, individual goals and values, and so on). He argues that people in this original position would choose two principles. The first principle would guarantee equal liberty to all. The second would permit social and economic inequalities so long as they were to the advantage of the least well off (the difference principle) and attached to positions open to all under fair conditions of equal opportunity. People in the original position would give priority to the first principle, forbidding a reduction of basic liberties for the sake of economic gains.[6]

Rawls also draws a distinction between ideal and nonideal theory. In ideal theory one assumes that, even after the "veil of ignorance" is lifted, people will accept and generally abide by the principles chosen in the original position and that there are no historical obstacles to the realization of just institutions. In nonideal theory, one takes account of both historical obstacles and the unjust actions of others. Nonideal theory is thus more immediately relevant to practical problems, but ideal theory is more fundamental, establishing the ultimate goal of social reform and a basis for judging the relative importance of departures from the ideal (e.g., the priority of liberty).[7]

Like a number of other commentators, I want to claim that many of the reasons that make the original position useful in thinking about questions of justice within a given society also make it useful for thinking about justice across different societies.[8] Cases like migration and trade, where people interact across governmental boundaries, raise questions about whether the background conditions of the interactions are fair. Moreover, anyone who wants to be moral will feel obliged to justify the use of force against other human beings, whether they are members of the same society or not. In thinking about these matters we don't want to be biased by self-interested or partisan considerations, and we don't want existing injustices (if any) to warp our reflections. Moreover, we can take it as a basic presupposition that we should treat all human beings, not just members of our own society, as free and equal moral persons.[9]

The original position offers a strategy of moral reasoning that helps to address these concerns. The purpose of the "veil of ignorance" is "to nullify the effects of specific contingencies which put men at odds" because natural and social contingencies are "arbitrary from a moral point of view" and therefore are factors which ought not to influence the choice of principles of justice.[10] Whether one is a citizen of a rich nation or a poor one, whether one is already a citizen of a particular state or an alien who wishes to become a citizen—this is the sort of specific contingency that could set people at odds. A fair procedure for choosing principles of justice must therefore exclude knowledge of these circumstances, just as it excludes knowledge of one's race or sex or social class. We should therefore take a global, not a national, view of the original position.

One objection to this global approach is that it ignores the extent to which Rawls's use of the original position and the "veil of ignorance" depends upon a particular understanding of moral personality that is characteristic of modern democratic societies but may not be shared by other societies.[11] Let us grant the objection and ask whether it really matters.

The understanding of moral personality in question is essentially the view that all people are free and equal moral persons. Even if this view of moral personality is not shared by people in other societies, it is not a view that applies only to people who share it. Many members of our own society do not share it, as illustrated by the recent demonstrations by white racists in Forsythe County, Georgia. We criticize the racists and reject their views but do not deprive them of their status as free and equal citizens because of their beliefs. Nor is our belief in moral equality limited to members of our own society. Indeed our commitment to civic equality is derived from our convictions about moral equality, not vice versa. So, whatever we think about the justice of borders and the limitations of the claims of aliens, our views must be compatible with a respect for all other human beings as moral persons.

A related objection emphasizes the "constructivist" nature of Rawls's theory, particularly in its later formulations.[12] The theory only makes sense, it is said, in a situation where people already share liberal-democratic values. But if we presuppose a context of shared values, what need have we for a "veil of ignorance?" Why not move directly from the shared values to an agreement on principles of justice and corresponding institutions? The "veil of ignorance" offers a way of thinking about principles of justice in a context where people have deep, unresolvable disagreements about matters of fundamental importance and yet still want to find a way to live together in peaceful cooperation on terms that are fair to all. That seems to be just as appropriate a context for considering the problem of worldwide justice as it is considering the problem of domestic justice.

To read Rawls's theory only as a constructive interpretation of existing social values is to undermine its potential as a constructive critique of those values. For example, racism has deep roots in American public culture, and in the not-too-distant past people like those in Forsythe County constituted a majority in the United States. If we think the racists are wrong and Rawls is right about our obligation to treat all members of our society as free and equal moral persons, it is surely not just because the public culture has changed and the racists are now in the minority. I gladly concede that I am using the original position in a way that Rawls himself does not intend, but I think that this extension is warranted by the nature of the questions I am addressing and the virtues of Rawls's approach as a general method of moral reasoning.

Let us therefore assume a global view of the original position. Those in the original position would be prevented by the "veil of ignorance" from knowing their place of birth or whether they were members of one particular society rather than another. They would presumably choose the same two principles of justice. (I will simply assume that Rawls's argument for the two principles is correct, though the point is disputed.) These principles would apply globally, and the next task would be to design institutions to implement the principles—still from the perspective of the original position. Would these institutions include sovereign states as they currently exist? In ideal theory, where we can assume away historical obstacles and the dangers of injustice, some of the reasons for defending the integrity of existing states disappear. But ideal theory does not require the elimination of all linguistic, cultural, and historical differences. Let us assume that a general case for decentralization of power to respect these sorts of factors would justify the existence of autonomous political communities comparable to modern states.[13] That does not mean that all the existing features of state sovereignty would be justified. State sovereignty would be (morally) constrained by the principles of justice. For example, no state could restrict religious freedom and inequalities among states would be restricted by an international difference principle.

What about freedom of movement among states? Would it be regarded as a basic liberty in a global system of equal liberties, or would states have the right to limit entry and exit? Even in an ideal world people might have powerful reasons to want to migrate from one state to another. Economic opportunities for particular individuals might vary greatly from one state to another even if economic inequalities among states were reduced by an international difference principle. One might fall in love with a citizen from another land, one might belong to a religion which has few followers in one's native land and many in another, one might seek cultural opportunities that are only available in another society. More generally, one has only to ask whether the right to migrate freely *within* a given society is an important liberty. The same sorts of considerations make migration across state boundaries important.[14]

Behind the "veil of ignorance," in considering possible restrictions on freedom, one adopts the perspective of the one who would be most disadvantaged by the restrictions, in this case the perspective of the alien who wants to immigrate. In the original position, then, one would insist that the right to migrate be included in the system of basic liberties for the same reasons that one would insist that the right to religious freedom be included: it might prove essential to one's plan of life. Once the "veil of ignorance" is lifted, of course, one might not make use of the right, but that is true of other rights and liberties as well. So, the basic agreement among those in the original position would be to permit no restrictions on migration (whether emigration or immigration).

There is one important qualification to this. According to Rawls, liberty may be restricted for the sake of liberty even in ideal theory and all liberties depend on the existence of public order and security.[15] (Let us call this the public order restriction.) Suppose that unrestricted immigration would lead to chaos and the breakdown of order. Then all would be worse off in terms of their basic liberties. Even adopting the perspective of the worst-off and recognizing the priority of liberty, those in the original position would endorse restrictions on immigration in such circumstances. This would be a case of restricting liberty for the sake of liberty and every individual would agree to such restrictions even though, once the "veil of ignorance" was lifted, one might find that it was one's own freedom to immigrate which had been curtailed.

Rawls warns against any attempt to use this sort of public order argument in an expansive fashion or as an excuse for restrictions on liberty undertaken for other reasons. The hypothetical possibility of a threat to public order is not enough. Restrictions would be justified only if there were a "reasonable expectation" that unlimited immigration would damage the public order and this expectation would have to be based on "evidence and ways of reasoning acceptable to all."[16] Moreover, restrictions would be justified only to the extent necessary to preserve public order. A need for some restrictions would not justify any level of restrictions whatsoever.

Finally, the threat to public order posed by unlimited immigration could not be the product of antagonistic reactions (e.g., riots) from current citizens. This discussion takes place in the context of ideal theory and in this context it is assumed that people try to act justly. Rioting to prevent others from exercising legitimate freedoms would not be just. So, the threat to public order would have to be one that emerged as the unintended cumulative effect of individually just actions.

In ideal theory, we face a world of just states with an international difference principle. Under such conditions, the likelihood of mass migrations threatening to the public order of any particular state seems small. So, there is little room for restrictions on immigration in ideal theory. But what about nonideal theory, where one takes into account both historical contingencies and the unjust actions of others?

In the nonideal, real world there are vast economic inequalities among nations (presumably much larger than would exist under an international difference principle). Moreover, people disagree about the nature of justice and often fail to live up to whatever principles they profess. Most states consider it necessary to protect themselves against the possibility of armed invasion or covert subversion. And many states deprive their own citizens of basic rights and liberties. How does all this affect what justice requires with regard to migration?

First, the conditions of the real world greatly strengthen the case for state sovereignty, especially in those states that have relatively just domestic institutions. National security is a crucial form of public order. So, states are clearly entitled to prevent the entry of people (whether armed invaders or subversives) whose goal is the overthrow of just institutions. On the other hand, the strictures against an expansive use of the public order argument also apply to claims about national security.

A related concern is the claim that immigrants from societies where liberal democratic values are weak or absent would pose a threat to the maintenance of a just public order. Again the distinction between reasonable expectations and hypothetical speculations is crucial. These sorts of arguments were used during the nineteenth century against Catholics and Jews from Europe and against all

Asians and Africans. If we judge those arguments to have been proven wrong (not to say ignorant and bigoted) by history, we should be wary of resurrecting them in another guise.

A more realistic concern is the sheer size of the potential demand. If a rich country like the United States were simply to open its doors, the number of people from poor countries seeking to immigrate might truly be overwhelming, even if their goals and beliefs posed no threat to national security or liberal democratic values.[17] Under these conditions, it seems likely that some restrictions on immigration would be justified under the public order principle. But it is important to recall all the qualifications that apply to this. In particular, the need for some restriction would not justify any level of restriction whatsoever or restrictions for other reasons, but only that level of restriction essential to maintain public order. This would surely imply a much less restrictive policy than the one currently in force, which is shaped by so many other considerations besides the need to maintain public order.

Rawls asserts that the priority accorded to liberty normally holds under nonideal conditions as well. This suggests that, if there are restrictions on immigration for public order reasons, priority should be given to those seeking to immigrate because they have been denied basic liberties over those seeking to immigrate simply for economic opportunities. There is a further complication, however. The priority of liberty holds absolutely only in the long run. Under nonideal conditions it can sometimes be justifiable to restrict liberty for the sake of economic gains, if that will improve the position of the worst-off and speed the creation of conditions in which all will enjoy equal and full liberties. Would it be justifiable to restrict immigration for the sake of the worst-off?

We have to be wary of hypocritical uses of this sort of argument. If rich states are really concerned with the worst-off in poor states, they can presumably help more by transferring resources and reforming international economic institutions than by restricting immigration. Indeed, there is reason to suppose more open immigration would help some of the worst-off, not hurt them. At the least, those who immigrate presumably gain themselves and often send money back home as well.

Perhaps the ones who come are not the worst-off, however. It is plausible to suppose that the worst-off don't have the resources to leave. That is still no reason to keep others from coming unless their departure hurts those left behind. But let's suppose it does, as the brain-drain hypothesis suggests. If we assume some restrictions on immigration would be justified for public order reasons, this would suggest that we should give priority to the least skilled among potential immigrants because their departure would presumably have little or no harmful effect on those left behind. It might also suggest that compensation was due to poor countries when skilled people emigrate. But to say that we should actually try to keep people from emigrating (by denying them a place to go) because they represent a valuable resource to their country of origin would be a dramatic departure from the liberal tradition in general and from the specific priority that Rawls attaches to liberty even under nonideal conditions.[18]

Consider the implications of this analysis for some of the conventional arguments for restrictions on immigration. First, one could not justify restrictions on the grounds that those born in a given territory or born of parents who were citizens were more entitled to the benefits of citizenship than those born elsewhere or born of alien parents. Birthplace and parentage are natural contingencies that are "arbitrary from a moral point of view." One of the primary goals of the original position is to minimize the effects of such contingencies upon the distribution of social benefits. To assign citizenship on the basis of birth might be an acceptable procedure, but only if it did not preclude individuals from making different choices later when they reached maturity.

Second, one could not justify restrictions on the grounds that immigration would reduce the economic well-being of current citizens. That line of argument is drastically limited by two considerations: the perspective of the worst-off and the priority of liberty. In order to establish the current citizens' perspective as the relevant worst-off position, it would be necessary to show that immigration would reduce the economic well-being of current citizens below the level the potential immigrants would enjoy if they were not permitted to immigrate. But even if this could be established, it would not justify restrictions on immigration because of the priority of liberty. So, the economic concerns of current citizens are essentially rendered irrelevant.

Third, the effect of immigration on the particular culture and history of the society would not be a relevant moral consideration, so long as there was no threat to basic liberal democratic values. This conclusion is less apparent from what I have said so far, but it follows from what Rawls says in his discussion of perfectionism.[19] The principle of perfectionism would require social institutions to be arranged so as to maximize the achievement of human excellence in art, science, or culture regardless of the effect of such arrangements on equality and freedom. (For example, slavery in ancient Athens has sometimes been defended on the grounds that it was essential to Athenian cultural achievements.) One variant of this position might be the claim that restrictions on immigration would be necessary to preserve the unity and coherence of a culture (assuming that the culture was worth preserving). Rawls argues that in the original position no one would accept any perfectionist standard because no one would be willing to risk the possibility of being required to forgo some important right or freedom for the sake of an ideal that might prove irrelevant to one's own concerns. So, restrictions on immigration for the sake of preserving a distinctive culture would be ruled out.

In sum, nonideal theory provides more grounds for restricting immigration than ideal theory, but these grounds are severely limited. And ideal theory holds up the principle of free migration as an essential part of the just social order toward which we should strive.

Aliens in the Calculus

A utilitarian approach to the problem of immigration can take into account some of the concerns that the original position excludes but even utilitarianism does not provide much support for the sorts of restrictions on immigration that are common today. The fundamental principle of utilitarianism is "maximize utility," and the utilitarian commitment to moral equality is reflected in the assumption that everyone is to count for one and no one for more than one when utility is calculated. Of course, these broad formulations cover over deep disagreements among utilitarians. For example, how is "utility" to be defined? Is it subjective or objective? Is it a question of happiness or welfare as in classical utilitarianism or preferences or interests as in some more recent versions?[20]

However these questions are answered, any utilitarian approach would give more weight to some reasons for restricting immigration than Rawls's approach would. For example, if more immigration would hurt some citizens economically, that would count against a more open immigration policy in any utilitarian theory I am familiar with. But that would not settle the question of whether restrictions were justified, for other citizens might gain economically from more immigration and that would count in favor of a more open policy. More importantly, the economic effects of more immigration on noncitizens would also have to be considered. If we focus only on economic consequences, the best immigration policy from a utilitarian perspective would be the one that maximized overall economic gains. In this calculation, current citizens would enjoy no privileged position. The gains and losses of aliens would count just as much. Now the dominant view among both classical and neoclassical economists is that the free mobility of capital and labor is essential to the maximization of overall economic gains. But the free mobility of labor requires open borders. So, despite the fact that the economic costs to current citizens are morally relevant in the utilitarian framework, they would probably not be sufficient to justify restrictions.

Economic consequences are not the only ones that utilitarians consider. For example, if immigration would affect the existing culture or way of life in a society in ways that current citizens found undesirable, that would count against open immigration in many versions of utilitarianism. But not in all. Utilitarians disagree about whether all pleasures (or desires or interests) are to count or only some. For example, should a sadist's pleasure be given moral weight and balanced against his victim's pain or should that sort of pleasure be disregarded? What about racial prejudice? That is clearly relevant to the question of immigration. Should a white racist's unhappiness at the prospect of associating with people of color be counted in the calculus of utility as an argument in favor of racial exclusion as reflected, say, in the White Australia policy? What about the desire to preserve a distinctive local culture as a reason for restricting immigration? That is sometimes linked to racial prejudice but by no means always.

Different utilitarians will answer these sorts of questions in different ways. Some argue that only long-term, rational, or otherwise refined pleasures (or desires or interests) should count. Others insist that we should not look behind the raw data in making our calculations. Everyone's preferences should count, not merely the preferences someone else finds acceptable. I favor the former approach, a reconstructive or filtering approach to utility, but I won't try to defend that here. Even if one takes the raw data approach, which seems to leave more room for reasons to restrict immigration, the final outcome is still likely to favor much more open immigration than is common today. Whatever the method of calculation, the concerns of aliens must be counted too. Under current conditions, when so many millions of poor and oppressed people feel they have so much to gain from migration to the advanced industrial states, it seems hard to believe that a utilitarian calculus which took the interests of aliens seriously would justify significantly greater limits on immigration than the ones entailed by the public order restriction implied by the Rawlsian approach.

The Communitarian Challenge

The three theories I have discussed conflict with one another on many important issues but not (deeply) on the question of immigration. Each leads on its own terms to a position far more favorable to open immigration than the conventional moral view. It is true that, in terms of numbers, even a public order restriction might exclude millions of potential immigrants given the size of the potential demand. Nevertheless, if the arguments I have developed here were accepted, they would require a radical transformation both of current immigration policies and of conventional moral thinking about the question of immigration.

Some may feel that I have wrenched these theories out of context. Each is rooted in the liberal tradition. Liberalism, it might be said, emerged with the modern state and presupposes it. Liberal theories were not designed to deal with questions about aliens. They assumed the context of the sovereign state. As a historical observation this has some truth, but it is not clear why it should have normative force. The same wrenching out of context complaint could as reasonably have been leveled at those who first constructed liberal arguments for the extension of full citizenship to women and members of the working class. Liberal theories also assumed the right to exclude them. Liberal theories focus attention on the need to justify the use of force by the state. Questions about the exclusion of aliens arise naturally from that context. Liberal principles (like most principles) have implications that the original advocates of the principles did not entirely foresee. That is part of what makes social criticism possible.

Others may think that my analysis merely illustrates the inadequacy of liberal theory, especially its inability to give sufficient weight to the value of community.[21] That indictment of liberal theory may or may not be correct, but my findings about immigration rest primarily on assumptions that I think no defensible moral theory can reject: that our social institutions and public policies must respect all human beings as moral persons and that this respect entails recognition, in some form, of the freedom and equality of every human being. Perhaps some other approach can accept these assumptions while still making room for greater restrictions on immigration. To test that possibility, I will consider the views of the theorist who has done the most to translate the communitarian critique into a positive alternative vision: Michael Walzer.

Unlike Rawls and the others, Walzer treats the question of membership as central to his theory of justice, and he comes to the opposite conclusion about immigration from the one that I have defended:

> Across a considerable range of the decisions that are made, states are simply free to take strangers in (or not).[22]

Walzer differs from the other theorists I have considered not only in his conclusions but also in his basic approach. He eschews the search for universal principles and is concerned instead with "the particularism of history, culture, and membership."[23] He thinks that questions of distributive justice should be addressed not from behind a "veil of ignorance" but from the perspective of membership in a political community in which people share a common culture and a common understanding about justice.

I cannot do full justice here to Walzer's rich and subtle discussion of the problem of membership, but I can draw attention to the main points of his argument and to some of the areas of our disagreement. Walzer's central claim is that exclusion is justified by the right of communities to self-determination. The right to exclude is constrained in three important ways, however. First, we have an obligation to provide aid to others who are in dire need, even if we have no established bonds with them, provided that we can do so without excessive cost to ourselves. So, we may be obliged to admit some needy strangers or at least to provide them with some of our resources and perhaps even territory. Second, once people are admitted as residents and participants in the economy, they must be entitled to acquire citizenship, if they wish. Here the constraint flows from principles of justice not mutual aid. The notion of permanent "guest workers" conflicts with the underlying rationale of communal self-determination which justified the right to exclude in the first place. Third, new states or governments may not expel existing inhabitants even if they are regarded as alien by most of the rest of the population.[24]

In developing his argument, Walzer compares the idea of open states with our experience of neighborhoods as a form of open association.[25] But in thinking about what open states would be like, we have a better comparison at hand. We can draw upon our experience of cities, provinces, or states in the American sense. These are familiar political communities whose borders are open. Unlike neighborhoods and like countries, they are formally organized communities with boundaries, distinctions between citizens and noncitizens, and elected officials who are expected to pursue policies that benefit the members of the community that elected them. They often have distinctive cultures and ways of life. Think of the differences between New York City and Waycross, Georgia, or between California and Kansas. These sorts of differences are often much greater than the differences across nation-states. Seattle has more in common with Vancouver than it does with many American communities. But cities and provinces and American states cannot restrict immigration (from other parts of the country). So, these cases call into question Walzer's claim that distinctiveness depends on the possibility of formal closure. What makes for distinctiveness and what erodes it is much more complex than political control of admissions.

This does not mean that control over admissions is unimportant. Often local communities would like to restrict immigration. The people of California wanted to keep out poor Oklahomans during the Great Depression. Now the people of Oregon would like to keep out the Californians. Internal migrations can be substantial. They can transform the character of communities. (Think of the migrations from the rural South to the urban North.) They can place strains on the local economy and make it difficult to maintain locally funded social programs. Despite all this, we do not think these political communities should be able to control their borders. The right to free migration takes priority.

Why should this be so? Is it just a choice that we make as a larger community (i.e., the nation state) to restrict the self-determination of local communities in this way? Could we legitimately permit them to exclude? Not easily. No liberal state restricts internal mobility. Those states that do restrict internal mobility are criticized for denying basic human freedoms. If freedom of movement within the state is so important that it overrides the claims of local political communities, on what grounds can we restrict freedom of movement across states? This requires a stronger case for the *moral* distinctiveness of the nation-state as a form of community than Walzer's discussion of neighborhoods provides.

Walzer also draws an analogy between states and clubs.[26] Clubs may generally admit or exclude whomever they want, although any particular decision may be criticized through an appeal to the character of the club and the shared understandings of its members. So, too, with states. This analogy ignores the familiar distinction between public and private, a distinction that Walzer makes use of elsewhere.[27] There is a deep tension between the right of freedom of association and the right to equal treatment. One way to address this tension is to say that in the private sphere freedom of association prevails and in the public sphere equal treatment does. You can pick your friends on the basis of whatever criteria you wish, but in selecting people for offices you must treat all candidates fairly. Drawing a line between public and private is often problematic, but it is clear that clubs are normally at one end of the scale and states at the other. So, the fact that private clubs may admit or exclude whomever they choose says nothing about the appropriate admission standards for states. When the state acts it must treat individuals equally.

Against this, one may object that the requirement of equal treatment applies fully only to those who are already *members* of the community. That is accurate as a description of practice but the question is why it should be so. At one time, the requirement of equal treatment did not extend fully to various groups (workers, blacks, women). On the whole, the history of liberalism reflects a tendency to expand both the definition of the public sphere and the requirements of equal treatment. In the United States today, for example, in contrast to earlier times, both public agencies and private corporations may not legally exclude women simply because they are women (although private clubs still may). A white shopkeeper may no longer exclude blacks from his store (although he may exclude them from his home). I think these recent developments, like the earlier extension of the franchise, reflect something fundamental about the inner logic of liberalism.[28] The extension of the right to immigrate reflects the same logic: equal treatment of individuals in the public sphere.

As I noted at the beginning of this section, Walzer asserts that the political community is constrained by principles of justice from admitting permanent guest workers without giving them the opportunity to become citizens. There is some ambiguity about whether this claim is intended to apply to all political communities or only to ones like ours. If states have a right to self-determination, broadly conceived, they must have a right to choose political forms and political practices different from those of liberal democracies. That presumably includes the right to establish categories of second-class citizens (or, at least, temporary guest workers) and also the right to determine other aspects of admissions policy in accordance with their own principles.[29] But if the question is what *our* society (or one with the same basic values) ought to do, then the matter is different both for guest workers and for other aliens. It is right to assert that *our* society ought to admit guest workers to full citizenship. Anything else is incompatible with our liberal democratic principles. But so is a restrictive policy on immigration.

Any approach like Walzer's that seeks its ground in the tradition and culture of *our* community must confront, as a methodological paradox, the fact that liberalism is a central part of our culture. The enormous intellectual popularity of Rawls and Nozick and the enduring influence of utilitarianism attest to their ability to communicate contemporary understandings and shared meanings in a language that has legitimacy and power in our culture. These theories would not make such sense to a Buddhist monk in medieval Japan. But their individualistic assumptions and their language of universal ahistorical reason makes sense to us because of *our* tradition, *our* culture, *our* community. For people in a different moral tradition, one that assumed fundamental moral differences between those inside the society and those outside, restrictions on immigration might be easy to justify. Those who are *other* simply might not count, or at least not count as much. But we cannot dismiss the aliens on the ground that they are other, because *we* are the products of a liberal culture.

The point goes still deeper. To take *our* community as a starting point is to take a community that expresses its moral views in terms of universal principles. Walzer's own arguments reflect this. When he asserts that states may not expel existing inhabitants whom the majority or the new government regards as alien, he is making a claim about what is right and wrong for *any* state not just our own or one that shares our basic values. He develops the argument by drawing on Hobbes. That is an argument from a particular tradition, one that may not be shared by new states that want to expel some of their inhabitants. Nonetheless, Walzer makes a universal claim (and one I consider correct). He makes the same sort of argument when he insists that states may not legitimately restrict emigration.[30] This applies to all political communities not just those that share our understanding of the relation of individual and collective.

Recognition of the particularity of our own culture should not prevent us from making these sorts of claims. We should not try to force others to accept our views, and we should be ready to listen to others and learn from them. But respect for the diversity of communities does not require us to abandon all claims about what other states ought to do. If my arguments are correct, the general case for open borders is deeply rooted in the fundamental values of our tradition. No moral argument will seem acceptable to *us*, if it directly challenges the assumption of the equal moral worth of all individuals. If restrictions on immigration are to be justified, they have to be based on arguments that respect that principle. Walzer's theory has many virtues that I have not explored here, but it does not supply an adequate argument for the state's right to exclude.

Conclusion

Free migration may not be immediately achievable, but it is a goal toward which we should strive. And we have an obligation to open our borders much more fully than we do now. The current restrictions on immigration in Western democracies—even in the most open ones like Canada and the United States—are not justifiable. Like feudal barriers to mobility, they protect unjust privilege.

Does it follow that there is no room for distinctions between aliens and citizens, no theory of citizenship, no boundaries for the community? Not at all. To say that membership is open to all who wish to join is not to say that there is no distinction between members and nonmembers. Those who choose to cooperate together in the state have special rights and obligations not shared by noncitizens. Respecting the particular choices and commitments that individuals make flows naturally from a commitment to the idea of equal moral worth. (Indeed, consent as a justification for political obligation is least problematic in the case of immigrants.) What is not readily compatible with the idea of equal moral worth is the exclusion of those who want to join. If people want to sign the social contract, they should be permitted to do so.

Open borders would threaten the distinctive character of different political communities only because we assume that so many people would move if they could. If the migrants were few, it would not matter. A few immigrants could always be absorbed without changing the character of the community. And, as Walzer observes, most human beings do not love to move.[31] They normally feel attached to their native land and to the particular language, culture, and community in which they grew up and in which they feel at home. They seek to move only when life is very difficult where they are. Their concerns are rarely frivolous. So, it is right to weigh the claims of those who want to move against the claims of those who want to preserve the community as it is. And if we don't unfairly tip the scales, the case for exclusion will rarely triumph.

People live in communities with bonds and bounds, but these may be of different kinds. In a liberal society, the bonds and bounds should be compatible with liberal principles. Open immigration would change the character of the community but it would not leave the community without any character. It might destroy old ways of life, highly valued by some, but it would make possible new ways of life, highly valued by others. The whites in Forsythe County who want to keep out blacks are trying to preserve a way of life that is valuable to them. To deny such communities the right to exclude does limit their ability to shape their future character and destiny, but it does not utterly destroy their capacity for self-determination. Many aspects of communal life remain potentially subject to collective control. Moreover, constraining the kinds of choices that people and communities may make is what principles of justice are for. They set limits on what people seeking to abide by these principles may do. To commit ourselves to open borders would not be to abandon the idea of communal character but to reaffirm it. It would be an affirmation of the liberal character of the community and of its commitment to principles of justice.

Notes

This paper was first written for an APSA seminar on citizenship directed by Nan Keohane. Subsequent versions were presented to seminars at the University of Chicago, the Institute for Advanced Study, and Columbia University. I would like to thank the members of these groups for their comments. In addition I would like to thank the following individuals for helpful comments on one of the many drafts: Sot Barber,

Charles Beitz, Michael Doyle, Amy Gutmann, Christine Korsgaard, Charles Miller, Donald Moon, Jennifer Nedelsky, Thomas Pogge, Peter Schuck, Rogers Smith, Dennis Thompson, and Michael Walzer.

1. The conventional assumption is captured by the Select Commission on Immigration and Refugee Policy: "Our policy—while providing opportunity to a portion of the world's population—must be guided by the basic national interests of the people of the United States." From *U.S. Immigration Policy and the National Interest: The Final Report and Recommendations of the Select Commission on Immigration and Refugee Policy to the Congress and the President of the United States* (1 March 1981). The best theoretical defense of the conventional assumption (with some modifications) is Michael Walzer, *Spheres of Justice* (New York: Basic Books, 1983), pp. 31–63. A few theorists have challenged the conventional assumption. See Bruce Ackerman, *Social Justice in the Liberal State* (New Haven: Yale University Press, 1980), pp. 89–95; Judith Lichtenberg, "National Boundaries and and Moral Boundaries: a Cosmopolitan View," in *Boundaries: National Autonomy and Its Limits*, ed. Peter G. Brown and Henry Shue (Totowa, NJ: Rowman and Littlefield, 1981), pp. 79–100, and Roger Nett, "The Civil Right We Are Not Ready For: The Right of Free Movement of People on the Face of the Earth," *Ethics* 81:212–27. Frederick Whelan has also explored these issues in two interesting unpublished papers.

2. Robert Nozick, *Anarchy, State, and Utopia* (New York: Basic Books. 1974), pp. 10–25, 88–119.

3. Ibid., pp. 108–113. Citizens, in Nozick's view, are simply consumers purchasing impartial, efficient protection of preexisting natural rights. Nozick uses the terms "citizen," "client," and "customer" interchangeably.

4. Nozick interprets the Lockean proviso as implying that property rights in land may not so restrict an individual's freedom of movement as to deny him effective liberty. This further limits the possibility of excluding aliens. See p. 55.

5. Ibid., pp. 320–23.

6. John Rawls, *A Theory of Justice* (Cambridge, MA.: Harvard University Press, 1971), pp. 60–65, 136–42, 243–48.

7. Ibid., pp. 8–9, 244–48.

8. The argument for a global view of the original position has been developed most fully in Charles Beitz, *Political Theory and International*

Relations (Princeton, NJ: Princeton University Press, 1979), pp 125–76, especially 129–36 and 143–53. For earlier criticisms of Rawls along the same lines, see Brian Barry, *The Liberal Theory of Justice* (Oxford: Clarendon Press, 1973), pp. 128–33 and Thomas M. Scanlon, "Rawls's Theory of Justice," *University of Pennsylvania Law Review* 121, no. 5 (May 1973): 1066–67. For more recent discussions, see David A. J. Richards, "International Distributive Justice," in *Ethics, Economics, and the Law,* eds. J. Roland Pennock and John Chapman (New York: New York University Press, 1982), pp. 275–99 and Charles Beitz, "Cosmopolitan Ideals and National Sentiments," *The Journal of Philosophy* 80, no. 10 (October 1983): 591–600. None of these discussions fully explores the implications of a global view of the original position for the issue of immigration, although the recent essay by Beitz touches on the topic.

9. Respecting others as free and equal moral persons does not imply that one cannot distinguish friends from strangers or citizens from aliens. See the conclusion for an elaboration.

10. Rawls, *Justice,* pp. 136, 72.

11. John Rawls, "Kantian Constructivism in Moral Theory," *The Journal of Philosophy* 77, no. 9 (September 1980): 515–72.

12. Ibid. See also John Rawls, "Justice as Fairness: Political not Metaphysical," *Philosophy and Public Affairs* 14 (Summer 1985): 223–51.

13. Compare Beitz, *Political Theory,* p. 183.

14. For more on the comparison of mobility within a country and mobility across countries, see Joseph H. Carens, "Migration and the Welfare State" in *Democracy and the Welfare State,* ed. Amy Gutmann (Princeton: Princeton University Press, 1987).

15. Rawls, *Justice,* pp. 212–13.

16. Ibid., p. 213.

17. For statistics on current and projected levels of immigration to the U.S., see Michael S. Teitelbaum, "Right Versus Right: Immigration and Refugee Policy in the United States," *Foreign Affairs* 59 (1980): 21–59.

18. For the deep roots of the right to emigrate in the liberal tradition, see Frederick Whelan, "Citizenship and the Right to Leave," *American Political Science Review* 75, no. 3 (September 1981): 636–53.

19. Rawls, *Justice,* pp. 325–32.

20. For recent discussions of utilitarianism, see Richard Brandt, *A Theory of the Good and the Right* (Oxford: Oxford University Press, 1979); Peter Singer, *Practical Ethics* (Cambridge: Cambridge University Press, 1979); R. M. Hare, *Moral Thinking* (Oxford: Oxford University Press, 1981); and Amartya Sen and Bernard Williams, eds., *Utilitarianism and Beyond* (Cambridge: Cambridge University Press, 1982).

21. For recent communitarian critiques of liberalism, see Alasdair MacIntyre, *After Virtue* (Notre Dame: Notre Dame University Press, 1981) and Michael Sandel, *Liberalism and the Limits of Justice* (New York: Cambridge University Press, 1982). For a critique of the critics, see Amy Gutmann, "Communitarian Critics of Liberalism," *Philosophy and Public Affairs* 14 (Summer 1985): 308–322.

22. Walzer, *Spheres*, p. 61.

23. Ibid., p. 5.

24. Ibid., pp. 33, 45–48, 55–61, 42–44.

25. Ibid., pp. 36–39.

26. Ibid., pp. 39–41.

27. Ibid., pp. 129–64.

28. I am not arguing that the changes in treatment of women, blacks, and workers were *brought about* by the inner logic of liberalism. These changes resulted from changes in social conditions and from politcal struggles including ideological struggles in which arguments about the implications of liberal principles played some role, though not necessarily a decisive one. But from a philosophical perspective, it is important to understand where principles lead, even if one does not assume that people's actions in the world will always be governed by the principles they espouse.

29. Compare Walzer's claim that the caste system would be just if accepted by the villages affected (ibid., pp. 313–15).

30. Ibid., pp. 39–40.

31. Ibid., p. 38.

— 9 —

Citizenship and National Identity: Some Reflections on the Future of Europe

Jürgen Habermas

Until the middle of the eighties, history seemed to be gradually entering that crystalline state known as *posthistoire*, to use Arnold Gehlen's term to describe that strange feeling that *tout ça change mais rien ne va plus*. In the iron grip of systemic constraints, all possibilities seemed to have been exhausted, all alternatives frozen dead, and all avenues still open to have become meaningless. This mood has changed in the meantime. History has become mobilized; it is accelerating, even overheating. The new problems are shifting old perspectives and, what is more important, opening up new perspectives for the future, points of view that restore our ability to perceive alternative courses of action.

Three historical currents of our contemporary period, once again in flux, touch upon the relation between citizenship and national identity. First, the issue of the future of the nation state has unexpectedly become topical in the wake of German unification, the liberation of the East Central European states and the nationality conflicts that are breaking out throughout Eastern Europe. Second, the fact that the states of the European Community are gradually growing together, especially with the impending *caesura* which will be created by the introduction of a common market in 1993, sheds some light on the relation between nation-state and democracy, for the democratic processes that have gone hand in hand with the nation-state lag hopelessly behind the supranational form taken by economic integration. Third, the tremendous influx of immigration from the poor regions of the East and South with which Europe will be increasingly confronted in the coming years lend the problem of asylum-seekers a new significance and urgency. This process exacerbates the conflict between the universalistic principles of constitutional democracies on the one hand and the particularistic claims of communities to preserve the integrity of their *habitual* ways of life on the other.

These topics offer an occasion for the conceptual clarification of some normative perspectives through which we can hopefully gain a better understanding of the complex relation between citizenship and national identity.

I.

The Past and Future of the Nation-State

Recent events in Germany and the Eastern European countries have given a new twist to the discussion in the former Federal Republic on the gradual development of postnational society.[1] Many German intellectuals have complained about the democratic deficit incurred by a process of unification that has been effected more at an administrative and economic level than by enlisting the participation of the citizens; they now find themselves accused of "postnational arrogance." The controversy as to the form and speed of unification has not only been fueled by contradictory feelings, but also by confusing thoughts and concepts. One side conceived of the five new states' joining the Federal Republic as restoring the unity of a nation-state torn apart four decades ago. From this viewpoint, the nation constitutes the prepolitical unity of a community with a shared common historical destiny. The other side conceived of the political unification as restoring democracy and a constitutional state in a territory where civil rights had been suspended in one form or another since 1933. From this viewpoint, what used to be West Germany was no less a nation of citizens than is the new Federal Republic. With this republican usage, the term "nation-state" is stripped of precisely those prepolitical connotations with which the expression was laden in modern Europe. Loosening the semantic connections between national citizenship and national identity takes into account that the classic form of the nation-state is at present disintegrating. This is confirmed by a glance back to its rise in early modern times.

In modern Europe, the premodern form of *empire*, which used to unite numerous peoples, remained rather unstable—as in the cases of the Holy Roman Empire or the Russian and Ottoman empires.[2] A different, federal form of state emerged from the belt of Central European cities in what was formerly Lorraine, the heart of the Carolingian Empire. It was, in particular, in Switzerland where a *federation* sprang up strong enough to balance the ethnic tensions within a multicultural association of citizens. However, it was only the *territorial states* with a central administration that exerted a structuring influence on the system of European states. In the sixteenth century, kingdoms gave birth to those territorial states— such as England, France, Portugal, Spain, and Sweden—which were later on, in the course of democratization in line with the French example, gradually transformed into *nation-states*. This state formation secured the overall conditions under which capitalism was then able to develop worldwide. The nation-state provided both the infrastructure for rational administration and the legal frame for free individual and collective action. Moreover, and it is this which shall interest us here, the nation-state laid the foundations for cultural and ethnic homogeneity on the basis of which it then proved possible to push ahead with the democratization of government since the late eighteenth century, although this was achieved at the cost of excluding ethnic minorities. The nation-state and democracy are twins born out of the French Revolution. From a cultural point of view, both have been growing in the shadow of *nationalism*.

Nationalism is the term for a specifically modern phenomenon of cultural integration. This type of national consciousness is formed in social movements and emerges from modernization processes at a time when people are at once both mobilized and isolated as individuals. Nationalism is a form of collective consciousness which both presupposes a reflexive appropriation of cultural traditions that have been filtered through historiography and which spreads only via the channels of modern mass communication. Both elements lend to nationalism the artifical traits of something that is to a certain extent a construct, thus rendering it by definition susceptible to manipulative misuse by political elites.

The history of the term "nation" mirrors in a peculiar way the emergence of the nation-state.[3] For the Romans, *natio* is the Goddess of Birth and Origin. *Natio* refers, like *gens* and *populus* and unlike *civitas*, to peoples and tribes who were not yet organized in political associations; indeed, the Romans often used it to refer to "savage," "barbaric," or "pagan" peoples. In this classic usage, therefore, nations are communities of people of the same descent, who are integrated geographically, in the form of settlements or neighborhoods, and culturally by their common language, customs, and traditions, but who are not yet politically integrated in the form of state organization. This meaning persists throughout the Middle Ages and indeed in early modern times. Even Kant still maintains that "that group which recognizes itself as being gathered together in a society due to common descent shall be called a nation (*gens*)." Yet, since the middle of the eighteenth century, the differences in meaning between *''Nation''* and *''Staatsvolk,''* that is, "nation" and "politically organized people," have gradually been disappearing. With the French Revolution, the nation even became the source of state sovereignty, for example, in the thought of Sieyès. Each nation is now supposed to be granted the right to political self-determination. Indeed, in the nineteenth century, the conservative representatives of the German Historical School equated the principle of nationality with the "principle of revolution."

The meaning of the term "nation" thus changed from designating a prepolitical entity to something that was supposed to play a constitutive role in defining the political identity of the citizen within a democratic polity. In the final instance, the manner in which national identity determines citizenship can in fact be reversed. Thus, the gist of Ernest Renan's famous saying, "the existence of a nation is. . .a daily plebiscite," is already directed *against* nationalism. After 1871, Renan was only able to counter the German Empire's claims to the Alsace by referring to the inhabitants' French nationality because he could conceive of the "nation" as a nation of citizens. The nation of citizens does not derive its identity from some common ethnic and cultural properties, but rather from the *praxis* of citizens who actively exercise their civil rights. At this juncture, the republican strand of "citizenship" completely parts company with the idea of belonging to a prepolitical community integrated on the basis of descent, a shared tradition and a common language. Viewed from this end, the initial fusion of republicanism with nationalism only functioned as a catalyst.

Nationalism, which was inspired by the works of historians and romantic writers, founded a collective identity that played a *functional role* for the implementation of the citizenship that arose in the French Revolution. In the melting pot of national consciousness, the ascriptive features of one's origin were now transformed into just so many achieved properties, resulting from a reflexive appropriation of tradition. Hereditary nationality gave way to an acquired nationalism, that is, to a product of one's own conscious striving. This nationalism was able to foster people's identification with a role which demanded a high degree of personal commitment, even to the point of self-sacrifice; in this respect, general conscription was only the other side of the civil rights coin. Nationalism and republicanism combine in the willingness to fight and, if necessary, die for one's country. This explains the complementary relation of mutual reinforcement that originally obtains between nationalism and republicanism, the one becoming the vehicle for the emergence of the other.

However, this socio-psychological connection does not mean that the two are linked in conceptual terms. Compare "freedom" in the sense of national independence, that is, collective self-assertion vis-à-vis other nations, with "freedom" in the sense of those political liberties the individual citizen enjoys within a country; the two notions are so different in meaning that, at a later point, the modern understanding of republican freedom can cut its umbilical links to the womb of the national consciousness which had originally given birth to it. Only briefly did the democratic nation-state forge a close link between "ethnos" and "demos."[4] Citizenship was never conceptually tied to national identity.

The concept of citizenship developed out of Rousseau's notion of self-determination. Initially, "popular sovereignty" had been understood as a delimitation or as the reversal of royal sovereignty and was judged to rest on a contract between a people and its government. Rousseau and Kant, by contrast, did not conceive of popular sovereignty as the transfer of political power from above to below or as its distribution among two contracting parties. Popular sovereignty rather signified the transformation of authoritarian into *self-legislated* power. The social contract is no longer conceived of as an historical pact; it provides an abstract model for the very mode of how political authority is constituted and legitimated. The intention is to purge the remaining strands of *violentia* from the *auctoritas* of the state's powers. In this conception, to take Kant's words, "legislation can only issue from the concurring and unified will of everyone, to the extent that each decides the same about all and that all decide the same about each...."

This concept of popular sovereignty does not refer to some substantive collective will which would owe its identity to a prior homogeneity of descent or form of life. The consensus achieved in the course of argument in an association of free and equal citizens stems in the final instance from an identically applied *procedure* recognized by all. This procedure for political will formation assumes a differentiated form in the constitution of a democratic state. Thus, in a pluralistic society, the constitution lends expression to a *formal* consensus. The citizens wish to organize their peaceful coexistence in line with principles which meet with the justified agreement of all because they are in the equal interest of all. Such an association is structured by relations of mutual recognition, and given these relations, everyone can expect to be respected by everybody else as free and equal. Everyone should be in a position to expect that all will receive equal protection and respect in his or her inviolable integrity as a unique individual, as a member of an ethnic or cultural group and as a citizen, that is, as a member of a polity. This idea of a self-determining political community has taken on concrete legal shape in a variety of constitutions, in fact, in all political systems of Western Europe and the United States.

For a long time, however, *"Staatsbürgerschaft," "citoyenneté"* or "citizenship" all only meant, in the language of the law, political membership. It is only recently that the concept has been expanded to cover the status of citizens defined in terms of civil rights.[5] Citizenship as membership in a state only assigns a particular person to a particular nation whose existence is recognized in terms of international law. This definition of membership serves, along with the territorial demarcation of the country's borders, the purpose of a social delimitation of the state. In democratic states, which understand themselves as an association of free and equal citizens, membership depends on the principle of voluntariness. Here the usual ascriptive characteristics of domicile and birth (*jus soli* and *jus sanguinis*) by no means justify a person's being irrevocably subjected to the sovereign authority of that country. They function merely as administrative criteria for attributing to citizens an assumed, implicit concurrence, to which the right to emigrate or to renounce one's citizenship corresponds.[6]

Today, however, the expressions "*Staatsbürgerschaft*" or "citizenship" are not only used to denote membership in a state but also for the status defined by civil rights. The German Basic Law has no parallel to the Swiss notion of active citizenship ("*Aktivbürgerschaft*").[7] However, taking Article 33, 1, of the Basic Law as its starting point, mainstream German legal thought has expanded the package of civil rights and duties to generate an overall status of a similar kind.[8] The republican meaning of citizenship is, for example, captured by R. Gawert's work; for him, citizenship has as its reference point the problem of societal self-organization and at its core the political rights of participation and communication. He conceives of citizenship as "the legal institution via which the individual member of a nation takes part as an active agent in the concrete nexus of state actions."[9] The status of citizen is constituted above all by those democratic rights to which the individual can reflexively lay claim in order to alter his material legal status.

Two mutually contradictory interpretations of such a capacity for active citizenship vie with each other for pride of place in the philosophy of law. The role of the citizen is given an individualist and instrumentalist reading in the liberal tradition of natural law starting with Locke, whereas a communitarian and ethical understanding of the same has emerged in the tradition of political philosophy that draws upon Aristotle. From the first perspective, citizenship is conceived in analogy with the model of received membership in an organization which secures a legal status. From the second, it is conceived in analogy with the model of achieved membership in a self-determining ethical community. In the one interpretation, the individuals remain external to the state, contributing only in a certain manner to its reproduction in return for the benefits of organizational membership. In the other, the citizens are integrated into the political community like parts into a whole, that is, in such a manner that they can only form their personal and social identity in this horizon of shared traditions and inter-subjectively recognized institutions. In the former, the citizens are no different than private persons who bring their prepolitical interests to bear vis-à-vis the state apparatus, whereas in the latter, citizenship can only be realized as a joint practice of self-determination. Charles Taylor has described these two competing concepts of citizenship as follows:

> One (model) focuses mainly on individual rights and equal treatment, as well as on a government performance which takes account of citizen's preferences. This is what has to be secured. Citizen capacity consists mainly in the power to retrieve these rights and ensure equal treatment, as well as to influence the effective decision-makers. . . .These institutions have an entirely instrumental significance. . . .No value is put on participation in rule for its own sake. . . .The other model, by contrast, defines participation in self-rule as of the essence of freedom, as part of what must be secured. This is. . .an essential component of citizen capacity. . . .Full participation in self-rule is seen as being able, at least part of the time, to have some part in the forming of a ruling consensus, with which one can identify along with others. To rule and be ruled in turn means that at least some of the time the governors can be "us" and not always "them."[10]

The holist model of a polity in which each citizen is completely bound up is inadequate if one bears in mind many of the aspects of modern politics. Nevertheless, it has an advantage over the organization model, for the latter sets isolated individuals against a state apparatus, the two being linked only via a relation of membership that regulates an exchange of benefits for functionally specified contributions. The holist model emphasizes that political autonomy is a purpose in itself, to be realized not by single persons in the private pursuit of their particular interests but rather only by all together in an intersubjectively shared *praxis*. In this reading, the citizen's status is constituted by a web of egalitarian relations of mutual recognition. It assumes that everyone can adopt the second person and first person plural perspective of participants—

that is, not merely the observer perspective of an observer or actor oriented toward his or her own success.

Legally guaranteed relations of recognition do not, however, reproduce themselves of their own accord, but rather require the cooperative efforts of the active *praxis* of citizens, something in which no one can be compelled by legal norms to take part. There are good reasons why modern compulsory law does not apply to the motives and beliefs of its addressees. A legal duty to make active use of democratic rights would have something totalitarian about it; we would feel it to be alien to modern law. As a consequence, the legally constituted status of the citizen is dependent on the *forthcomingness* of a kindred background of motives and beliefs of citizenship geared toward the commonweal—motives and beliefs that cannot be enforced legally. In this regard, the republican model of citizenship reminds one that the institutions of constitutional freedom are only worth as much as a population makes of them, and this would be a population *accustomed* to political freedom and well-versed in adopting the we-perspective of active self-determination. Therefore, the legally institutionalized role of a citizen had to be embedded in the context of a political culture imbued with the concept of freedom. The necessity of such a background seems to justify the communitarians in their insistence that the citizen must identify himself "patriotically" with his particular form of life. Taylor himself emphasizes the requirement of a collective consciousness which arises from identification with the consciously accepted traditions of one's own particular ethical and cultural community: "The issue is, can our patriotism survive the marginalization of a participatory self-rule? As we have seen, a patriotism is a common identification with a historical community founded on certain values. . . . But it must be one whose core values incorporate freedom."[11]

With this, Taylor appears to contradict my proposition that there is only an historically contingent and not a conceptual connection between republicanism and nationalism. Studied more closely, Taylor's remarks boil down to the statement that the universalist principles of democratic states need an anchoring in the political culture of each country. The principles laid down in the constitution can neither take shape in social practices nor become the driving force for the project of creating an association of free and equal

persons until they are *situated* in the horizon of the history of a nation
of citizens in such a way as to be connected with their motives and
convictions.

However, examples of multicultural societies like Switzerland
and the United States demonstrate that a political culture in the
seedbed of which constitutional principles are rooted by no means
has to be based on all citizens sharing the same language or the
same ethnic and cultural origins. Rather, the political culture must
serve as the common denominator for a constitutional patriotism
which simultaneously sharpens an awareness of the multiplicity
and integrity of the different forms of life which coexist in a
multicultural society. In a future Federal Republic of European States,
the same legal principles would also have to be interpreted from
the vantage point of different national traditions and histories. One's
own national tradition will, in each case, have to be appropriated
in such a manner that it is related to and relativized by the vantage
points of the other national cultures. It must be connected with the
overlapping consensus of a common, supranationally shared
political culture of the European Community. Particularist anchoring
of *this sort* would in no way impair the universalist meaning of
popular sovereignty and human rights.

II.

Nation State and Democracy in a Unified Europe

The political future of the European Community sheds light
on the relation between national citizenship and national identity
in yet another respect. The concept of national citizenship as
developed from Aristotle to Rousseau was, after all, originally
tailored to the size of cities and city-states. The transformation of
populations into nations which formed states occurred, as we have
seen, under the sign of a nationalism which apparently succeeded
in reconciling republican ideas with the larger dimensions of modern
territorial states. It was, moreover, in the political forms created by
the nation-state that modern trade and commerce arose. And, like
the bureaucratic state apparatus, the capitalist economy also
developed a systemic entelechy of its own. The markets for goods,

capital, and labor obey their own logic, independent of the intentions of persons involved. Alongside administrative power, money has thus become an anonymous medium of societal integration that functions beyond the minds of individual actors. Now this *system integration* competes with another form of integration running through the consciousness of the actors involved, that is, *social integration* through values, norms, and processes of reaching understanding. Just one such aspect of social integration is political integration via citizenship. As a consequence, although liberal theories often deny the fact, the relation between capitalism and democracy is fraught with tension.

Examples from Third World countries confirm that there is no linear connection between the emergence of democratic regimes and capitalist modernization. Even the welfare state compromise practised in Western democracies since the end of World War II did not come into being automatically. And, finally, the development of the European Community brings, in its own way, the tension between democracy and capitalism to the fore. Here, it is expressed in the vertical divide between the systemic integration of economy and administration at the supranational level and the political integration that thus far works only at the level of the nation-state. The technocratic shape taken by the European Community reinforces doubts as to whether the normative expectations one associates with the role of the democratic citizen have not actually always been a mere illusion. Did the temporary symbiosis of republicanism and nationalism not merely mask the fact that the exacting concept of citizenship is at best suited for the less-complex relations within an ethnically and culturally homogeneous community?

The "European Economic Community" has meanwhile become a "European Community" that proclaims the political will to create a "European Union." Leaving India aside, the United States provides the only example for such a large edifice of 320 million inhabitants. Having said that, however, let me add that the United States is a multicultural society united by the same political culture and (at least at present) the same language, whereas the European Union would be a multilingual state of different nations. This association would still have to exhibit some similarities with de Gaulle's "Europe of Fatherlands," even if—and this is to be hoped—it were to be more like a Federal Republic than a loose federation of semi-sovereign individual states. The sort of nation-states we have seen to date would continue to exert a strong structural force in such a Europe.

That nation-states constitute a problem along the thorny path to a European Union is, however, due less to their insurmountable claims to sovereignty than to another fact: democratic processes have hitherto only functioned within national borders. So far the political public sphere is fragmented into national units. The question thus arises whether there can ever be such a thing as European citizenship. And by this I mean not only the possibilities for collective political action across national borders but also the consciousness of "an obligation toward the European common-weal."[12] As late as 1974, Raymond Aron answered this question with a resolute "no." To date, genuine civil rights do not reach beyond national borders.

The administration of justice by the European Court takes the "Five Freedoms of the Common Market" as its point of orientation and interprets the free exchange of goods, the free movement of labor, the freedom of entrepreneurial domicile, the freedom of service transactions, and the freedom of currency movements as basic rights. This corresponds to the powers the Treaty of Rome conferred upon the Council of Ministers and the High Commission in Article 3. This, in turn, is to be explained in terms of the goal set out in Article 9: "The basis of the Community shall be a customs union which extends to include the exchange of all goods." This goal will be reached with the advent of the currency union and the establishment of an autonomous central bank. The new level of economic interdependence will give rise to a growing need for coordination in other policy fields as well, such as environmental policy, fiscal and social policy, education policy, and so forth. And the need for new regulations will again be assessed primarily by criteria of economic rationality—such as securing equal conditions for competition. These tasks will be accomplished by European organizations which have meanwhile meshed to form a dense administrative network. The new elites of bureaucrats are, formally speaking, still accountable to the governments and institutions in their respective countries of origin; factually, however, they have outgrown their national context. In this respect, the Brussels authorities can best be equated with the German Central Bank. Professional civil servants form a bureaucracy that is aloof from democratic processes.

For the citizen, this translates into an ever greater gap between being affected by something and participating in changing it. An increasing number of measures decided at a supranational level affect more and more citizens over an ever increasing area of life. Given that the role of citizen has hitherto only been institutionalized at the level of nation-states, citizens have no effective means of debating European decisions and influencing the decision-making processes. M. R. Lepsius's terse statement sums it up: "There is no European public opinion."[13] Now, what interests me is the question whether this disparity is just a passing imbalance that can be set right by the parliamentarization of the Brussels expertocracy or whether these suprastate bureaucracies with their orientation towards sheer economic criteria of rationality merely highlight a general trend that has for a long time also been gaining momentum within the nation-states. I am thinking of the fact that economic imperatives have gradually become independent of all else, and that politics has gradually become a matter of administration, of processes that undermine the status of the citizen and deny the republican meat of such status.

Taking England as his example, T. H. Marshall[14] has studied the expansion of civil rights and duties in connection with capitalist modernization. His division into *civil, political* and *social* rights is modeled on the well-known legal classification of basic rights. Here, liberal negative rights protect the private legal subject against the state illegally infringing on his or her individual freedom and property; the rights of political participation enable the active citizen to take part in the democratic processes of opinion and will formation; social rights secure for the client of the welfare state a minimum of social security. Marshall's analysis supports the thesis that the status of the citizen in modern societies has been expanded and buttressed step-by-step. The negative rights of individual freedom have been first supplemented by democratic rights and then the two classical types by social rights in such a way that ever greater sections of the population have gradually acquired full membership.

Even leaving the historical details aside, this suggestion of a more or less linear development only holds for what sociologists term "inclusion." In a functionally ever more differentiated society, an ever greater number of persons acquire an ever larger number of rights of access to and participation in an ever greater number of subsystems, be these markets, factories and places of work, government offices, courts and standing armies, schools and hospitals, theaters and museums, insurance, public services and goods, political associations and public communications media, political parties, or parliaments. For each individual, the number of memberships in organizations therewith multiplies, and the range of options expands. However, this image of linear progress arises from a description that remains neutral toward increases or losses in autonomy, it says nothing about the actual use made of active citizenship by means of which the individual can himself bring influence to bear on democratic changes of his own status. It is indeed only political rights of participation which endow the citizen with this kind of self-referential competence. The negative rights of liberty and social or positive rights of participation can also be conferred by a paternalistic authority. In principle then, the rule of law and the welfare state can exist without the concommitant existence of democracy. These negative and social rights remain ambiguous even in countries where all three categories of rights are institutionalized, as in the category of a "democratic and social constitutional state."

Liberal rights, which have—viewed historically—crystallized around private ownership, can be grasped from a *functionalist* viewpoint as the institutionalization of a market-steered economy, whereas, from a *normative* viewpoint, they guarantee individual freedoms. Social rights signify from a *functionalist* viewpoint the installation of a welfare bureaucracy, while, from the *normative* viewpoint, they grant the compensatory claims individuals make to a supposedly just distribution of social wealth. It is true that both individual freedom and social security can be considered as the legal basis for the social independence necessary for an effective exercise of political rights in the first place. Yet, this link is contingent. For rights of individual freedom and social security can just as well facilitate a privatist retreat from citizenship and a particular "clientelization" of the citizen's role.

The occurrence of this syndrome, that is, of citizenship reduced to the interests of a client, becomes all the more probable the more the economy and the state apparatus—which have been institutionalized in terms of the same rights—develop a systemic autonomy and push citizens into the periphery of organizational membership. As self-regulated systems, economy and administration tend to cut themselves off from their environments and obey only their internal imperatives of money and power. They no longer fit into the model of a self-determining community of citizens. The classic republican idea of the self-conscious political integration of a community of free and equal persons is evidently too concrete and simple a notion to remain applicable to modern conditions, especially if one has in mind a nation, indeed an ethnically homogeneous community which is held together by common traditions and a shared history.

Fortunately, modern law is a medium which allows for a much more abstract notion of the citizen's autonomy. Nowadays, the sovereignty of the people has constrained itself to become a procedure of more or less discursive opinion and will formation. Still on a normative level, I assume a networking of different communication flows which, however, should be organized in such a way that these can be supposed to bind the public administration to more or less rational premises and in this way enforce social and ecological discipline on the economic system without nonetheless impinging on its intrinsic logic. This provides a model of a deliberative democracy that no longer hinges on the assumption of macro-subjects like the "people" of "the" community but on anonymously interlinked discourses or flows of communication. The model shifts the brunt of fulfilling normative expectations to the infrastructure of a political public sphere that is fueled by spontaneous sources. Citizenship can today only be enacted in the paradoxical sense of compliance with the procedural rationality of a political will-formation, the more or less discursive character of which depends on the vitality of the informal circuit of public communication. An inclusive public sphere cannot be organized as a whole; it depends rather on the stabilizing context of a liberal and egalitarian political culture. At the same time, such a communicative pluralism would still be ineffective unless further conditions could be met. In the first place, deliberations within the decision-making bodies should be open for and sensitive to the influx of issues, value orientations, contributions, and programs originating from their informal environments. Only if such an interplay between institutionalized processes of opinion and will formation and those informal networks of public communication occurs can citizenship today mean more than the aggregation of prepolitical individual interests and the passive enjoyment of rights bestowed upon the individual by the paternalistic authority of the state.

I cannot go into this model in any further detail here.[15] Yet when assessing the chances for a future European citizenship, some empirical hints can at least be gleaned from the historical example of the institutionalization of citizenship within the nation-states. Clearly, the view that sees the rights of citizenship essentially as the product of class struggle is too narrow in focus.[16] Other types of social movements, above all migrations and wars, were the driving force behind the development of a full-fledged status for citizens. In addition, factors that prompted the juridification of new relations of inclusion also had an impact on the political mobilization of a population and thus on the active exercise of given rights of citizenship.[17] These and other related findings allow us to extrapolate with cautious optimism the course European developments could take; thus we are at least not condemned to resignation from the outset.

The single market will set in motion even more extensive horizontal mobility and multiply the contacts between members of different nationalities. Immigration from Eastern Europe and the poverty-stricken regions of the Third World will intensify the multicultural diversity of these societies. This will give rise to social tensions. However, if those tensions are processed productively, they will enhance political mobilization in general, and might particularly encourage the new, endogenous type of new social movements—I am thinking of the peace, ecological and women's movements. These tendencies would strengthen the relevance public issues have for the lifeworld. The increasing pressure of these problems is, furthermore, to be expected—problems for which coordinated solutions are available only at a European level. Given these conditions, communication networks of European-wide public spheres may emerge, networks that may form a favorable context both for new parliamentary bodies of regions that are now in the process of merging and for a European Parliament furnished with greater competence.

To date, the member states have not made the legitimation of EC policy an object of controversy. By and large, the national public spheres are culturally isolated from one another. They are anchored in contexts in which political issues only gain relevance against the background of national histories and national experiences. In the future, however, differentiation could occur in a European culture between a common *political* culture and the branching *national* traditions of art and literature, historiography, philosophy, and so forth. The cultural elites and the mass media would have an important role to play in this regard. Unlike the American variant, a European constitutional patriotism would have to grow out of different interpretations of the same universalist rights and constitutional principles which are marked by the context of different national histories. Switzerland is an example of how a common politico-cultural self-image stands out against the cultural orientations of the different nationalities.

In this context, our task is less to reassure ourselves of our common origins in the European Middle Ages than to develop a new political self-confidence commensurate with the role of Europe in the world of the twenty-first century. Hitherto, world history has accorded the empires that have come and gone but *one* appearance on the stage. This is not only true of the rise and fall of empires in the Old World, but also for modern states like Portugal, Spain, England, France, and Russia. It now appears as if Europe as a whole is being given a second chance. It will not be able to make use of this in terms of the power politics of yesteryear, but only under changed premises, namely, a non-imperial process of reaching understanding with, and learning from, other cultures.

III.

Immigration and the Chauvinism of Prosperity: A Debate

Hannah Arendt's analysis that stateless persons, refugees, and those deprived of rights would determine the mark of this century has turned out to be frighteningly correct. The displaced persons who World War II had left in the midst of a Europe in ruins have been replaced by asylum-seekers and immigrants flooding into a peaceful and wealthy Europe from the South and the East. The old refugee camps cannot accommodate the flood of new immigration. In coming years, statisticians anticipate 20 to 30 million immigrants from Eastern Europe. This problem can be solved only by the joint action of the European states involved. This process would repeat a dialectic that has already taken place, on a smaller scale, during the process of German unification. The transnational immigrants' movements function as sanctions which force western Europe to act responsibly in the aftermath of the bankruptcy of state socialism. Europe must make a great effort to quickly improve conditions in the poorer areas of middle and eastern Europe or it will be flooded by asylum-seekers and immigrants.

The experts are debating the capacity of the economic system to absorb these people, but the readiness to politically integrate the asylum-seekers depends more upon how citizens *perceive* the social and economic problems posed by immigration. Throughout Europe, right-wing xenophobic reaction against the "estrangement" (*Überfremdung*) caused by foreigners has increased. The relatively deprived classes, whether they feel endangered by social decline or have already slipped into segmented marginal groups, identify quite openly with the ideologized supremacy of their own collectivity and reject everything foreign. This is the underside of a chauvinism of prosperity which is increasing everywhere. Thus, the asylum problem as well brings to light the latent tension between citizenship and national identity.

One example is the nationalistic and anti-Polish sentiments in the new German state. The newly acquired status of German citizenship is bound together with the hope that the Republic's frontier of prosperity will be pushed toward the Oder and Neiße. Their newly gained citizenship also gives many of them the ethnocentric satisfaction that they will no longer be treated as second class Germans. They forget that citizenship rights guarantee liberty because they contain a core composed of universal human rights. Article Four of the Revolutionary Constitution of 1793, which defined the status of the citizen, gave to *every* adult foreigner who lived for one year in France not just the right to remain within the country but also the active rights of a citizen.

In the Federal Republic, as in most Western legal systems, the legal status of aliens, homeless foreigners and the stateless has been adjusted to the status of citizens. Since the structure of the *Grundgesetz* (Basic Law) is founded on the idea of human rights, *every* inhabitant enjoys the protection of the Constitution. Foreigners share equal duties with citizens, as well as certain benefits and legal protections. With a few exceptions, they also receive equal treatment with regard to economic status. The great number of laws which are indifferent to citizenship status only tempers the real meaning of passive citizenship. The human rights component of citizenship will be intensified and strengthened through supranational rights, and especially through European Civil Rights, which might even effect core political exercise of influence. The Federal German Constitutional Court's decision of 31 October 1990 is notable in this context. Though it declared unconstitutional the right of foreigners to vote in municipal and district elections, that is the communal voting right of foreigners, it recognized the principles raised by the petitioners: "Behind this interpretation obviously stands the notion that it corresponds to the democratic idea, especially as it contains the idea of liberty, that there is a congruence between the possessor of democratic political rights and those subject to a specific state power. This is the proper starting point. . . ."[18]

These tendencies signify only that a concept of citizenship, the normative content of which has been dissociated from that of national identity, cannot allow arguments for restrictive and obstructionist asylum or immigration policies. It remains an open question whether the European Community today, in expectation of great and turbulent migrations, can and ought to adopt even such liberal foreigner and immigration policies as the Jacobins did in their time. Today the pertinent *moral-theoretical discussion* regarding the definition of "special duties" and special responsibilities is restricted to the social boundaries of a community. Thus, the state, too, forms a concrete legal community which imposes special duties on its citizens. Asylum-seekers and immigrants generally present the European States with the problem of whether special citizenship-related duties are to be privileged above those universal, transnational duties which transcend state boundaries. I will outline this discussion in five steps.

A.

Special duties are those which specific persons owe to others to whom they are obligated by virtue of being "connected" to them as dependents, thus as members of a family, as friends, as neighbors, and as comembers of a political community or nation. Parents have special obligations toward their children—and vice versa. Consulates in foreign countries have special obligations to those of their citizenry who need protection—these in turn are obligated to the institutions and laws of their own land. In this context, we think above all of positive duties, which remain undetermined, insofar as they demand acts of solidarity, engagement, and care in measures which cannot be accurately determined. Help cannot always be expected by everyone. Special duties are those which result from the relationship between the concrete community and a part of its membership, and can be understood as social attributes and factual specifications of such intrinsically undetermined duties.

From the utilitarian point of view, one could try to establish these special duties by indicating the mutual benefit a community would gain through the reciprocal performances of some act. Nations and states would thus be defined as "mutual benefit societies."[19] According to this model, every member of the society can expect that the profit gained by interacting with other members through exchange is proportional to their performances. With this, utilitarianism justifies a prohibition against the exploitation of guest workers through the reciprocity of special duties and rights. Of course, this model cannot determine the obligations owed to those members of the community who cannot contribute as much as others (e.g. the handicapped, the sick, and the old) or who are needy (e.g. asylum-seekers and foreigners). The instrumental ethnocentrism of utilitarianism would permit an immigration policy allowing foreigners to enter a country only when it could be justifiably guaranteed that the existing balance of performances and claims, and thus the expectations of all, would not be disturbed by them.

B.

This counterintuitive result is a reason to reject the utilitarian position, and adopt in its place a model wherein special duties cannot be explained through the reciprocal actions of exchanging performers but rather through the coordinative achievements of a division of labor.[20] Special duties do not vary only in equal proportion with the social distance between individuals so that the claims of those who are near have priority over those who are far. This intuition applies within the close confines of family and neighborhood. But it is confusing insofar as all those persons beyond these intimate circles are equally close and far. We perceive these "strangers" as "others" whether they are citizens of our nation or not. A special duty toward these "others" does not result primarily from their membership in a concrete community. It results more from the abstract coordinating tendencies of *judicial* institutions, which specify, according to certain attributes, certain categories of persons or agents; this process, in turn, specifies and legally enforces those positive social and factual obligations which would have been undetermined otherwise. According to this interpretation, institutionally mediated responsibilities determine those specific obligations owed to certain others active in a moral division of labor. Within such a judicially regulated moral economy, the social boundaries of a legal community only have the function of regulating the distribution of responsibilities throughout the community. That does not mean that our responsibility ends at this boundary. More must be done by the national government so that the citizenry fulfills its duties toward its nonmembers—to the asylum-seekers, for example. Still, with this argument the question, "What are these duties?" has not yet been answered.

C.

The moral point of view commits us to assess this problem impartially, and thus not just from the one-sided perspective of those living in prosperous regions but also from the perspective of the immigrants, those who search for grace. Let us say that they seek not only political asylum but a free and dignified human existence.

John Rawls's well-known thought experiment proposed an original position in which individuals, under the "veil of ignorance," did not know the society they were born into and the position they would have in it. In view of our problem, the result of a moral test with regards to a world society is obvious:

> Behind the "veil of ignorance," in considering possible restrictions of freedom, one adopts the perspective of the one who would be most disadvantaged by the restrictions, in this case the perspective of the alien who wants to immigrate. In the original position, then, one would insist that the right to migrate be included in the system of basic liberties for the same reasons one would insist that the right to religious freedom would be included: it might prove essential to one's plan of life.[21]

Legitimate restrictions of immigration rights would then be established by competing viewpoints, such as consideration to avoid the enormity of claims, social conflicts, and burdens that might seriously endanger the public order or the economic reproduction of society. The criteria of ethnic origin, language, and education—or an "acknowledgement of belonging to the cultural community" of the land of migration, in the case of those who have Germanic status—could not establish privileges in the process of immigration and naturalization.

D.

Against this position the communitarians point to an issue which the above mentioned individualistic arguments overlook: The social borders of a political community do not just have a *functional* meaning, as suggested by the model of a judicially organized moral division of labor. They regulate rather one's belonging to a distinct historical community united by a common fate and a political life form that constitutes the identity of its citizens: "Citizenship is an answer to the questions 'Who am I?' and 'What should I do?' when posed in the public sphere."[22] Membership in a political community confirms special duties, behind which stands a patriotic identity. This kind of loyalty reaches beyond the validity claims of institutionally prescribed legal duties. "Each member recognizes a loyalty to the community expressed in a willingness to sacrifice personal gains to advance its interests."[23] We have already discerned considerations against the communitarian notion of citizenship and thus against an exclusive moral and juridical consideration of this problem. Such conceptions are no longer appropriate for complex social relations, but they raise an *ethical* issue which should not be overlooked.

The modern state also presents a political way of life which cannot be exhausted through the abstract form of an institutionalization of legal principles. The way of life builds a political-cultural context in which basic universalistic constitutional principles must be implemented. Then and only then will a population, because it is *accustomed* to freedom, also secure and support free institutions. For that reason, Michael Walzer is of the opinion that the right of immigration is limited by the political right of a community to protect the integrity of its life form. According to him, the right of citizens to self-determination implies the right of self-assertion to each particular way of life.[24]

E.

This argument, of course, can be read in two opposed ways. In the communitarian version, liberal immigration rights should be placed under added normative restrictions. In addition to functional restrictions, which result from the conditions of reproduction of the administrative and economic systems of a community, are those which would secure the ethnic-cultural substance of a way of life. With this the *particularistic* meaning of the argument triumphs, wherein citizenship is limited not according to national identity but according to a historically defined cultural identity. Completely in the spirit of Hannah Arendt's analysis, H. R. van Gunsteren specifies the following conditions for permitting citizenship to a democratic community:

> The prospective citizen must be capable and willing to be a member of this particular historical community, its past and future, its forms of life and institutions within which its members think and act. In a community that values autonomy and judgement

of its members, this is obviously not a requirement of pure conformity. But it is a requirement of knowledge of the language and the culture and of acknowledgement of those institutions that foster the reproduction of citizens who are capable of autonomous and responsible judgement.[25]

The requisite competence "to act as citizens of a special political community (this particular polity)" is to be understood in another sense completely—namely, the *universalistic* sense—as soon as the political community itself implements universalistic basic laws. The identity of a political community, which may not be touched by immigration, depends primarily upon the constitutional principles rooted in a political culture and not upon an ethical-cultural form of life as a whole. That is why it must be expected that the new citizens will readily engage in the political culture of their new home, without necessarily giving up the cultural life specific to their country of origin. The *political acculturation* demanded of them does not include the entirety of their socialization. With immigration, new forms of life are imported which expand and multiply the perspective of all, and on the basis of which the common political constitution is always interpreted:

> People live in communities with bonds and bounds, but these may be of different kinds. In a liberal society, the bonds and bounds should be compatible with liberal principles. Open immigration would change the character of the community, but it should not leave the community without any character.[26]

From the discussion which we followed from steps A. to E., we can draw the following normative conclusion: The European states should agree upon a liberal immigration policy. They should not draw their wagons around themselves and their chauvinism of prosperity, hoping to ignore the pressures of those hoping to immigrate or seek asylum. The democratic right of self-determination includes, of course, the right to preserve one's own *political* culture, which includes the concrete context of citizen's rights, though it does not include the self-assertion of a privileged *cultural* life form. Only within the constitutional framework of a democratic legal system can different ways of life coexist equally. These must, however, overlap within a common political culture, which again implies an impulse to open these ways of life to others.

Only democratic citizenship can prepare the way for a condition of world citizenship which does not close itself off within particularistic biases, and which accepts a worldwide form of political communication. The Vietnam War, the revolutionary changes in eastern and middle Europe, as well as the war in the Persian Gulf are the first *world political* events in a strict sense. Through the electronic mass media, these events were made instantaneous and ubiquitous. In the context of the French Revolution, Kant speculated on the role of the participating public. He identified a world public sphere, which today will become a political reality for the first time with the new relations of global communication. Even the superpowers must recognize worldwide protests. The obsolescence of the state of nature between bellicose states has begun, implying that states have lost some sovereignty. The arrival of world citizenship is no longer merely a phantom, though we are still far from achieving it. State citizenship and world citizenship form a continuum that already shows itself, at least, in outline form.

Notes

I thank Inge Mous and Klaus Günther for critical suggestions and commentary.

1. Peter Glotz, *Der Irrweg des Nationalstaats* (Stuttgart, 1990).

2. M. R. Lepsius, "Der europäische Nationalstaat," *Interessen, Ideen und Institutionen* (Opladen, 1990), p. 256 ff.

3. See the article on "Nation" in *Historisches Wörterbuch der Philosophie*, Vol. 6, pp. 406–14.

4. M. R. Lepsius, "Ethnos und Demos," *Interessen*, pp. 247–55.

5. See on what follows R. Grawert, "Staatsangehörigkeit und Staatsbürgerschaft," *Der Staat*, 23 (1984): pp. 179–204.

6. P. H. Schuck & R. M. Smith, *Citizenship without Consent* (New Haven, 1985), Chapter 1. Admittedly, not everywhere is the normative meaning of national citizenship consistently uncoupled from ascriptive characteristics. Article 116 of the German Basic Law, for example, intro-

duces a notion of so-called German by status, someone who belongs to the German people according to an objectively confirmed "attestation of membership in the cultural community," without at the same time being a German citizen. Such a person enjoys the privilege of being able to become a German citizen, although this is now contested by some constitutional experts.

7. R. Winzeler, *Die politischen Rechte des Aktivbürgers nach Schweizerischem Bundesrecht* (Berne, 1983).

8. K. Hesse, *Grundzüge des Verfassungsrechts* (Heidelberg, 1990), p. 113, states: "In their function as subjective rights, the basic rights detemine and secure the foundations of the individual's legal status. In their function as objective basic components of a democratic and constitutional social order, they insert the individual in this order, which can itself only become a reality if these rights are given real shape. The status of the individual in terms of constitutional law, as grounded in and guaranteed by the basic rights laid out in the Basic Law, is thus a material legal status, i.e. a status with concretely determined contents, a status which neither the individual not the state's powers can unrestrictedly adopt at will. This status in constitutional law forms the core of the general status of national citizenship, which, along with the basic rights,...is laid down in law."

9. R. Gawert, "Staatsvolk und Staatsangehörigkeit," *Handbuch des Staatsrechts*, ed. J. Isensee & P. Kirchhof (Heidelberg, 1987), p. 684 ff.

10. C. Taylor, "The Liberal-Communitarian Debate," *Liberalism and the Moral Life*, ed. N. Rosenblum (Cambridge, Mass., 1989), p. 178 f.

11. Taylor, "The Liberal-Communitarian Debate," p. 178.

12. P. Kielmannsegg "Ohne historisches Vorbild," in *Frankfurter Allgemeine Zeitung*, 7 (December, 1990).

13. M. R. Lepsius, "Die Europäische Gemeinschaft," contribution to the 20th Congress of German Sociologists, Frankfurt on Main, 1990.

14. T. H. Marshall, *Citizenship and Social Class* (Cambridge, 1950).

15. J. Habermas, "Volkssouveränität als Verfahren," *Die Moderne—ein unvollendetes Projekt* (Leipzig, 1990), p. 180 ff.

16. B. S. Turner, *Citizenship and Capitalism* (London, 1986).

17. J. M. Barbalet, *Citizenship* (Stratford, England, 1988).

18. EuGRZ, 1990, 443.

19. R. Goodin, "What Is So Special about Our Fellow Countrymen?", *Ethics* 98 (July 1988): 663–686.

20. H. Shue, "Mediating Duties," *Ethics* 98 (July 1988): 687–704.

21. J. H. Carens, "Aliens and Citizens: The Case for Open Borders," *Review of Politics* 49 (1987): 258.

22. H. R. van Gunsteren, "Admission to Citizenship," *Ethics* 98 (July 1988): 752.

23. D. Miller, "The Ethical Significance of Nationality," *Ethics* 98 (July 1988): 648.

24. M. Walzer, *Spheres of Justice* (New York, 1983), 31–63.

25. van Gunsteren, "Admission to Citizenship," 736.

26. Carens, "Aliens and Citizens," 271.

— 10 —

Return of the Citizen: A Survey of Recent Work on Citizenship Theory

Will Kymlicka and Wayne Norman

I.

Introduction

There has been an explosion of interest in the concept of citizenship among political theorists. In 1978, it could be confidently stated that "the concept of citizenship has gone out of fashion among political thinkers" (van Gunsteren 1978, p. 9). Fifteen years later, citizenship has become the "buzz word" among thinkers on all points of the political spectrum (Heater 1990, p.293; Vogel and Moran 1991, p. x).

There are a number of reasons for this renewed interest in citizenship in the 1990s. At the level of theory it is a natural evolution in political discourse because the concept of citizenship seems to integrate the demands of justice and community membership—the central concepts of political philosophy in the 1970s and 1980s, respectively. Citizenship is intimately linked to ideas of individual entitlement on the one hand and of attachment to a particular community on the other. Thus, it may help clarify what is really at stake in the debate between liberals and communitarians.

Interest in citizenship has also been sparked by a number of recent political events and trends throughout the world—increasing voter apathy and long-term welfare dependency in the United States, the resurgence of nationalist movements in Eastern Europe, the stresses created by an increasingly multicultural and multiracial population in Western Europe, the backlash against the welfare state in Thatcher's England, the failure of environmental policies that rely on voluntary citizen cooperation, and so forth.

These events have made clear that the health and stability of a modern democracy depends, not only on the justice of its "basic structure" but also on the qualities and attitudes of its citizens,[1] for example, their sense of identity and how they view potentially competing forms of national, regional, ethnic, or religious identities; their ability to tolerate and work together with others who are different from themselves; their desire to participate in the political process in order to promote the public good and hold political authorities accountable; their willingness to show self-restraint and exercise personal responsibility in their economic demands and in personal choices which affect their health and the environment. Without citizens who possess these qualities, democracies become difficult to govern, even unstable.[2] As Habermas notes, "the institutions of constitutional freedom are only worth as much as a population makes of them" (Habermas 1992, p. 7).

It is not surprising, then, that there should be increasing calls for "a theory of citizenship" that focuses on the identity and conduct of individual citizens, including their responsibilities, loyalties, and roles. There are, however, at least two general hazards in this quest. First, the scope of a "theory of citizenship" is potentially limitless—almost every problem in political philosophy involves relations among citizens or between citizens and the state. In this survey, we try to avoid this danger by concentrating on two general issues that citizenship theorists claim have been neglected due to the overemphasis in recent political philosophy on structures and institutions—namely, civic virtues and citizenship identity.[3]

The second danger for a theory of citizenship arises because there are two different concepts which are sometimes conflated in these discussions: citizenship-as-legal-status, that is, as full membership in a particular political community; and citizenship-as-desirable-activity, where the extent and quality of one's citizenship is a function of one's participation in that community.

As we shall see in the next section, most writers believe that an adequate theory of citizenship requires greater emphasis on responsibilities and virtues. Few of them, however, are proposing that we should revise our account of citizenship-as-legal-status in a way that would, say, strip apathetic people of their citizenship. Instead, these authors are generally concerned with the requirements of being a "good citizen." But we should expect a theory of the good citizen to be relatively independent of the legal question of what it is to be a citizen, just as a theory of the good person is distinct from the metaphysical (or legal) question of what it is to be a person. While most theorists respect this distinction in developing their own theories, we shall discuss in section IV a fairly widespread tendency to ignore it when criticizing others' theories of citizenship, for example, by contrasting their own "thick" conception of citizenship-as-activity with an opponent's "thin" conception of citizenship-as-status.

II.

The Postwar Orthodoxy

Before describing the new work on citizenship, it is necessary to outline quickly the view of citizenship that is implicit in much postwar political theory and that is defined almost entirely in terms of the possession of rights.

The most influential exposition of this postwar conception of citizenship-as-rights is T. H. Marshall's "Citizenship and Social Class," written in 1949.[4] According to Marshall, citizenship is essentially a matter of ensuring that everyone is treated as a full and equal member of society. And the way to ensure this sense of membership is through according people an increasing number of citizenship rights.

Marshall divides citizenship rights into three categories which he sees as having taken hold in England in three successive centuries: civil rights, which arose in the eighteenth century; political rights, which arose in the nineteenth century; and social rights, for example, to public education, health care, unemployment insurance, and old-age pension, which have become established in this century (Marshall 1965, pp. 78 ff.)[5] And with the expansion of the rights of citizenship, he notes, there was also an expansion of the class of citizens. Civil and political rights that had been restricted to white property-owning Protestant men were gradually extended to women, the working class, Jews and Catholics, blacks, and other previously excluded groups.

For Marshall, the fullest expression of citizenship requires a liberal-democratic welfare state. By guaranteeing civil, political, and social rights to all, the welfare state ensures that every member of society feels like a full member of society, able to participate in and enjoy the common life of society. Where any of these rights are withheld or violated, people will be marginalized and unable to participate.

This is often called "passive" or "private" citizenship, because of its emphasis on passive entitlements and the absence of any obligation to participate in public life. It is still widely supported,[6] and with good reason: "the benefits of private citizenship are not to be sneezed at: they place certain basic human goods (security, prosperity, and freedom) within the grasp of nearly all, and that is nothing less than a fantastic human achievement" (Macedo 1990, p. 39).

Nevertheless, this orthodox postwar conception of citizenship has come increasingly under attack in the past decade. For the purposes of this article, we can identify two sets of criticisms. The first set focuses on the need to supplement (or replace) the passive acceptance of citizenship responsibilities and virtues, including economic self-reliance, political participation, and even civility. These issues are discussed in section III.

The second set focuses on the need to revise the current definition of citizenship to accommodate the increasing social and cultural pluralism of modern societies. Can citizenship provide a common experience, identity and allegiance for the members of society? Is it enough simply to include historically excluded groups on an equal basis, or are special measures sometimes required? This issue is discussed in section IV.

III.

The Responsibilities and Virtues of Citizenship

A.   The New Right Critique of Social Citizenship and the Welfare State

The first, and most politically powerful, critique of the postwar orthodoxy came from the New Right's attack on the idea of "social rights." These rights had always been resisted by the right, on the grounds that they were (*a*) inconsistent with the demands of (negative) freedom or (desert-based) justice, (*b*) economically inefficient, and (*c*) steps down "the road to serfdom." But in the public's eye, these arguments were seen as either implausible or, at any rate, as justifiably outweighed by considerations of social justice or by a citizenship-based welfare state such as Marshall's.

One of the revolutions in conservative thinking during the Thatcher/Reagan years was the willingness to engage the left in battle over the domain of social citizenship itself. Whereas Marshall had argued that social rights enable the disadvantaged to enter the mainstream of society and effectively exercise their civil and political rights, the New Right argues that the welfare state has promoted passivity among the poor, without actually improving their life chances, and created a culture of dependency. Far from being the solution, the welfare state has itself perpetuated the problem by reducing citizens to passive dependents who are under bureaucratic tutelage. According to Norman Barry, there is no evidence that welfare programs have in fact promoted more active citizenship (Barry 1990, pp. 43–53).

The New Right believes that the model of passive citizenship underestimated the extent to which fulfilling certain obligations is a precondition for being accepted as a full member of society. In particular, by failing to meet the obligation to support themselves, the long-term unemployed are a source of shame for society as well as themselves (Mead 1986, p. 240).[7] Failure to fulfill common obligations is as much of an obstacle to full membership as the lack of equal rights. In these circumstances, "to obligate the dependent as others are obligated is essential to equality, not opposed to it. An effective welfare [policy] must include recipients in the common obligations of citizens rather than exclude them" (Mead 1986, pp. 12–13).

According to the New Right, to ensure the social and cultural integration of the poor we must go "beyond entitlement," and focus instead on their responsibility to earn a living. Since the welfare state discourages people from becoming self-reliant, the safety net should be cut back and any remaining welfare benefits should have obligations tied to them. This is the idea behind one of the principal reforms of the welfare system in the 1980s: "workfare" programs, which require welfare recipients to work for their benefits, to reinforce the idea that citizens should be self-supporting.

This New Right vision of citizenship has not gone unchallenged. For example, the claim that the rise of an unemployed welfare-underclass is due to the availability of welfare ignores the impact of global economic restructuring, and sits uncomfortably with the fact that many of the most extensive welfare states (in Scandinavia, e.g.) have traditionally enjoyed among the lowest unemployment rates.

Moreover, critics charge, it is difficult to find any evidence that the New Right reforms of the 1980s have promoted responsible citizenship. These reforms aimed to extend the scope of markets in people's lives—through freer trade, deregulation, tax cuts, the weakening of trade unions, and the tightening of unemployment benefits—in part in order to teach people the virtues of initiative, self-reliance, and self-sufficiency (Mulgan 1991, p. 43).

Instead, however, many market deregulations arguably made possible an era of unprecedented greed and economic irresponsibility, as evidenced by the savings and loan and junk bond scandals in America (Mulgan 1991, p. 39). Also, cutting welfare benefits, far from getting the disadvantaged back on their feet, has expanded the underclass. Class inequalities have been exacerbated, and the working poor and unemployed have been effectively "disenfranchised," unable to participate in the new economy of the New Right (Fierlbeck 1991, p. 579; Hoover and Plant 1988, chap. 12).[8]

For many, therefore, the New Right program is most plausibly seen not as an alternative account of citizenship but as an assault on the very principle of citizenship. As Plant puts it, "Instead of accepting citizenship as a political and social status, modern Conservatives have sought to reassert the role of the market and have rejected the idea that citizenship confers a status independent of economic standing" (Plant 1991, p. 52; cf. Heater 1990, p. 303; King 1987, pp. 196-98).

B. Rethinking Social Citizenship

Given these difficulties with the New Right critique of welfare entitlements, most people on the left continue to defend the principle that full citizenship requires social rights. For the left, Marshall's argument that people can be full members and participants in the common life of society only if their basic needs are met "is as strong now...as it ever was" (Ignatieff 1989, p. 72). However, many on the left accept that the existing institutions of the welfare state are unpopular, in part because they seem to promote passivity and dependence, and to "facilitate a privatist retreat from citizenship and a particular 'clientalization' of the citizen's role" (Habermas 1992, pp. 10–11; cf. King 1987, pp. 45–46).

How then should the state foster self-reliance and personal responsibility? The left has responded ambivalently to issues such as "workfare." On the one hand, the principle of personal responsibility and social obligation has always been at the heart of socialism (Mulgan 1991, p. 39). A duty to work is, after all, implicit in Marx's famous slogan, "From each according to his talents, to each according to his needs." Some people on the left, therefore, express qualified acceptance of workfare, if it "gives both responsibility and the power to use it" (Mulgan 1991, p. 46).

On the other hand, most people on the left remain uncomfortable with imposing obligations as a matter of public policy. They believe that the dependent are kept out of the mainstream of society because of a lack of opportunities, such as jobs, education, and training, not because of any desire to avoid work. Imposing obligations, therefore, is futile if genuine opportunities are absent, and unnecessary if those opportunities are present, since the vast majority of people on welfare would prefer not to be (King 1987, pp. 186–91; Fullinwider 1988, pp. 270–78). Rather than impose an obligation to work, the left would try to achieve full employment through, for example, worker-training programs. So while the left accepts the general principle that citizenship involves both rights and responsibilities, it feels that rights to participate must, in a sense, precede the responsibilities—that is, it is only appropriate to demand fulfillment of the responsibilities after the rights to participate are secured.

A similar rejection of the New Right's view of citizenship can be found in recent feminist discussions of citizenship. Many feminists accept the importance of balancing rights and responsibilities—indeed, Carol Gilligan's findings suggest that women, in

their everyday moral reasoning, prefer the language of responsibility to the language of rights (Gilligan 1982, p. 19). But feminists
have grave doubts about the New Right rhetoric of economic self-
sufficiency. Gender-neutral talk about "self-reliance" is often a code
for the view that men should financially support the family, while
women should look after the household and care for the elderly,
the sick, and the young. This reinforces, rather than eliminates, the
barriers to women's full participation in society.[9]

When the New Right talks about self-reliance, the boundaries
of the "self" include the family—it is families that should be self-
reliant. Hence, greater "self-reliance" is consistent with, and may
even require, greater dependency within the family. Yet women's
dependence on men within the family can be every bit as harmful
as welfare dependency, since it allows men to exercise unequal
power over decisions regarding sex, reproduction, consumption,
leisure, and so on (King 1987, p. 47; Okin 1989, pp. 128–29).

Since perceptions of responsibility tend to fall unequally on
women, many feminists share the left's view that rights to participate
must, in a sense, precede responsibilities. Indeed, feminists wish
to expand the list of social rights, in order to tackle structural barriers
to women's full participation as citizens that the welfare state
currently ignores, or even exacerbates, such as the unequal distribution of domestic responsibilities (Phillips 1991a, 1991b; Okin 1992).
Given the difficulty of combining family and public responsibilities,
equal citizenship for women is impossible until workplaces and
career expectations are rearranged to allow more room for family
responsibilities and until men accept their share of domestic
responsibilities (Okin 1989, pp. 175–77).

However, if rights must precede responsibilities, it seems we
are back to the old view of passive citizenship. Yet the left, as much
as the right, accepts the need for change. The most popular proposal
is to decentralize and democratize the welfare state, for example,
by giving local welfare agencies more power and making them
accountable to their clients (Pierson 1991, pp. 200–207). Hence, the
now-familiar talk of "empowering" welfare recipients by supple-
menting welfare rights with democratic participatory rights in the
administration of welfare programs.

This is the central theme of the contemporary left view of social citizenship.[10] Whether it will work to overcome welfare dependency is difficult to say. Service providers have often resisted attempts to increase their accountability (Rustin 1991, p. 231; Pierson 1991, pp. 206–207). Moreover there may be some tension between the goal of increasing democratic accountability to the local community and increasing accountability to clients (Plant 1990, p. 30). As we discuss in the next section, the left may have excessive faith in the ability of democratic participation to solve the problems of citizenship.

C. The Need for Civic Virtues

Many classical liberals believed that a liberal democracy could be made secure, even in the absence of an especially virtuous citizenry, by creating checks and balances. Institutional and pro-cedural devices such as the separation of powers, a bicameral legislature, and federalism would all serve to block would-be oppressors. Even if each person pursued her own self-interest, without regard for the common good, one set of private interests would check another set of private interests.[11] However, it has become clear that procedural-institutional mechanisms to balance self-interest are not enough, and that some level of civic virtue and public-spiritedness is required (Galston 1991, pp. 217, 244; Macedo 1990, pp. 138–39).

Consider the many ways that public policy relies on responsible personal life-style decisions: the state will be unable to provide adequate health care if citizens do not act responsibly with respect to their own health, in terms of a healthy diet, exercise, and the consumption of liquor and tobacco; the state will be unable to meet the needs of children, the elderly, or the disabled if citizens do not agree to share this responsibility by providing some care for their relatives; the state cannot protect the environment if citizens are unwilling to reduce, reuse, and recycle in their own homes; the ability of the government to regulate the economy can be undermined if citizens borrow immoderate amounts or demand excessive wage increases; attempts to create a fairer society will flounder if citizens are chronically intolerant of difference and generally lacking in what Rawls calls a sense of justice (Rawls 1971, pp. 114–16, 335). Without cooperation and self-restraint in these areas, "the ability of liberal societies to function successfully progressively diminishes" (Galston 1991, p. 220; Macedo 1990, p. 39).

In short, we need "a fuller, richer and yet more subtle understanding and practice of citizenship," because "what the state needs from the citizenry cannot be secured by coercion, but only cooperation and self-restraint in the exercise of private power" (Cairns and Williams 1985, p. 43). Yet there is growing fear that the civility and public-spiritedness of citizens of liberal democracies may be in serious decline (Walzer 1992, p. 90).[12]

An adequate conception of citizenship, therefore, seems to require a balance of rights and responsibilities. Where do we learn these virtues? The New Right relies heavily on the market as a school of virtue. But there are other answers to this question.

1. *The left and participatory democracy.*—As we just noted, one of the left's responses to the problem of citizen passivity is to "empower" citizens by democratizing the welfare state and, more generally, by dispersing state power through local democratic institutions, regional assemblies, and judicable rights. However, emphasizing participation does not yet explain how to ensure that citizens participate responsibly—that is, in a public-spirited, rather than self-interested or prejudiced, way.

Indeed, as Mulgan notes, "by concentrating too narrowly on the need to devolve power and on the virtues of freedom, issues of responsibility have been pushed to the margins" (Mulgan 1991, pp. 40–41). Empowered citizens may use their power irresponsibly by pushing for benefits and entitlements they cannot ultimately afford, or by voting themselves tax breaks and slashing assistance to the needy, or by "seeking scapegoats in the indolence of the poor, the strangeness of ethnic minorities, or the insolence and irresponsibility of modern women" (Fierlbeck 1991, p. 592).

Following Rousseau and J. S. Mill, many modern participatory democrats assume that political participation itself will teach people responsibility and toleration. As Oldfield notes, they place their faith in the activity of participation "as the means whereby individuals may become accustomed to perform the duties of citizenship. Political participation enlarges the minds of individuals, familiarizes them with interests which lie beyond the immediacy of personal circumstance and environment, and encourages them to acknowledge that public concerns are the proper ones to which they should pay attention" (Oldfield 1990b, p. 184).

Many people on the left have tried in this way to bypass the issue of responsible citizenship "by dissolving [it] into that of democracy itself," which in turn has led to the "advocacy of collective decision-making as a resolution to all the problems of citizenship" (Held 1991, p. 23; cf. Pierson 1991, p. 202).[13] Unfortunately, this faith in the educative function of participation seems overly optimistic (Oldfield 1990b, p. 184; Mead 1986, p. 247; Andrews 1991, p. 216).

Hence, there is increasing recognition that citizenship responsibilities should be incorporated more explicitly into left-wing theory (Hoover and Plant 1988, pp. 289–91; Vogel and Moran 1991, p. xv; Mouffe, 1992b). But it seems clear that the left has not yet found a language of responsibility that it is comfortable with, or a set of concrete policies to promote these responsibilities.[14]

2. *Civic republicanism.*—The modern civic republican tradition is an extreme form of participatory democracy largely inspired by Machiavelli and Rousseau (who were in turn enamored with the Greeks and Romans). It is not surprising that the recent upsurge of interest in citizenship has given civic republicans a wider audience.

The feature that distinguishes civic republicans from other participationists, such as the left-wing theorists discussed above, is their emphasis on the intrinsic value of political participation for the participants themselves. Such participation is, in Oldfield's words, "the highest form of human living-together that most individuals can aspire to" (Oldfield 1990a, p. 6). On this view, political life is superior to the merely private pleasures of family, neighborhood, and profession and so should occupy the center of people's lives. Failure to participate in politics makes one a "radically incomplete and stunted being" (Oldfield 1990b, p.187; cf. Pocock 1992, pp. 45, 53; Skinner 1992; Beiner 1992).

As its proponents admit, this conception is markedly at odds with the way most people in the modern world understand both citizenship and the good life. Most people find the greatest happiness in their family life, work, religion, or leisure, not in politics. Political participation is seen as an occasional, and often burdensome, activity needed to ensure that government respects and supports their freedom to pursue these personal occupations and attachments. This assumption that politics is a means to private life is shared by most people on the left (Ignatieff 1989, pp. 72–73) and right (Mead 1986, p. 254), as well as by liberals (Rawls 1971, pp. 229–30), civil society theorists (Walzer 1989, p. 215), and feminists (Elshtain 1981, p. 327), and defines the modern view of citizenship.

In order to explain the modern indifference to political partici-pation, civic republicans often argue that political life today has become impoverished compared to the active citizenship of, say, ancient Greece. Political debate is no longer meaningful and people lack access to effective participation.

But it is more plausible to view our attachment to private life as a result not of the impoverishment of public life but of the enrichment of private life. We no longer seek gratification in politics because our personal and social life is so much richer than the Greeks'. There are many reasons for this historical change, including the rise of romantic love and the nuclear family (and its emphasis on intimacy and privacy), increased prosperity (and hence richer forms of leisure and consumption), the Christian commitment to the dignity of labor (which the Greeks despised), and the growing dislike for war (which the Greeks esteemed).

Those passive citizens who prefer the joys of family and career to the duties of politics are not necessarily misguided. As Galston has put it, republicans who denigrate private life as tedious and self-absorbed show no delight in real communities of people, and indeed are "contemptuous" of "everyday life" (Galston 1991, pp. 58–63).[15]

3. *Civil society theorists.*—We shall use the label "civil society theorists" to identify a recent development from communitarian thought in the 1980s. These theorists emphasize the necessity of civility and self-restraint to a healthy democracy but deny that either the market or political participation is sufficient to teach these virtues. Instead, it is in the voluntary organizations of civil society— churches, families, unions, ethnic associations, cooperatives, en-vironmental groups, neighborhood associations, women's support groups, charities—that we learn the virtues of mutual obligation. As Walzer puts it, "the civility that makes democratic politics possible

can only be learned in the associational networks" of civil society (Walzer 1992, p. 104).

Because these groups are voluntary, failure to live up to the responsibilities that come with them is usually met simply with disapproval rather than legal punishment. Yet because the disapproval comes from family, friends, colleagues, or comrades, it is in many ways a more powerful incentive to act responsibly than punishment by an impersonal state. It is here that "human character, competence, and capacity for citizenship are formed," for it is here that we internalize the idea of personal responsibility and mutual obligation and learn the voluntary self-restraint which is essential to truly responsible citizenship (Glendon 1991, p. 109).

It follows, therefore, that one of the first obligations of citizenship is to participate in civil society. As Walzer notes, "Join the association of your choice" is "not a slogan to rally political militants, and yet that is what civil society requires" (Walzer 1992, p. 106).

The claim that civil society is the "seedbed of civic virtue" (Glendon 1991, p. 109) is essentially an empirical claim, for which there is little hard evidence one way or the other. It is an old and venerable view, but it is not obviously true. It may be in the neighborhood that we learn to be good neighbors, but neighborhood associations also teach people to operate on the "NIMBY" (not in my backyard) principle when it comes to the location of group homes or public works. Similarly, the family is often "a school of despotism" that teaches male dominance over women (Okin 1992, p. 65); churches often teach deference to authority and intolerance of other faiths; ethnic groups often teach prejudice against other races; and so on.

Walzer recognizes that most people are "trapped in one or another subordinate relationship, where the 'civility' they learned was deferential rather than independent and active." In these circumstances, he says, we have to "reconstruct" the associational network "under new conditions of freedom and equality." Similarly, when the activities of some associations "are narrowly conceived, partial and particularist," then "they need political correction." Walzer calls his view "critical associationalism" to signify that the associations of civil society may need to be reformed in the light of principles of citizenship (Walzer 1992, pp. 106–07).

But this may go too far in the other direction. Rather than supporting voluntary associations, this approach may unintentionally license wholesale intervention in them. Governments must of course intervene to protect the rights of people inside and outside the group if these rights are threatened. But do we want governments to reconstruct churches, for example, to make them more internally democratic, or to make sure that their members learn to be independent rather than deferential? And, in any event, wouldn't reconstructing churches, families, or unions to make them more internally democratic start to undermine their essentially uncoerced and voluntary character, which is what supposedly made them the seedbeds of civic virtue?

Civil society theorists demand too much of these voluntary associations in expecting them to be the main school for, or small-scale replica of, democratic citizenship. While these associations may teach civic virtue, that is not their raison d'être. The reason why people join churches, families, or ethnic organizations is not to learn civic virtue. It is, rather, to honor certain values and enjoy certain human goods, and these motives may have little to do with the promotion of citizenship.

Joining a religious or ethnic association may be more a matter of withdrawing from the mainstream of society than of learning how to participate in it. To expect parents, priests, or union members to organize the internal life of their groups to promote citizenship maximally is to ignore why these groups exist in the first place. (Some associations, like the Boy Scouts, are designed to promote citizenship, but they are the exception, not the rule.)[16]

A similar issue arises with theorists of "maternal citizenship," who focus on the family, and mothering in particular, as the school of responsibility and virtue. According to Jean Elshtain and Sara Ruddick, mothering teaches women about the responsibility to conserve life and protect the vulnerable, and these lessons should become the guiding principles of political life as well. For example, mothering involves a "metaphysical attitude" of "holding," which gives priority to the protection of existing relationships over the acquisition of new benefits (Elshtain 1981, pp. 326–27, 349–53; Ruddick 1987, p. 242). This has obvious implications for decisions about war or the environment.

However, some critics argue that mothering does not involve the same attributes or virtues as citizenship and that there is no evidence that maternal attitudes such as "holding" promote democratic values such as "active citizenship, self-government, egalitarianism, and the exercise of freedom" (Dietz 1985, p. 30; Nauta 1992, p. 31). As Dietz puts it, "An enlightened despotism, a welfare-state, a single-party bureaucracy and a democratic republic may all respect mothers, protect children's lives and show compassion for the vulnerable" (Dietz 1992, p. 76).

This criticism parallels that of civil society theories. Both maternal feminists and civil society theorists define citizenship in terms of the virtues of the private sphere. But while these virtues may sometimes be necessary for good citizenship, they are not sufficient, and may sometimes be counterproductive.

4. *Liberal virtue theory.*—Liberals are often blamed for the current imbalance between rights and responsibilities, and not without reason. Liberal theorists in the 1970s and 1980s focused almost exclusively on the justification of rights and of the institutions to secure these rights, without attending to the responsibilities of citizens. Many critics believe that liberals are incapable of righting this imbalance, since the liberal commitment to liberty or neutrality or individualism renders the concept of civic virtue unintelligible (Mouffe 1992b).

However, some of the most interesting work on the importance of civic virtue is in fact being done by liberals such as Amy Gutmann, Stephen Macedo, and William Galston. According to Galston, the virtues required for responsible citizenship can be divided into four groups: (*i*) general virtues: courage, law-abidingness, loyalty; (*ii*) social virtues: independence, open-mindedness; (*iii*) economic virtues: work ethic, capacity to delay self-gratification, adaptability to economic and technological change; and (*iv*) political virtues: capacity to discern and respect the rights of others, willingness to demand only what can be paid for, ability to evaluate the performance of those in office, willingness to engage in public discourse (Galston 1991, pp. 221–24).

It is the last two virtues—the ability to question authority and the willingness to engage in public discourse—which are the most distinctive components of liberal virtue theory. The need to question authority arises in part from the fact that citizens in a representative democracy elect representatives who govern in their name. Hence, an important responsibility of citizens is to monitor those officials and judge their conduct.

The need to engage in public discourse arises from the fact that the decisions of government in a democracy should be made publicly, through free and open discussion. But as Galston notes, the virtue of public discourse is not just the willingness to participate in politics or to make one's views known. Rather, it "includes the willingness to listen seriously to a range of views which, given the diversity of liberal societies, will include ideas the listener is bound to find strange and even obnoxious. The virtue of political discourse also includes the willingness to set forth one's own views intelligibly and candidly as the basis for a politics of persuasion rather than manipulation or coercion" (Galston 1991, p. 227).

Macedo calls this the virtue of "public reasonableness." Liberal citizens must give reasons for their political demands, not just state preferences or make threats. Moreover, these reasons must be "public" reasons, in the sense that they are capable of persuading people of different faiths and nationalities. Hence, it is not enough to invoke Scripture or tradition.[17] Liberal citizens must justify their political demands in terms that fellow citizens can understand and accept as consistent with their status as free and equal citizens. It requires a conscientious effort to distinguish those beliefs which are matters of private faith from those which are capable of public defense and to see how issues look from the point of view of those with differing religious commitments and cultural backgrounds (cf. Phillips 1991b, pp. 57–59).[18]

Where do we learn these virtues? Other theorists we have examined relied on the market, the family, or the associations of civil society to teach civic virtue. But it is clear that people will not automatically learn to engage in public discourse or to question authority in any of these spheres, since these spheres are often held together by private discourse and respect for authority.

The answer, according to many liberal virtue theorists, is the system of education. Schools must teach children how to engage in the kind of critical reasoning and moral perspective that defines public reasonableness. As Amy Gutmann puts it, children at school "must learn not just to behave in accordance with authority but to think critically about authority if they are to live up to the democratic ideal of sharing political sovereignty as citizens." People who "are ruled only by habit and authority...are incapable of constituting a society of sovereign citizens" (Gutmann 1987, p. 51)[19].

However, this idea that schools should teach children to be skeptical of political authority and to distance themselves from their own cultural traditions when engaging in public discourse is controversial. Traditionalists object to it on the grounds that it inevitably leads children to question tradition and parental or religious authority in private life. And that is surely correct. As Gutmann admits, education for democratic citizenship will necessarily involve "equipping children with the intellectual skills necessary to evaluate ways of life different from that of their parents," because "many if not all of the capacities necessary for choice among good lives are also necessary for choice among good societies" (Gutmann 1987, pp. 30, 40).

Hence, those groups which rely heavily on an uncritical acceptance of tradition and authority, while not strictly ruled out, "are bound to be discouraged by the free, open, pluralistic, progressive" attitudes which liberal education encourages (Macedo 1990, pp. 53–54). This is why groups such as the Amish have sought to remove their children from the school system.

This creates a dilemma for liberals, many of whom wish to accommodate law-abiding groups like the Amish. Some liberals view the demise of such groups as regrettable but sometimes inevitable in a democratic society (Rawls 1975, p. 551; but see Rawls 1988, pp. 267–68). Other liberals, however, want to adjust citizenship education to minimize the impact on parental and religious authority. Galston, for example, argues that the need to teach children how to engage in public discourse and to evaluate political leaders "does not warrant the conclusion that the state must (or may) structure public education to foster in children skeptical reflection on ways of life inherited from parents or local communities" (Galston 1991, p. 253). However, he admits that it is not easy for schools to promote a child's willingness to question political authority without undermining her "unswerving belief in the correctness" of her parents' way of life.

This parallels the dilemma facing civil society theorists. They face the question of when to intervene in private groups in order to make them more effective schools of civic virtue; liberal virtue theorists, on the other hand, face the question of when to modify civic education in the schools in order to limit its impact on private associations. Neither group has, to date, fully come to grips with these questions.

D. Conclusion: Responsible Citizenship and Public Policy

In most postwar political theory, the fundamental normative concepts were democracy (for evaluating procedures) and justice (for evaluating outcomes). Citizenship, if it was discussed at all, was usually seen as derivative of democracy and justice—that is, a citizen is someone who has democratic rights and claims of justice. There is increasing support, however, from all points of the political spectrum, for the view that citizenship must play an independent normative role in any plausible political theory and that the promotion of responsible citizenship is an urgent aim of public policy.

And yet a striking feature of the current debate is the timidity with which authors apply their theories of citizenship to questions of public policy. As we have seen, there are some suggestions about the sorts of institutions or policies that would promote or enforce the virtues and responsibilities of good citizenship. But these tend to be the same policies which have long been defended on grounds of justice or democracy. The left favored democratizing the welfare state long before they adopted the language of citizenship, just as feminists favored day-care and the New Right opposed the welfare state. It is not clear whether adopting the perspective of citizenship really leads to different policy conclusions than the more familiar perspectives of justice and democracy.

We can imagine more radical proposals to promote citizenship. If civility is important, why not pass Good Samaritan laws, as many European countries have done? If political participation is important, why not require mandatory voting, as in Australia or Belgium? If public-spiritedness is important, why not require a period of mandatory national service, as in most European countries? If public schools help teach responsible citizenship, because they require children of different races and religions to sit together and learn to respect each other, why not prohibit private schools?

These are the kinds of policies which are concerned specifically with promoting citizenship, rather than justice or democracy. Yet few authors even contemplate such proposals. Instead, most citizenship theorists either leave the question of how to promote citizenship unanswered (Glendon 1991, p. 138) or focus on "modest" or "gentle and relatively unobtrusive ways" to promote civic virtues (Macedo 1990, pp. 234, 253).[20] While citizenship theorists bemoan the excessive focus given to rights, they seem reluctant to propose any policies that could be seen as restricting those rights.

There may be good reasons for this timidity, but it sits uneasily with the claim that we face a crisis of citizenship and that we urgently need a theory of citizenship. As a result, much recent work on citizenship virtues seems quite hollow. In the absence of some account of legitimate and illegitimate ways to promote or enforce good citizenship, many works on citizenship reduce to a platitude: namely, society would be better if the people in it were nicer and more thoughtful.[21]

Indeed, it is not clear how urgent the need to promote good citizenship is. The literature on citizenship is full of dire predictions about the decline of virtue, but as Galston admits, "cultural pessimism is a pervasive theme of human history, and in nearly every generation" (Galston 1991, p. 237).[22] If there are increasing crime and decreasing voting rates, it is equally true that we are more tolerant, more respectful of others' rights, and more committed to democracy and constitutionalism than were previous generations (Macedo 1990, pp. 6–7). So it remains unclear how we should be promoting good citizenship and how urgent it is to do so.

IV.

Citizenship, Identity, and Difference

Citizenship is not just a certain status, defined by a set of rights and responsibilities. It is also an identity, an expression of one's membership in a political community. Marshall saw citizenship as a shared identity that would integrate previously excluded groups within British society and provide a source of national unity. He was particularly concerned to integrate the working classes, whose lack of education and economic resources excluded them from the "common culture" which should have been a "common possession and heritage" (Marshall 1965, pp. 101–102).[23]

It has become clear, however, that many groups—blacks, women, Aboriginal peoples, ethnic and religious minorities, gays and lesbians—still feel excluded from the "common culture," despite possessing the common rights of citizenship. Members of these groups feel excluded not only because of their socioeconomic status but also because of their sociocultural identity—their "difference."

An increasing number of theorists, whom we will call "cultural pluralists," argue that citizenship must take account of these differences. Cultural pluralists believe that the common rights of citizenship, originally defined by and for white men, cannot accommodate the special needs of minority groups. These groups can only be integrated into the common culture if we adopt what Iris Marion Young calls a conception of "differentiated citizenship" (Young 1989, p. 258).

On this view, members of certain groups would be incorporated into the political community not only as individuals but also through the group, and their rights would depend, in part, on their group membership. For example, some immigrant groups are demanding special rights or exemptions to accommodate their religious practices; historically disadvantaged groups, such as women or blacks, are demanding special representation in the political process; and many national minorities (Québécois, Kurds, Catalans) are seeking greater powers of self-government within the larger country, if not outright secession.

These demands for "differentiated citizenship" pose a serious challenge to the prevailing conception of citizenship. Many people regard the idea of group-differentiated citizenship as a contradiction in terms. On the orthodox view, citizenship is, by definition, a matter of treating people as individuals with equal rights under the law. This is what distinguishes democratic citizenship from feudal and other premodern views that determined people's political status by their religious, ethnic, or class membership. Hence "the organization of society on the basis of rights or claims that derive from group membership is sharply opposed to the concept of society based on citizenship" (Porter 1987, p. 128). The idea of differentiated citizenship, therefore, is a radical development in citizenship theory.

One of the most influential theorists of cultural pluralism is Iris Marion Young. According to Young, the attempt to create a universal conception of citizenship which transcends group differences is fundamentally unjust because it oppresses historically excluded groups: "In a society where some groups are privileged while others are oppressed, insisting that as citizens persons should leave behind their particular affiliations and experiences to adopt a general point of view serves only to reinforce the privilege; for the perspective and interests of the privileged will tend to dominate this unified public, marginalizing or silencing those of other groups" (Young 1989, p. 257).[24] Young gives two reasons why genuine equality requires affirming rather than ignoring group differences. First, culturally excluded groups are at a disadvantage in the political process, and "the solution lies at least in part in providing institutionalized means for the explicit recognition and representation of oppressed groups" (Young 1989, p. 259). These procedural measures would include public funds for advocacy groups, guaranteed representation in political bodies, and veto rights over specific policies that affect a group directly (Young 1989, pp. 261–62; 1990, pp. 183–91).

Second, culturally excluded groups often have distinctive needs which can only be met through group-differentiated policies. These include language rights for Hispanics, land rights for Aboriginal groups, and reproductive rights for women (Young 1990, pp. 175–83). Other policies which have been advocated by cultural pluralists include group libel laws for women or Muslims, publicly funded schools for certain religious minorities, and exemptions from laws that interfere with religious worship, such as Sunday closing, animal-slaughtering legislation for Jews and Muslims, or motorcycle helmet laws for Sikhs (Parekh 1990, p. 705; 1991, pp. 197–204; Modood 1992).

Much has been written regarding the justification for these rights and how they relate to broader theories of justice and democracy. Young herself defends them as a response to "oppression," of which she outlines five forms: exploitation, marginalization, powerlessness, cultural imperialism, and "random violence and harassment motivated by group hatred or fear" (Young 1989, p. 261). It would take us too far afield to consider these justifications or the various objections to them.[25] Instead, we will focus on the impact of these rights on citizenship identity.

Critics of differentiated citizenship worry that if groups are encouraged by the very terms of citizenship to turn inward and focus on their "difference" (whether racial, ethnic, religious, sexual, and so on), then "the hope of a larger fraternity of all Americans will have to be abandoned" (Glazer 1983, p. 227). Citizenship will cease to be "a device to cultivate a sense of community and a common sense of purpose" (Heater 1990, p. 295; Kristeva 1993, p. 7; Cairns 1993). Nothing will bind the various groups in society together and prevent the spread of mutual mistrust or conflict (Kukathas 1993, p. 156).

Critics also worry that differentiated citizenship would create a "politics of grievance." If, as Young implies, only oppressed groups are entitled to differentiated citizenship, this may encourage group leaders to devote their political energy to establishing a perception of disadvantage—rather than working to overcome it—in order to secure their claim to group rights.

These are serious concerns. In evaluating them, however, we need to distinguish three different kinds of groups and three different kinds of group rights, which both Young and her critics tend to run together: (a) special representation rights (for disadvantaged groups); (b) multicultural rights (for immigrant and religious groups); and (c) self-government rights (for national minorities). Each of these has very different implications for citizenship identity.

Special representation rights.—For many of the groups on Young's list, such as the poor, elderly, African-Americans, and gays, the demand for group rights takes the form of special representation within the political process of the larger society. Since Young views these rights as a response to conditions of oppression, they are most plausibly seen as a temporary measure on the way to a society where the need for special representation no longer exists. Society should seek to remove the oppression, thereby eliminating the need for these rights.

Self-government rights.—In some of Young's examples, such as the reservation system of the American Indians, the demand for group rights is not seen as a temporary measure, and it is misleading to say that group rights are a response to a form of oppression that we hope someday to eliminate. Aboriginal peoples and other national minorities like the Québécois or Scots claim permanent and inherent rights, grounded in a principle of self-determination. These groups are "cultures," "peoples," or "nations," in the sense of being historical communities, more or less institutionally complete, occupying a given homeland or territory, sharing a distinct language and history. These nations find themselves within the boundaries of a larger political community, but claim the right to govern themselves in certain key matters, in order to ensure the full and free development of their culture and the best interests of their people. What these national minorities want is not primarily better representation in the central government but, rather, the transfer of power and legislative jurisdictions from the central government to their own communities.

Multicultural rights.—The case of Hispanics and other immigrant groups in the United States is different again. Their demands include public support of bilingual education and ethnic studies in schools and exemptions from laws that disadvantage them, given their religious practices. These measures are intended to help immigrants express their cultural particularity and pride without its hampering their success in the economic and political institutions of the dominant society. Like self-government rights, these rights need not be temporary, because the cultural differences they promote are not something we hope to eliminate. But unlike self-government rights, multicultural rights are intended to promote integration into the larger society, not self-government.

Obviously, these three kinds of rights can overlap, in the sense that some groups can claim more than one kind of group right.

If differentiated citizenship is defined as the adoption of one or more of these group-differentiated rights, then virtually every modern democracy recognizes some form of it. Citizenship today "is a much more differentiated and far less homogeneous concept than has been presupposed by political theorists" (Parekh 1990, p. 702). Nevertheless, most cultural pluralists demand a degree of differentiation not present in almost any developed democracy.

Would adopting one or more of these group rights undermine the integrative function of citizenship? A closer look at the distinction between the three kinds of rights suggests that such fears are often misplaced. The fact is that, generally speaking, the demand for both representation rights and multicultural rights is a demand for inclusion. Groups that feel excluded want to be included in the larger society, and the recognition and accommodation of their "difference" is intended to facilitate this.

The right to special representation is just a new twist on an old idea. It has always been recognized that a majoritarian democracy can systematically ignore the voices of minorities. In cases where minorities are regionally concentrated, democratic systems have responded by intentionally drawing the boundaries of federal units, or of individual constituencies, to create seats where the minority is in a majority (Beitz 1989, chap. 7). Cultural pluralists simply extend this logic to nonterritorial minorities, who may equally be in need of representation (e.g., women, the disabled, or gays and lesbians).

There are enormous practical obstacles to such a proposal. For example, how do we decide which groups are entitled to such representation,[26] and how do we ensure that their "representatives" are in fact accountable to the group?[27] But the basic impulse underlying representation rights is integration, not separation.

Similarly, most multicultural demands are evidence that members of minority groups want to get into the mainstream of society. Consider the case of Canadian Sikhs who wanted to join the Royal Canadian Mounted Police (RCMP) but, because of their religious requirement to wear a turban, could not do so unless they were exempted from the usual dress code regarding headgear. The fact that these men wanted to be a part of the RCMP, one of Canada's "national symbols," is ample evidence of their desire to participate in the larger community. The special right they were requesting could only be seen as promoting, not discouraging, their integration.[28]

Some people fear that multicultural rights impede the process of integration for immigrants by creating a confusing halfway house between their old nation and citizenship in the new one. But these worries seem empirically unfounded. Experience in countries with extensive multicultural programs, such as Canada and Australia, suggest that first- and second-generation immigrants who remain proud of their heritage are also among the most patriotic citizens of their new country (Kruhlak 1992).[29] Moreover, their strong affiliation with their new country seems to be based in large part on its willingness not just to tolerate but to welcome cultural difference.[30]

Self-government rights, however, do raise deep problems for traditional notions of citizenship identity. While both representation and multicultural rights take the larger political community for granted and seek greater inclusion in it, demands for self-government reflect a desire to weaken the bonds with the larger community and, indeed, question its very nature, authority, and permanence. If democracy is the rule of the people, group self-determination raises the question of who "the people" really are. National minorities claim that they are distinct peoples, with inherent rights of self-determination which were not relinquished by their (sometimes involuntary) federation with other nations within a larger country. Indeed, the retaining of certain powers is often explicitly spelled out in the treaties or constitutional agreements which specified the terms of federation.

Self-government rights, therefore, are the most complete case of differentiated citizenship, since they divide the people into separate "peoples," each with its own historic rights, territories, and powers of self-government, and each, therefore, with its own political community.

It seems unlikely that differentiated citizenship can serve an integrative function in this context. If citizenship is membership in a political community, then in creating overlapping political communities, self-government rights necessarily give rise to a sort of dual citizenship and to potential conflicts about which community citizens identify with most deeply (Vernon 1988). Moreover, there seems to be no natural stopping point to the demands for increasing self-government. If limited autonomy is granted, this may simply fuel the ambitions of nationalist leaders who will be satisfied with nothing short of their own undifferentiated nation-state. Democratic multination states are, it would seem, inherently unstable for this reason.

It might seem tempting, therefore, to ignore the demands of national minorities, keep any reference to particular groups out of the constitution, and insist that citizenship is a common identity shared by all individuals without regard to group membership. This is often described as the American strategy for dealing with cultural pluralism. But with a few exceptions—such as the (mostly outlying or isolated) American Indian, Inuit, Puerto Rican, and native Hawaiian populations—the United States is not a multination state. It faced the problem of assimilating voluntary immigrants, not of incorporating historically self-governing communities whose homeland has become part of the larger community. And where it was applied to national minorities—for example, American Indians—the "common citizenship" strategy has often been a spectacular failure, as even its supporters admit (Walzer 1982, p. 27; cf. Kymlicka 1991). Hence, many of these groups are now accorded self-government rights within the United States.

Indeed, there are very few democratic multination states that follow the strict "common citizenship" strategy. This is not surprising, because refusing demands for self-government rights may simply aggravate alienation among these groups and increase the desire for secession (Taylor 1992a, p. 64).[31]

Hence, demands for self -government raise a problem for proponents of both common citizenship and differentiated citizenship. Yet remarkably little attention has been paid, by either defenders or critics, to this form of differentiated citizenship (or to the most common arrangement for instantiating self-government rights, namely, federalism).[32]

What, then, is the source of unity in a multination country? Rawls claims that the source of union in modern societies is a shared conception of justice: "Although a well-ordered society is divided and pluralistic... public agreement on questions of political and social justice supports ties of civic friendship and secures the bonds of association" (Rawls 1980, p. 540). But the fact that two national groups share the same principles of justice does not necessarily give them any strong reason to join (or remain) together, rather than remaining (or splitting into) two separate countries. The fact that people in Norway and Sweden share the same principles of justice is no reason for them to regret the secession of Norway in 1905. Similarly, the fact that the anglophones and francophones in Canada share the same principles of justice is not a strong reason to remain together, since the Québécois rightly assume that their own national state could respect the same principles. A shared conception of justice throughout a political community does not necessarily generate a shared identity, let alone a shared citizenship identity that will supersede rival identities based on ethnicity (Nickel 1990; Norman 1993a).[33]

It seems clear, then, that this is one place where we really do need a theory of citizenship, not just a theory of democracy or justice. How can we construct a common identity in a country where people not only belong to separate political communities but also belong in different ways—that is, some are incorporated as individuals and others through membership in a group? Taylor calls this "deep diversity" and insists that it is "the only formula" on which a multination state can remain united (Taylor 1991). However, he admits that it is an open question what holds such a country together.[34]

Indeed, the great variance in historical, cultural, and political situations in multination states suggests that any generalized answer to this question will likely be overstated. It might be a mistake to suppose that one could develop a general theory about the role of either a common citizenship identity or a differentiated citizenship identity in promoting or hindering national unity (Taylor 1992b, pp. 65–66). Here, as with the other issues we have examined in this survey, it remains unclear what we can expect from a "theory of citizenship."

Notes

1. Rawls says that the "basic structure" of society is the primary subject of a theory of justice (Rawls 1971, p. 7; Rawls 1993, pp. 257–89).

2. This may account for the recent interest in citizenship promotion among governments (e.g., Britain's Commission on Citizenship, *Encour-*

aging Citizenship [1990]; Senate of Australia, *Active Citizenship Revisited* [1991]; Senate of Canada, *Canadian Citizenship: Sharing the Responsibility* [1993]).

3. One issue we will not discuss is immigration and naturalization policy (e.g., Brubaker 1989; van Gunsteren 1988).

4. Reprinted in Marshall (1965). For a concise introduction to the history of citizenship, see Heater (1990) and Walzer (1989).

5. It is often noted how idiosyncratically English this history is. In many European countries most of this progress occurred only in the past fifty years, and often in reverse order. Even in England, the historical evidence supports an "ebb and flow model" of citizenship rights, rather than a "unilinear" model (Heater 1990, p. 271; Parry 1991, p. 167; Held 1989, p. 193; Turner 1989).

6. When asked what citizenship means to them, people are much more likely to talk about rights than responsibilities. This is true in Britain as well as the United States, although the British tend to emphasize social rights (e.g., to public education and health care), whereas Americans usually mention civil rights (e.g., freedom of speech and religion) (King and Waldron 1988: Conover et al. 1991, p. 804). For most people, citizenship is, as the U.S. Supreme Court once put it, "the right to have rights" (Trop v. Dulles 356 U.S. 86, 102 [1958]).

7. For evidence that there is a set of social expectations that Americans have of each other, and of themselves, that must be fulfilled if people are to be perceived as full members of society, see Mead (1986, p. 243); Shklar (1991, p. 413); Moon (1988, pp. 34–35); Dworkin (1992, p. 131).

8. Some people on the right have recognized this danger with a purely market-based conception of citizenship and have sought to supplement it with an emphasis on volunteerism and charity. See the discussion of the British Conservative party's citizenship rhetoric in Fierlbeck (1991, p. 589), Andrews (1991, p. 13), and Heater (1990, p. 303).

9. The New Right's emphasis on self-reliance puts women in a double bind. If they stay home and care for their children, they are accused of failing to live up to their duty to be self-supporting. (Hence the stereotype of irresponsible welfare mothers.) If they seek to earn a living, however, they are accused of failing to live up to their family responsibilities.

10. Another theme in recent left writing on citizenship is the importance of constitutional rights. Indeed, the left's reconciliation with

liberal rights "is one of the major theoretical phenomena of our times" (Phillips 1991b, p. 13; Andrews 1991, pp. 207–11; Sedley 1991, p. 226).

11. Kant thought that the problem of good government "can be solved even for a race of devils" (quoted in Galston 1991, p. 215). Of course, other liberals recognized the need for civic virtue, including Locke, Mill, and the British Idealists (see Vincent and Plant 1984, chap. 1). See also Carens (1986) and Deigh (1988), who argue that basic liberal rights and principles ground a fairly extensive range of positive social duties and responsibilities, including the obligation to make good use of one's talents, to vote, to fulfill the responsibilities of one's office, and to aid in the defense of one's country, as well as the duty to protect and educate one's children.

12. According to a recent survey, only 12 percent of American teenagers said voting was important to being a good citizen. Moreover, this apathy is not just a function of youth—comparisons with similar surveys from the previous fifty years suggest that "the current cohort knows less, cares less, votes less, and is less critical of its leaders and institutions than young people have been at any time over the past five decades" (Glendon 1991, p. 129). The evidence from Great Britain is similar (Heater 1990, p. 215).

13. See Arneson (1992, pp. 488–92) for a range of potential conflicts between democratic procedures and socialist goals. As Dworkin notes, there is a danger of making democracy "a black hole into which all other political virtues collapse" (1992, p. 132).

14. The left neglected many of these issues for decades, on the ground that a concern with "citizenship" was bourgeois ideology. The very language of citizenship was "alien" (Selbourne 1991, p.94; van Gunsteren 1978, p.9; Dietz 1992, p. 70; Wolin 1992, p. 241; Andrews 1991, p. 13).

15. Civic republicans rarely defend their conception of value at length. For example, after asserting that political life is "the highest form of human living-together that most individuals can aspire to," Oldfield goes on to say, "I shall not argue for this moral point. It has in any case been argued many times within the corpus of civic republican writing" (1990a, p. 6). But many critics have argued that these earlier defenses rest on sexism and denigration of the private sphere (e.g., Vogel 1991, p. 68; Young 1989, p. 253: Phillips 1991b, p. 49) or on ethnic exclusiveness (Habermas 1992, p. 8). Skinner's argument seems to be that while political participation may only have instrumental value for most people, we must get people to view it as if it has intrinsic value, or else they will not withstand internal or external threats to democracy (Skinner 1992, pp. 219–21). For discussions

of the relationship between republican conceptions of the good and liberalism, see Dworkin (1989, pp. 499–504), Taylor (1989, pp. 177–81), Hill (1993, pp. 67–84), and Sinopoli (1992, pp. 163–71).

16. Also, it is difficult to see how even reconstructed groups could teach what some regard as an essential aspect of citizenship—namely, a common identity and sense of purpose (Phillips 1991b, pp. 117–18). We discuss this in sec. IV below.

17. See the discussion of the "principle of secular motivation" in Audi (1989, p. 284).

18. This shows why civil society theorists are mistaken to think that good citizenship can be based on essentially private virtues. The requirement of public reasonableness in political debate is unnecessary and undesirable in the private sphere. It would be absurd to ask church-goers to abstain from appealing to Scripture in deciding how to run their church.

19. Public schools teach these virtues not only through their curriculum but also "by insisting that students sit in their seats (next to students of different races and religions), raise their hands before speaking, hand in their homework on time...be good sports on its playing field" (Gutmann 1987, p. 53).

20. For other accounts of the "unobtrusive" promotion of citizenship, see Habermas (1992, pp. 6–7), Hill (1993), and Rawls (1993, pp. 216–20).

21. For example, Mouffe criticizes liberalism for reducing citizenship "to a mere legal status, setting out the rights that the individual holds against the state" (1992b, p. 227) and seeks to "reestablish the lost connection between ethics and politics," by understanding citizenship as a form of "political identity that is created through the identification with the *res publica*" (p. 230). Yet she offers no suggestions about how to promote or compel this public-spirited participation, and insists (against civic republicans) that citizens must be free to choose not to give priority to their political activities. Her critique of liberalism, therefore, seems to reduce to the claim that the liberal conception of citizenship-as-legal-status is not an adequate conception of good citizenship, which liberals would readily accept. Many critiques of liberal citizenship amount to the same unenlightening claim.

22. Indeed, we can find similar worries about political apathy in 1950s political sociologists, and even in Tocqueville.

23. See the discussion of citizenship's "integrative function" in Barbalet (1988, p. 93).

24. See also Pateman's discussion of how citizenship is currently "constructed from men's attributes, capacities and activities," so that citizenship can only be extended to women "as lesser men" (1988, pp. 252–253; cf. James 1992, pp. 52–55; Pateman 1992).

25. Critics have objected that differentiated citizenship (*a*) violates equality: granting rights to some people but not others on the basis of their group membership sets up a hierarchy in which some citizens are "more equal" than others; (*b*) violates liberal neutrality: the role of the state in matters of culture should be limited to maintaining a fair cultural marketplace; and (*c*) is arbitrary: there is no principled way to determine which groups are entitled to differential status. For a discussion of these objections, see Glazer (1983), Taylor (1991; 1992a, pp. 51–61), Hindess (1993), Kymlicka (1989, 1991), Phillips (1992), and Van Dyke (1985).

26. According to Young, "Once we are clear that the principle of group representation refers only to oppressed social groups, then the fear of an unworkable proliferation of group representation should dissipate" (1990, p. 187). However, her list of "oppressed groups" would seem to include 80 percent of the population—she says that "in the United States today, at least the following groups are oppressed in one or more of these ways: women, blacks, Native Americans, Chicanos, Puerto Ricans and other Spanish-speaking Americans, Asian Americans, gay men, lesbians, working-class people, poor people, old people, and mentally and physically disabled people" (1989, p. 261). In short, everyone but healthy, relatively well-off, relatively young, heterosexual white males. Even then, it is hard to see how this criterion would avoid an "unworkable proliferation" since each of these groups has subgroups that might claim their own rights. In the case of Britain, for example, "the all-embracing concept of 'black' people rapidly dissolved into a distinction between the Asian and Afro-Caribbean communities, and then subsequently into finer distinctions between a wide variety of ethnic groups. What in this context then counts as 'adequate' ethnic representation?" (Phillips 1992, p. 89). Nevertheless, many political parties and trade unions have allowed for special group representation without entering an escalating spiral of demands and resentment (Young 1989, pp. 187–89).

27. "There are few mechanisms for establishing what each group wants. . . . Accountability is always the other side of representation, and, in the absence of procedures for establishing what any group wants or thinks, we cannot usefully talk of their political representation" (Phillips 1992, pp. 86–88). In the absence of accountability, it might be more appropriate to talk of consultation than representation.

28. This is in contrast to many Aboriginal communities in Canada who, as part of their self-government, have been trying to remove the RCMP from their reserves and replace it with a Native police force. Of course, some demands for multicultural rights also take the form of withdrawal from the larger society, although this is more likely to be true of religious sects (e.g., the Amish) than of ethnic communities per se.

29. Moreover, a proliferation of such demands is unlikely, since they usually involve clear and specific cases of unintended conflict between majority rules and minority religious practices. And since proof of oppression is neither necessary nor sufficient to claim these rights, there is little risk that they will promote a politics of grievance.

30. Of course, liberals cannot accept a group's demand to practice its religious or cultural customs if these violate the basic rights of the members of these groups (e.g., clitoridectomy, restrictions on exit). It is important to distinguish what we can call "internal" and "external" group rights. Internal rights are rights of a group against its own members, used to force individuals within the group to obey traditional customs or authority. External rights are rights of the group against the larger society, used to provide support for the group against economic or political pressure from outside for cultural assimilation. In western democracies, group-differentiated rights are almost always external rights, since internal rights are clearly inconsistent with liberal democratic norms. See Kukathas (1992) and the reply in Kymlicka (1992).

31. In any event, the state cannot avoid giving public recognition to particular group identities. After all, governments must decide which language(s) will serve as the official language of the schools, courts, and legislatures.

32. For a survey of philosophical work on federalism, see Norman (1993b).

33. If governments wish to use citizenship identity to promote national unity, therefore, they will have to identify citizenship, not only with acceptance of principles of justice but also with an emotional-affective sense of identity, based perhaps on a manipulation of shared symbols or historical myths. For a discussion of this strategy, see Norman (1993a).

34. European philosophers are confronting increasingly these dilemmas as they seek to understand the nature of the European Community and the form of citizenship it requires. Habermas and his followers argue that European unity cannot be based on the shared traditions, cultures, and languages that characterized successful nation-

states. Instead, European citizenship must be founded on a "postnational" constitutional patriotism based on shared principles of justice and democracy (Habermas 1992; Berten 1992; Ferry 1992). Others, however, argue that such a basis for unity is too "thin." As Taylor notes, even the model experiments in constitutional patriotism, France and the United States, have always also required many of the trappings of nation-states, including founding myths, national symbols, and ideals of historical and quasi-ethnic membership (Taylor 1992b, p. 61; cf. Lenoble 1992; Smith 1993). According to Taylor, it is not for philosophers to define a priori the form of citizenship that is legitimate or admissible. Rather, we should seek forms of identity which appear significant to the people themselves (Taylor 1992b, p. 65; Berten 1992, p. 64).

References

Andrews, Geoff. 1991. *Citizenship*. London: Lawrence & Wishart.

Arneson, Richard. 1992. Is Socialism Dead? A Comment on Market Socialism and Basic Income Capitalism. *Ethics* 102:485–511.

Audi, Robert. 1989. The Separation of Church and State and the Obligations of Citizenship. *Philosophy and Public Affairs* 18:259–96.

Barbalet, J. M. 1988. *Citizenship: Rights, Struggle and Class Inequality*. Minneapolis: University of Minnesota Press.

Barry, Norman. 1990. Markets, Citizenship and the Welfare State: Some Critical Reflections. In Raymond Plant and Norman Barry, *Citizenship and Rights in Thatcher's Britain: Two Views*. London: IEA Health and Welfare Unit.

Beiner, Ronald. 1992. Citizenship. In *What's the Matter With Liberalism?* Berkeley: University of California Press.

Beitz, Charles. 1989. *Political Equality*. Princeton, N.J.: Princeton University Press.

Berten, André. 1992. Identité Européenne, Une ou Multiple? In *L'Europe au soir du siècle: Identité et démocratie*, ed. Jacques Lenoble and Nicole Dewandre. Paris: Éditions Esprit.

Brubaker, William Rogers, ed. 1989. *Immigration and the Politics of Citizenship in Europe and North America*. Lanham, Md.: University Press of America.

Cairns, Alan. 1993. The Fragmentation of Canadian Citizenship. In *Belonging: The Meaning and Future of Canadian Citizenship*, ed. William Kaplan. Montreal: McGill-Queen's Press.

Cairns, Alan, and Williams, Cynthia. 1985. *Constitutionalism, Citizenship, and Society in Canada*. Toronto: University of Toronto Press.

Carens, Joseph. 1986. Rights and Duties in an Egalitarian Society. *Political Theory* 14:31–49.

Conover, Pamela; Crewe, Ivor; and Searing, Donald. 1991. The Nature of Citizenship in the United States and Great Britain: Empirical Comments on Theoretical Themes. *Journal of Politics* 53:800–832.

Deigh, John. 1988. On Rights and Responsibilities. *Law and Philosophy* 7:147–78.

Dietz, Mary. 1985. Citizenship with a Feminist Face: The Problem with Maternal Thinking. *Political Theory* 13:19–35.

———. 1992. Context is All: Feminism and Theories of Citizenship. In Mouffe. *Dimensions of Radical Democracy*.

Dworkin, Ronald. 1989. Liberal Community. *California Law Review* 77:479–504.

———. 1992. Deux Conceptions de la Démocratie. In *L'Europe au soir du siècle: Identité et démocratie*, ed. Jacques Lenoble and Nicole Dewandre. Paris: Éditions Esprit.

Elshtain, Jean Bethke. 1981. *Public Man, Private Woman: Women in Social and Political Thought*. Princeton, N.J.: Princeton University Press.

Ferry, Jean-Marc. 1992. Identité et Citoyenneté Européennes. In *L'Europe au soir du siècle: Identité et démocratie*, ed. Jacques Lenoble and Nicole Dewandre. Paris: Éditions Esprit.

Fierlbeck, Katherine. 1991. Redefining Responsibilities: The Politics of Citizenship in the United Kingdom. *Canadian Journal of Political Science* 24:575–83.

Fullinwider, Robert. 1988. Citizenship and Welfare. In *Democracy and the Welfare State*, ed. Amy Gutmann. Princeton, N.J.: Princeton University Press.

Galston, William. 1991. *Liberal Purposes: Goods, Virtues, and Duties in the Liberal State.* Cambridge: Cambridge University Press.

Gilligan, Carol. 1982. *In a Different Voice: Psychological Theory and Moral Development.* Cambridge, Mass.: Harvard University Press.

Glazer, Nathan. 1983. *Ethnic Dilemmas: 1964–1982.* Cambridge, Mass.: Harvard University Press.

Glendon, Mary Ann. 1991. *Rights Talk: The Impoverishment of Political Discourse.* New York: Free Press.

Gutmann, Amy. 1987. *Democratic Education.* Princeton, N.J.: Princeton University Press.

Habermas, Jürgen. 1992. Citizenship and National Identity: Some Reflections on the Future of Europe. *Praxis International* 12:1–19.

Heater, Derek. 1990. *Citizenship: The Civic Ideal in World History, Politics, and Education.* London: Longman.

Held, David. 1989. Citizenship and Autonomy. In *Political Theory and the Modern State.* Stanford, Calif.: Stanford University Press.

———. 1991. Between State and Civil Society: Citizenship. In Andrews. *Citizenship* 1991, pp. 19–25.

Hill, Greg. 1993. Citizenship and Ontology in the Liberal State. *Review of Politics* 51:67–84.

Hindess, Barry. 1993. Multiculturalism and Citizenship. In *Multicultural Citizens: The Philosophy and Politics of Identity*, ed. Chandran Kukathas. St. Leonard's: Centre for Independent Studies.

Hoover, K., and Plant, R. 1988. *Conservative Capitalism in Britain and the United States.* London: Routledge.

Ignatieff, Michael. 1989. Citizenship and Moral Narcissism. *Political Quarterly* 60: 63–74. Reprinted in Andrews. *Citizenship.* 1991, pp. 26–37.

James, Susan. 1992. The Good-Enough Citizen: Citizenship and Independence. In *Beyond Equality and Difference: Citizenship, Feminist Politics, and Female Subjectivity*, ed. Gisela Bock and Susan James. London: Routledge.

King, Desmond. 1987. *The New Right: Politics, Markets and Citizenship.* London: Macmillan.

King, Desmond, and Waldron, Jeremy. 1988. Citizenship, Social Citizenship and the Defence of the Welfare State. *British Journal of Political Science* 18:415–43.

Kristeva, Julia. 1993. *Nations without Nationalism*, trans. Leon S. Roudiez. New York: Columbia University Press.

Kruhlak, Orest. 1992. Multiculturalism: Myth versus Reality. Institute for Research on Public Policy, Montreal, typescript.

Kukathas, Chandran. 1992. Are There Any Cultural Rights? *Political Theory* 20:105–39.

———. 1993. Multiculturalism and the Idea of an Australian Identity. In *Multicultural Citizens: The Philosophy and Politics of Identity*, ed. Chandran Kukathas. St. Leonard's: Centre for Independent Studies.

Kymlicka, Will. 1989. *Liberalism, Community, and Culture*. Oxford: Oxford University Press.

———. 1991. Liberalism and the Politicization of Ethnicity. *Canadian Journal of Law and Jurisprudence* 4:239–56.

———. 1992. The Rights of Minority Cultures: Reply to Kukathas. *Political Theory* 20:140–46.

Lenoble, Jacques. 1992. Penser l'identité et la démocratie en Europe. In *L'Europe au soir du siècle: Identité et démocratie*, ed. Jacques Lenoble and Nicole Dewandre. Paris: Éditions Esprit.

Macedo, Stephen. 1990. *Liberal Virtues: Citizenship, Virtue, and Community*. Oxford: Oxford University Press.

Marshall, T. H. 1965. *Class, Citizenship and Social Development*. New York: Anchor.

Mead, Lawrence. 1986. *Beyond Entitlement: The Social Obligations of Citizenship*. New York: Free Press.

Modood, Tariq. 1992. *Not Easy Being British: Colour, Culture and Citizenship*. London: Trentham.

Moon, J. Donald. 1988. The Moral Basis of the Democratic Welfare State. In *Democracy and the Welfare State*, ed. Amy Gutmann. Princeton, N.J.: Princeton University Press.

Mouffe, Chantal. 1992a. *Dimensions of Radical Democracy: Pluralism, Citizenship and Community*. London: Routledge.

Mouffe, Chantal. 1992b. Democratic Citizenship and the Political Community. In Mouffe. *Dimensions of Radical Democracy*.

Mulgan, Geoff. 1991. Citizens and Responsibilities. In Andrews. *Citizenship*. 1991, pp. 37–49.

Nauta, Lolle. 1992. Changing Conceptions of Citizenship. *Praxis International* 12:20–34.

Nickel, James. 1990. Rawls on Political Community and Principles of Justice. *Law and Philosophy* 9:205–16.

Norman, Wayne. 1993a. The Ideology of Shared Values. University of Ottawa, Department of Philosophy, typescript.

———. 1993b. Toward a Philosophy of Federalism. In *Group Rights*, ed. Judith Baker. Toronto: University of Toronto Press, in press.

Okin, Susan. 1989. *Justice, Gender, and the Family*. New York: Basic.

———. 1992. Women, Equality and Citizenship. *Queen's Quarterly* 99:56–71.

Oldfield, Adrian. 1990a. *Citizenship and Community: Civic Republicanism and the Modern World*. London: Routledge.

———. 1990b. Citizenship: An Unnatural Practice? *Political Quarterly* 61:177–87.

Parekh, Bhiku. 1990. The Rushdie Affair: Research Agenda for Political Philosophy. *Political Studies* 38:695–709.

———. 1991. British Citizenship and Cultural Difference. In Andrews. *Citizenship*. 1991, pp. 183–204.

Parry, Geraint. 1991. Paths to Citizenship. In Vogel and Moran, *The Frontiers of Citizenship*. 1991, pp. 167–96.

Pateman, Carole. 1988. The Patriarchal Welfare State. In *Democracy and the Welfare State*, ed. Amy Gutmann. Princeton, N.J.: Princeton University Press.

———. 1992. Equality, Difference and Subordination: The Politics of Motherhood and Women's Citizenship. In *Beyond Equality and Difference: Citizenship, Feminist Politics, and Female Subjectivity*, ed. Gisela Bock and Susan James. London: Routledge.

Phillips, Anne. 1991a. Citizenship and Feminist Theory. In Andrews. *Citizenship*. 1991, pp. 76–88.

———. 1991b. *Engendering Democracy*. University Park, Pa.: Pennsylvania State University Press.

———. 1992. Democracy and Difference: Some Problems for Feminist Theory. *Political Quarterly* 63:79–90.

Pierson, Christopher. 1991. *Beyond the Welfare State: The New Political Economy of Welfare*. University Park, Pa.: Pennsylvania State University Press.

Plant, Raymond. 1990. Citizenship and Rights. In *Citizenship and Rights in Thatcher's Britain: Two Views*. London: IEA Health and Welfare Unit.

———. 1991. Social Rights and the Reconstruction of Welfare. In Andrews. *Citizenship*. 1991, pp. 50–64.

Pocock, J. G. A. 1992. The Ideal of Citizenship since Classical Times. *Queen's Quarterly* 99:33–55.

Porter, John. 1987. *The Measure of Canadian Society*. Carleton University Press.

Rawls, John. 1971. *A Theory of Justice*. London: Oxford University Press.

———. 1975. Fairness to Goodness. *Philosophical Review* 84:536–54.

———. 1980. Kantian Constructivism in Moral Theory. *Journal of Philosophy* 77:515–72.

———. 1988. The Priority of Right and Ideas of the Good. *Philosophy and Public Affairs* 17:251–76.

———. 1993. *Political Liberalism*. New York: Columbia University Press.

Ruddick, Sara. 1987. Remarks on the Sexual Politics of Reason. In *Women and Moral Theory*, ed. Eva Kittay and Diana Meyers. Totowa, N.J.: Rowman & Allanheld.

Rustin, Michael. 1991. Whose Rights of Citizenship? In Andrews. *Citizenship*. 1991, pp. 228–34.

Sedley, Stephen. 1991. Charter 88: Wrongs and Rights. In Andrews. *Citizenship*. 1991, pp. 219–27.

Selbourne, David. 1991. Who Would Be a Socialist Citizen? In Andrews. *Citizenship.* 1991, pp. 91–104.

Shklar, Judith. 1991. *American Citizenship: The Quest for Inclusion.* The Tanner Lectures on Human Values, 10:386–439. Cambridge, Mass.: Harvard University Press.

Sinopoli, Richard. 1992. *The Foundations of American Citizenship: Liberalism, the Constitution, and Civic Virtue.* New York: Oxford University Press.

Skinner, Quentin. 1992. On Justice, the Common Good and the Priority of Liberty. In Mouffe. *Dimensions of Radical Democracy.* pp. 211–24.

Smith, Rogers. 1993. American Conceptions of Citizenship and National Service. *The Responsive Community* 3:14–27.

Taylor, Charles. 1989. The Liberal-Communitarian Debate. In *Liberalism and the Moral Life,* ed. N. Rosenblum. Cambridge, Mass.: Harvard University Press.

———. 1991. Shared and Divergent Values. In *Options for a New Canada,* ed. R. L. Watts and D. G. Brown. Toronto: University of Toronto Press.

———. 1992a. *Multiculturalism and "The Politics of Recognition,"* ed. Amy Gutmann. Princeton, N.J.: Princeton University Press.

———. 1992b. Quel principe d'identité collective. In *L'Europe au soir du siècle: Identité et démocratie,* ed. Jacques Lenoble and Nicole Dewandre. Paris: Éditions Esprit.

Turner, Bryan. 1989. Outline of a Theory of Citizenship. *Sociology* 24:189–217.

Van Dyke, Vernon. 1985. *Human Rights, Ethnicity, and Discrimination.* Westport, Conn.: Greenwood.

van Gunsteren, Herman. 1978. Notes towards a Theory of Citizenship. In *From Contract to Community,* ed. F. Dallmayr. New York: Marcel Decker.

van Gunsteren, Herman. 1988. Admission to Citizenship. *Ethics* 98:731–41.

Vernon, Richard. 1988. The Federal Citizen. In *Perspectives on Canadian Federalism,* ed. R. D. Olling and M. Westmacott. Scarborough: Prentice-Hall.

ALASDAIR MacINTYRE is McMahon/Hank Professor of Philosophy at the University of Notre Dame. His recent books include *Whose Justice? Which Rationality?* (1988) and *Three Rival Versions of Moral Enquiry* (1990).

WAYNE NORMAN is Associate Professor of Philosophy at the University of Ottawa. He is author of *Taking Freedom Too Seriously?* (1991).

J. G. A. POCOCK is Harry C. Black Professor of History at the Johns Hopkins University. His books include *The Machiavellian Moment* (1975) and *Virtue, Commerce, and History* (1988).

MICHAEL WALZER is Professor of Social Science at the Institute for Advanced Study, Princeton University. His recent books include *Interpretation and Social Criticism* (1987), *The Company of Critics* (1988), and *Thick and Thin: Moral Argument at Home and Abroad* (1994).

IRIS MARION YOUNG is Professor of Public and International Affairs at the University of Pittsburgh. Her books include *Justice and the Politics of Difference* (1990) and *Throwing Like a Girl and Other Essays in Feminist Philosophy and Social Theory* (1990).

Index